The Crisis of Expertise

The Crisis of Expertise

Gil Eyal

polity

First published in 2019 by Polity Press
Reprinted 2020

Polity Press
65 Bridge Street
Cambridge CB2 1UR, UK

Polity Press
101 Station Landing
Suite 300
Medford, MA 02155, USA

ISBN-13: 978-0-7456-6577-1 (hardback)
ISBN-13: 978-0-7456-6578-8 (paperback)

A catalogue record for this book is available from the British Library.

Typeset in 10.5 on 12 pt Sabon
by Toppan Best-set Premedia Limited
Printed and bound in the United States by LSC Communications

The publisher has used its best endeavours to ensure that the URLs for
external websites referred to in this book are correct and active at the time of
going to press. However, the publisher has no responsibility for the websites
and can make no guarantee that a site will remain live or that the content is
or will remain appropriate.

Every effort has been made to trace all copyright holders, but if any have been
overlooked the publisher will be pleased to include any necessary credits in
any subsequent reprint or edition.

For further information on Polity, visit our website: politybooks.com

Contents

Acknowledgments   *viii*

Introduction: The Crisis   1

1 Expertise   11

2 The Debate about Expertise   21

3 Trust   43

4 Risk   64

5 Crisis, Take 2   82

6 Inside the Vortex   104

7 Balaam's Blessing   130

Conclusions: Trans-Science as a Vocation   142

Notes   *150*

Index   *179*

Opinion, a pre-eminently social thing, is therefore a source of authority; and we can even speculate whether all authority is not the daughter of opinion. Some will object that science is often the combative antagonist of opinion, rectifying its errors. But science can succeed in this task only if it has sufficient authority and it can draw this authority only from opinion itself. All the scientific demonstrations in the world would have no influence if a people had no faith in science. Even today, if science happens to go against a strong current of public opinion, it risks losing its credibility.

Emile Durkheim, *The Elementary Forms of Religious Life*. 1912 (p. 156)

… as far as possible, our anti-intellectualism must be excised from the benevolent impulses upon which it lives by constant and delicate acts of intellectual surgery which spare these impulses themselves.

Richard Hofstadter, *Anti-Intellectualism in American Life*. 1962 (p. 23)

An expert is a specialist to whom one can put questions that he is unable to answer.

Niklas Luhmann, quoted in Gotthard Bechmann, "The Rise and Crisis of Scientific Expertise," in Gotthard Bechmann and Imre Hronzsky, eds, *Expertise and its Interfaces*. Berlin: Edition Sigma, 2003 (p. 23)

Acknowledgments

The idea for this book first emerged in conversations with John Thompson over coffee at the West Village. I have come to rely on John's good judgment, his polite but firm shooting down of ill-conceived trial balloons, and his unfailing patience throughout the process. I am indebted to my editor at Polity, Susan Beer, who has made sure all my errors of fact were corrected, while taking a more indulgent approach to my stylistic peculiarities. Evie Deavall shepherded the manuscript with professionalism and dispatch. My thanks to the John Simon Guggenheim Foundation, whose generosity allowed me to spend the academic year 2017–2018 researching and writing this book, unencumbered by other duties. The greatest debts were incurred at home, where the collateral damage of book writing is often most keenly felt, yet where I could always count on the home crowd to cheer me on through thick and thin. This book is dedicated to my wife, Johanna Shih, and my children, Benny, David and Lilly, whose loving support animates its every page.

Introduction
The Crisis

Michael Gove perhaps did not intend to ignite a firestorm. He did not wish, perhaps, to impugn the character of any specific expert or organization. Nor did he wish to dismiss all experts. All he wanted to say, he explained later, is that economics is a "profession in crisis" (and how could I, a sociologist, object to this characterization?) because the forecasts of economists have failed spectacularly in recent years, and none was able to predict (let alone forestall) the financial crisis of 2008. Their predictions and advice regarding the economic effects of Brexit, therefore, should be taken with a grain of salt. All he wanted to say – as he can indeed be heard saying underneath the Sky News interviewer's alarmed protestations – is that "people in this country have had enough of experts from organizations with acronyms saying that they know what is best and getting it consistently wrong." This was an altogether unexceptional, even predictable response, given that the interviewer, Faisal Islam, has just finished ticking off a long list of all these "organizations with acronyms" and challenged Gove to explain how he can ignore their warnings about the dire economic consequences of Brexit. It was an altogether predictable response, since Gove was trying to parry, in this Q&A session in front of a live audience, the arguments of anti-Brexit politicians – David Cameron appeared in the same session just before him – that economic experts were forecasting significant economic losses to Britain if it were to exit the EU. It was an altogether reasonable response, *sans* the populist pretense that this Oxford Upper Second Classman was speaking for "people in this country." The economists' past predictions *were* wrong. Economic forecasting *is* a tricky business. The acronyms *do* bespeak of elitism and deep attachment to the establishment. And after all, this was a televised debate, part of an intense political battle in which the experts' opinions were clearly mobilized by one side to attack the other. But poor Mr. Gove, he was never given the chance to sound or seem reasonable or at least unexceptional. The appalled interviewer cut him off mid-sentence: "had enough of experts? ... People ... in this country ... [raised pitch] had enough of experts?" and accused him of being an "Oxbridge Trump." So poor Michael Gove will go down in history with the next day's headline firmly tattooed on his forehead: "Britain has had Enough of Experts, says Gove."[1]

Mr. Islam, for his part, may be forgiven the shrillness of his response. Like the commentators agonizing in the following weeks, Mr. Islam could not but read a larger meaning into the exchange. Climate skeptics too "had enough" of the IPCC's forecasting based on models and simulations (which *by definition* "get it consistently wrong"). Anti-vaxxers too "had enough" of the CDC, the NIH, and the NHS (and other "organizations with acronyms") knowing what is best for children and telling parents what to do. Gove's quip seemed to take a page from the "merchants of doubt," who for years have plied their agnoto-genic (i.e. ignorance-producing) trade of "alternative facts," "false balance," and paid skepticism to protect the interests of corporations. Their techniques were now being deployed in the service of populist politicians, who were exploiting and thereby amplifying the mistrust of experts – due to the financial crisis, due to increasing inequality and the gap between the elite and the masses; due to the internet and social media; due to relativism and post-modernism; due to the experts' own inability to communicate in plain English; the list of guilty culprits is long – to dismiss and delegitimize their opponents. Ultimately, with the Trump Administration, the attacks on "phony experts" became a full-fledged "assault on science," as declared by the Union of Concerned Scientists (UCS): the hostile takeover of the Environmental Protection

Agency (EPA) and the gagging of its experts; the retreat from the Paris Climate accords; the decision by EPA Administrator Scott Pruitt not to ban the pesticide *Chlorpyrifos* despite the contrary recommendation by the Agency's own Science Advisory Panel; the revoking or delaying of health and environmental protections based on scientific research (the Methane decision, the stream protection rule); the "transparency rule" attacking so-called "secret science" at the EPA and requiring the Agency to rely only on research for which all data has been made public (thereby excluding many important health studies that are required by law to provide research subjects with strong privacy protections); the initial omission of any funds for the NSF in Trump's proposed budget; and, to complete a full circle and return to Gove's original target, the attack on the economic forecasting models of the Congressional Budget Office (CBO).[2]

So Mr. Islam may be forgiven for pouncing on poor Michael Gove as he did. The stakes couldn't have been higher. He sensed, rightly, that we are in the midst of an all-out assault on expertise, in which populist politicians are riding the crest of a longer-term wave of disaffection, yet doing their best to amplify doubt and mistrust. In the course of the debates about Brexit, as well as in political debates in the US, there has been a not-too-subtle change in the valence of the word "expert." While in ordinary talk we may still call someone an "expert," and use the word with conviction as a superlative ("she's an expert baker"), this is no longer the case in political discourse, where the term is most often used as a pejorative, accompanied by a dismissive snort, scare quotes, or a recitation of the failures of experts. Are we witnessing, therefore, the "death of expertise," as announced by a bestseller published immediately after the dust has settled? Or is it hyperbole, the hysterical reaction of threatened elites? After all, whenever a book is published with the title "the death of ... (common sense, books, money, white privilege, or what have you)," it's a fair bet that Twain's quip holds, the reports are greatly exaggerated, and the subject of the lament is gratefully invigorated by the renewed interest in its health.[3]   •

Amidst handwringing about declining trust in experts, disregard of scientific evidence and dismissal of expert opinion, we may need to recite the obvious: that there has never been a society more reliant on expertise than our own; that experts were never more numerous and more indispensable than in our own "post-industrial," computerized, medicalized society; that scientific evidence and methods were never more integrated into the very fabric of politics. To make sense of the current impasse, we need to be a little bit more "dialectical," even though this word is decidedly out of fashion. What needs to be explained is not a one-sided "death of expertise," "mistrust of experts," or "assault on science," but the two-headed *pushmi-pullyu* of unprecedented reliance on science and expertise coupled with increased suspicion, skepticism, and dismissal of scientific findings, expert opinion, or even of whole branches of investigation.[4]

More than half a century ago, Richard Hofstadter made essentially the same observation. Anti-intellectualism in American life, he said, is "a manifestation not of a decline in [the intellectual's] position but of his increasing prominence." Among the symptoms of anti-intellectualism he included the ridicule of "eggheads," "the old Jacksonian dislike of experts and specialists," assertions that common people are just as competent as the experts ("all of us are economists by necessity"), and other rhetoric that sounds eerily familiar today. What bound all of these together, he said, "is a resentment and suspicion of the life of the mind and of those who are considered to represent it; and a disposition constantly to minimize the value of that life." Precisely because "the citizen cannot cease to need or to be at the mercy of experts ... he can achieve a kind of revenge by ridiculing the wild-eyed professor, the irresponsible brain-truster, or the mad scientist, and by applauding the politicians as they pursue the subversive teacher, the suspect scientist, or the allegedly treacherous foreign policy adviser." Contemporary observers echo Hofstadter's diagnosis. Resentment is the fuel feeding the flames of anti-expert sentiment. They see "resentful laypeople demand[ing] that all marks of achievement, including expertise, be leveled and equalized in the name of 'democracy' and 'fairness.'" Behind it all they see C. S. Lewis' *Screwtape* gleefully chortling "*I'm as good as you* ... is a useful means for the destruction of democratic societies."[5]

Far be it from me to minimize the role of resentment in history, yet in this case the diagnosis is not only partial but counter-productive. To suspicion and misgivings it retorts with belittling accusations and pejoratives. Moreover, just as even paranoids can have real enemies, so the resentful grudge can have a real basis. After all, in the *locus classicus* of the diagnosis of resentment, Nietzsche's parable of the lambs and the birds of prey, the latter *do eat* the former, even if without evil intent. Similarly, expert advice has been proven wrong, misleading, even disastrous, countless times, even if behind it were not necessarily any ulterior motives or nefarious compromises (though sometimes there were). After being told for decades by the FDA that Cyclamate, an artificial sweetener, is "generally considered safe," only to have it banned as carcinogenic in the early 1970s, then told in the mid 1980s that perhaps it was not cancer-producing after all, then a year later told by the National Academy of Sciences that it is unsafe when used with Saccharin, is it irrational for laypeople to doubt the advice and expertise of nutritionists, doctors, and medical researchers? Must their doubt be evidence of resentment?[6]

To get to the bottom of our current malaise, we need, as Hofstadter himself advised, "constant and delicate acts of intellectual surgery" by which we excise what amounts to little more than name-calling from the true sense of crisis upon which it feeds. We need to begin by cleaning our language of certain proper names that do nothing but pose an obstacle to clear thinking. The first is "facts," the opposite of which is "fake." Both need to go. How could people ignore the facts, when they stare them in the face, we ask incredulously with respect to any number of issues – vaccines, climate change, GMOs, the economic impact of Brexit, or the price tag of cutting taxes. And we blame, therefore, "fake news," calculated misinformation and outright lies. "Many persons seem to suppose," said John Dewey long ago, "that facts carry their meaning along with themselves on their face. Accumulate enough of them, and their interpretation stares out at you." This is not the case. "No one is ever forced by just the collection of facts to accept a particular theory of their meaning, so long as one retains intact some other doctrine by which he can marshal them." Moreover, when it comes to the issues at the heart of current debates, to call them "facts" is an abuse of language. They are estimates, models, predictions, forecasts, guidelines, points on a graph, expert judgments, but they are not "facts." More than anything else, they are ways of assessing and managing *uncertainty*. To call them "facts" is to say that they are indisputably the case, but who of us could really check this for ourselves? The more general point is that facts – unlike their common image as "hard," "brute" and "bare" – are precarious things that can exist only in carefully controlled environments. Only in the laboratory a fact is indisputably the case. To circulate freely in the public sphere it needs to be transformed into something else – an interpretation supported by rhetorical defenses, by the credibility of those who utter it, by the prestige of the venue in which it is uttered, by the allies it is able to marshal. "Take away from physical science its laboratory apparatus and its mathematical technique, and the human imagination might run wild in its theories of interpretation even if we suppose the brute facts to remain the same."[7]

Dewey thought that while "the power of physical facts to coerce belief does not reside in the bare phenomena," it resides nonetheless in science itself. "It proceeds from method, from the technique of research and calculation."[8] Alas, this is the second proper name we need to learn to do without, namely "science," the opposite of which is the "assault on science." Invoking "science" conjures the whole history of dramatic confrontations between courageous truth and willful ignorance – from Galileo to the Scopes "monkey trial" – and leads to branding one's opponents "deniers." Denial is resentment's daughter, a self-imposed refusal to look at what the light of science exposes. Yet, as science studies have shown, *there is no single Science, nor a single "scientific method."* There are only different sciences, each producing a different type of facts oriented to radically different uses, and each striking a different trade-off between competing epistemic virtues (precision vs. standardization, generalization vs. observational depth, etc.) This is the rational kernel contained in Bruno Latour's provocative aphorism, which warns precisely against this appeal to "science": "'Science' – in quotation marks – does not exist. It is the name that has been pasted onto certain sections of certain networks, associations that are so sparse and fragile that they would have escaped attention altogether if everything had not been attributed to them."[9]

The appeal to "science" and the moral panic about the "assault on science" are, therefore, beside the point because not all of "science" is under assault. Nobody disputes quantum mechanics, nor, for that matter, is any solid state physics discipline under assault. If one surveys the entire terrain of contemporary struggles, it is clear that they mostly center on what is called "regulatory science" and "policy science," a collection of sub-disciplines, research programs and techniques that have in common the need to arrive at a policy recommendation.

Let me use the analogy of a three-lane highway to explain the significance of this distinction. The left, fast lane, belongs to law and policy. It is a fast lane – however much we complain that "the wheels of justice turn slowly" – because law and policy need to arrive at a decision about how to act. The right, slow lane, belongs to pure scientific research (of various kinds). It is slow not simply because it takes the long view, but fundamentally because it does not need to make a decision about how to act. Instead, scientific research is carried within a peculiar temporal frame, a sort of "reversible time." There is no clear end point marking an established present as against a consummated past. At least in principle, one can always roll time back and run the experiment again, modifying another element. Put differently, pure scientific research delivers facts that are open-forward, so to speak, constantly revisable, while legal or policy decisions deliver facts that are closed. They cannot be revised (even if they are manifestly wrong), unless the whole cumbersome process of collective decision-making is set in motion again. This is because legal facts serve as the basis for decision and action, and because one needs to preserve the fragile stability of the whole framework of which they are but one node. The facts upon which people are convicted in a Court of Law often do not stand up to scientific scrutiny. The touchstone of legal evidence, eyewitness testimony, is notoriously vulnerable to cognitive biases and to influence by interrogators. Yet, the opposite is also true. Courts often reject scientific facts as inadmissible because the distance separating observations from conclusions, the necessary chain of transcriptions and deductions, is too long.[10]

The middle lane, finally, where the fast and the slow must adjust to one another (horns blaring, curses muttered under breath), belongs to *regulatory science and policy science*. While the methods used in regulatory science may seem superficially similar to the methods used in pure research, they operate within a distinct temporal frame. To bridge open-forward scientific facts with closed, actionable legal and policy facts, regulatory facts take the form of cutoffs, thresholds, guidelines, surrogate end points, acceptable risk levels, consensus documents, expert assessments, simulations, stress tests. These can become near immutable, etched in regulations and backed by legal sanctions, yet they are also inherently provisional and convention-like. The middle lane of regulatory science is thus contentious and crisis-prone precisely because it serves as the interface between scientific research, law and policy. Scientists often resort to the "long-termism" defense when sociologists of science point out the crucial role played by social mechanisms – the reliance on judgment and interpretation, the resort to interpersonal trust – in scientific research. In the long term, they say, "it all comes out in the wash," meaning that whatever bias or arbitrariness is introduced in this way, they ultimately will be detected and removed by the collective work of scientists as they scrutinize each other's research and seek to improve it. It should be obvious that this defense falls completely flat when it comes to regulatory science, where one cannot wait for the long term, and where, therefore, the social mechanisms stand exposed in the glaring light of a decision taken in the here and now. To appeal to "Science" from the midst of this contention is to misrecognize that one is in the middle lane, at the seam of inevitable friction.[11]

If we cannot appeal to the facts or to science, surely we can appeal to *expertise*. This is the premise of books like *The Death of Expertise* (despite the ominous sounding title) or of Harry Collins and his collaborators' decade-long campaign to develop a set of criteria and tests by which those who possess it could be readily distinguished from those who don't. Recognizing that the facts do not speak for themselves, they emphasize that there is only a small circle of people to whose interpretations of the facts the public should listen. The advantage of talking in terms of "expertise" rather than "science" is that this circle need not be composed only of scientists, and that we need not be overly attached to certain credentials, proper names and lines of demarcation. If certain laypersons possess relevant "experience-based expertise," say Collins and Evans, then by all means they should have the public's ear. What distinguishes these people from others is not the possession of a credential, or being a "scientist," or even the attribution of expertise by others, but the fact that they "know what they are talking about" by virtue of being active participants in the production of these facts or similar ones. They possess "contributory expertise," a set of embodied and often tacit skills acquired at great pains by being socialized into a "core set" of contributing experts, and through the experience of doing the thing that needs doing. Beyond this group, which is often not altogether eloquent when speaking in public forums, the public should listen only to people who have seriously immersed themselves in the specific linguistic variant spoken by contributing experts. While their expertise is merely "interactional," they too "know what they are talking about" to such an extent that a Turing test cannot distinguish them from contributory experts. In comparison with these two relatively small groups, the ordinary layperson possesses no firsthand knowledge of the matters involved. She would do well to listen to their advice. Indeed, the public would do well to listen to knowledgeable interactional experts who are better equipped than anybody else to identify who truly possesses expertise in the matter at hand.[12]

Collins' argument echoes Dewey's interlocutor in the 1920s debate over the role of public opinion in modern democratic societies, Walter Lippmann, for whom the public was a "phantom." Ordinary people going about their everyday lives, said Lippmann, cannot be expected to form an opinion about how "to deal with the substance of a problem … [or] make technical decisions." With regard to most of these problems, they are merely "bystanders." Their knowledge of these problems is general and superficial, while the "agents," who are actually involved in these problems in their "executive capacity" either as officials or as interested private actors, possess firsthand, detailed, substantive knowledge. All we can expect of public opinion "is to align men during the crisis of a problem in such a way as to favor the action of those individuals who may be able to compose the crisis." Efforts to educate public opinion, therefore, should concentrate on developing "the power to discern those individuals." As if anticipating the hopes that Collins and his collaborators invest in their research program, Lippmann opined that the "aim of research designed to facilitate public action is the discovery of clear signs by which these individuals may be discerned." Lippmann, who from 1931 until 1967 wrote a column syndicated in more than 200 papers reaching an audience of more than ten million, clearly saw himself as one of these "interactional experts," especially regarding economic affairs.[13]

Yet, the word "expertise" is nowhere to be found in *The Phantom Public* (the closest synonym is the one mention of "inexpertness"), and the only reference to experts is to acknowledge that they are not "always expert." This should give us pause before we hasten to place our hopes in expertise and in the meta-expertise of discerning the experts from the impostors. Before we proceed we need to look a little bit more carefully at this word – expertise – and what it purports to signify.

1

Expertise

In 1891, John Earle, the Rawlinsonian Professor of Anglo-Saxon at Oxford, surveyed the transformation of English prose, how certain words and usages decline and new ones take their place. The best kinds of "word coining," he noted, are like "spring blossoms ... too slight, delicate and ephemeral." The coinage is so subtle and promptly adopted that with a couple of iterations readers no longer notice it is a new word. The opposite happened with a "more robust and coarser sort" of word invention, more jarring and strange to the ears of readers, who couldn't fail to recognize its novelty. Among this latter sort he counted "carnalization" (the diversion of human aspirations from spiritual to material concerns), "criticaster" (for critics who are fond of praising the dead at the expense of the living) and "dispeace" (conflict). And then there was also "expertise." He quoted its appearance in an article in *The Times* on March 20, 1876 as another example of this clumsier sort of word coining, easily recognizable as an innovation and somewhat artificial and discordant to the ear.[1]

More than a century later, a *Google* search of "expertise" returns 359 million entries in 0.3 seconds. Whatever the damage it originally inflicted on Earle's delicate ear, expertise is evidently no longer an innovation; evidently, it is one of the keywords of our time. It is at the center of many lively and vigorous debates, projects and explorations. There is a "philosophy of expertise," a "psychology of expertise," and the obligatory "neuroscience of expertise." There is an avid debate about the "politics of expertise." There is a huge legal literature about who can claim expertise when testifying as expert witness, and a no less voluminous sociological and anthropological literature on expertise as a social phenomenon including also "lay expertise." Finally, there is an immense mountain of investigations, articles, books, and experiments concerning the nature of expertise and how it may be developed, at the intersection of cognitive psychology, artificial intelligence, and management theory.[2]

In the process, the meaning of "expertise" has undergone a subtle change. "Expertise" was adopted into the English language from the French, where it meant not something that one *possesses*, but something that one *does*. *Une expertise* is translated to English as appraisal, evaluation, valuation; while the English word "expertise" is translated to the French as *compétences*. In the late nineteenth century, British merchants shipping their wares across the Channel took their disputes with the French Customs Authority to Court. They were incensed to find out, however, that the Court ordered *une expertise* to be conducted – namely an appraisal of the class, origin, quality, and value of their merchandise – by local "experts," who were none other than their very competitors, French merchants and manufacturers. When first taken up into English, "expertise" still meant something that experts do, such as an inspection of handwriting to determine the authenticity of a document; determining the authorship of a painting; estimating the value of a piece of land; or an examination by a medical doctor to determine cause of death, sanity, or other medico-legal questions. This original French meaning was still evident in various English language usages well into the first decades of the twentieth century. A 1936 edition of Mencken's *The American Language* still refers to a verb, "to expertise ... meaning a survey or valuation by experts" and reports that it "is in universal use among American art or antique dealers." At the same time, however, the word began to acquire a new meaning through slippage from designating the procedure of inspection or appraisal to a shorthand for the training and experience of the specialist conducting these. It was, finally, in the course of discussions in the 1920s that "expertise" came to mean narrow, specialized, technical knowhow as opposed to generalist judgment. But even then it was hardly in common parlance. When people wanted to speak about technical knowhow, or about what experts possessed, they were just as likely to use "expertness" (and "inexpertness"), however awkward it may now sound to us.[3]

In short, "expertise" is really a very recent word. As the reader can see in Figure 1, "expertise" finally came into widespread use only in the 1960s, when discussion about "expertise" exploded, increasing by a whopping 4,300 percent from 1955 to 2000. Over the same period, in comparison, the appearance of the word "expert" has only increased by about 30 percent, while the appearance of the term "professions" in books and articles actually declined somewhat. Expertise, in fact, is so recent that Mandarin Chinese, while it has an equivalent for "expert" (專家 *zhuan jia*) and can capture some of its meanings as "expert topic" (專題 *zhuan ti*) or "specialized knowledge" (專門知識 *zhuan men zhi shi*), does not yet have a direct translation to "expertise" that captures its multifold meanings.[4]

Why this sudden interest in expertise? Why did we not have much use for a word designating the specialized skills that experts possess in, say, 1880, but now seem unable to

Figure 1 Frequency of appearance of "expertise," "expert," and "professions" in *Google Books* from 1800 to 2000[5]

do without it? What kind of societal transformation has suddenly necessitated this word? I am confident that the increased usage of "expertise" is symptomatic. It is not idle fashion or mere figure of speech. But symptomatic of what? It is tempting to conjecture that it probably reflects the transformation of modern society from an industrial into a post-industrial "knowledge society" or indeed an "expert society." Surely, the explosion of interest in expertise reflects awareness of the outsized role that experts and "expert systems" have come to play in our politics, our economy, indeed our everyday life.[6] I am not convinced by this explanation. It is too facile. After all, as can be seen in Figure 1, we have been talking about *them*, about the "experts," for quite a while. More importantly, the whole idea that a certain word "reflects" what is happening in society is sloppy. The question should really be about *pragmatics* – how the term is used – while taking into account the historical context of usage: Who was talking? To whom? For what purpose? What work did the word "expertise" do in this context that other words (like "expert" or "profession") did not? When the question is posed this way, it becomes immediately clear that the word "expertise" is useful when one is asking what makes someone an expert, or how to distinguish experts from non-experts, or whether a particular claim to the status of expert is legitimate. To put it simply: when it is fairly clear who the experts are, and how to recognize them, there is little need for a word like "expertise," for a substance noun identifying what makes one an expert. The need only arises when these matters are not clear-cut or when one would like to question them.

Let me give an example that hopefully will clarify this point, while also advancing the argument. After scouring the literature and following all the leads provided by *Google Ngram*, I am fairly confident that the first instance when "expertise" was at the center of a focused discussion was in the course of legal debate in the United States about the limits of judicial review and the deference that should be accorded to the decisions of administrative agencies. While this debate began a few years before Roosevelt's election, it became part of the struggle over the New Deal and continued well into the 1940s. The main bones of contention were the independent commissions created by the Interstate Commerce Act of

1887 – the Interstate Commerce Commission (ICC), the Federal Trade Commission (FTC), the Securities and Exchange Commission (SEC), and so on. New Dealers wanted the deliberations of these agencies to be generally immune to judicial review because they were "applying trained specialized judgment to evidence of a technical character," and therefore should not "be subjected to revision by a non-expert body." In short, they were claiming for the commissions the same status as human experts, into whose judgment the courts typically did not inquire. More precisely, they wanted the commission to be treated as a collective expert, whose opinion and judgment was represented by its higher administrators, while the actual investigations and discretion exercised by lower, technically trained officials would not need to be presented at court.[7]

But how credible was it to treat a government agency or an independent commission as equivalent to a human expert? Even champions of the commissions recognized the difficulty: "In all that has been said the expertness of expert administrators has been taken for granted. As matters stand, it may be doubtful whether the assumption is fully in accord with the facts. A recent enumeration mentions a commissioner of health in an American city who was a harness-maker; a public utilities commissioner who was a barber; a commissioner of sanitation who was a house mover; and another commissioner of health who was an undertaker. ... before we insist that expert administration be relieved from hampering interference by the judges, we should make sure that its expertness is above suspicion."[8]

Beyond the qualifications of the commissioners, opponents of the New Deal adduced even more fundamental reasons to doubt the analogy. For somebody to be considered an expert, they argued, there must be "a specialized body of knowledge which can be acquired only by study and training, and which is not possessed by the ordinary run of men." They did not find the subject matter with which the commissions dealt, often problems of valuation and rate-setting, to be so specialized as to justify a restriction on judicial review. It is typically a matter of economic and political opinion about what is "fair and reasonable," needing no specific expertise (the New Dealers, in the person of the formidable Felix Frankfurter, retorted: "rate determination is the province of economics, not lawyers.") Secondly, for somebody to be considered expert, their knowledge "must be knowledge in a substantial sense," it must contain "some reasonably objective standard of certainty." Once again, the critics denied that this was true for the expertise claimed by the commissions, "which reveals, upon close examination, that it is little more than a new formula in words ... smoothly and confidently presented." What about the situation, they added, when "the expertness of one governmental agency clashes with the expertness of another?" Or for that matter, any cases in which there is a conflict of expert views? "What are we to say when we are faced with the dilemma of choosing between two experts, each of whom has made a judgment into which, because of his expertness, the court ought not to inquire? ... The Commission must then be not only more expert than the court but also more expert than any of the contending experts if its expertise is to be of any value in resolving the conflict of expert opinion."[9]

The frequent resort to the more archaic form – "expertness" – notwithstanding, it is clear that the attempt to pass the agencies as collective experts has raised the question of *expertise* – what makes somebody an expert? What body of knowledge qualifies as expert knowledge? Can an agency of government really be treated as equivalent to an expert? Critics and proponents both emphasized that there was nothing new about courts using experts to assist them by providing opinion testimony. What was radically new was the theory according to which "administrative agencies are expert bodies ... whose findings of fact, views as to statutory policy and, to some extent, conclusions of law, should ... evoke the special deference which is due to esoteric learning and skill." Justices and legal scholars fumbled to find the right word with which to characterize the new set of problems raised by this theory. They referred just as often, as we saw, to "expertness." The term "expertise" was so new, the spelling was not yet standardized, and just as often they spelled it "expertize." Ultimately, it came to be known as "the expertise theory" (always with a definite article). Thus, the first sustained discussion of expertise was occasioned by the difficulty presented by a new and confusing claim to expert status, a claim seeking to admit into the category of experts – previously consisting of private individuals, whether scientists, professionals or businessmen, engaged in a particular practice – the incongruent figure of an agency composed of public officials with technical knowledge derived from *regulating* this practice.[10]

This seems to me to be a pattern. The enormous increase in talk about "expertise" beginning in the 1960s, as documented in Figure 1, can be traced to contexts that share some characteristics with the early New Deal episode. First, these were contexts where claims were made on behalf of entities radically different from the prototypical expert of the time. Two examples come readily to mind. There is the debate about expert systems and artificial intelligence, which had begun already in the 1950s. AI advocates claimed that computers could mimic the work of human experts and ultimately surpass them. Critics countered by developing theories of *expertise* as embodied, tacit knowledge. Then there were the challenges to the medical establishment mounted by patients' rights groups and embodied health movements beginning in the 1970s. Activists claimed that patients possessed experiential knowledge of their diseases, which organized medicine ignored at its peril. Under pressure, public health authorities often responded by incorporating patients, advocates and other stakeholders into advisory bodies. This gave rise to a debate, ranging beyond the field of health, about whether something like "lay expertise" existed; whether experience-based knowledge was a legitimate basis for claims to expertise made by laypeople.[11]

Second, these were contexts in which intense discussion of "expertise" took place because it was not clear who the experts were and how to decide between competing claims. This is especially true of the debate about scientific expert testimony, as it coincided with the explosion in mass tort litigation about "risk," beginning in the late 1960s. I will take up the subject of risk in Chapter 4. For the moment, however, I will limit myself to considering how and why debates about risk destabilized the delicate *status quo* regarding expert testimony that prevailed up till the 1960s. In deciding whether or which expert testimony was credible, courts followed a body of somewhat contradictory precedents, rules, and tests. Increasingly, they came to rely on the early twentieth-century *Frye* ruling, which enjoined them to ask whether the witness or the method enjoyed "general acceptance in the particular field"

considered. Essentially, *Frye* delegated the job of vetting the experts to the various professional associations and disciplinary societies. Yet, once the question of assessing and managing risk came before the courts, the *Frye* standard became increasingly untenable. The assessment of risk is an interdisciplinary matter and requires the mobilization of different experts and methodologies. No less importantly, risk is typically produced by science or technology itself. Consequently, tort litigation about "accidents, technological breakdowns, dangerous drugs, industrial defects, environmental pollutants and other toxic substances" almost invariably pitted one group of experts against another, leading to accusations of "junk science" and research misconduct, and turning judicial attention to the methods and procedures of regulatory science. Intense debates about *expertise* followed in the legal literature, seeking a new standard for how to evaluate the credibility of competing claims. In the early 1990s, the *Frye* standard was finally replaced by the Supreme Court's *Daubert* ruling, issued in a case involving the claim that the morning sickness drug *Benedictin* caused birth defects. At least one of the scientists who conducted the research supporting the claim was later convicted of research fraud. The new *Daubert* guidelines empower judges to look beyond "general acceptability" and to determine for themselves whether the methods and knowledge claimed by expert witnesses stand up to scientific standards of testability, peer review, known error rate, and so on. In short, from relying on the professions to vet the *experts*, the law has burdened judges with the task of evaluating *expertise*.[12]

Third, most of these contexts were connected, as was the initial New Deal episode, with the expansion of the administrative state. The 1960s and 1970s witnessed an intensified debate, which is still with us, about the role that experts play in policy-making and about how to organize the relations between science and democratic institutions. As politics become dominated by technically complex issues (rate-setting, pollution, global warming, inflation, financial regulation, GMOs), is there a role for public opinion and democratic decision-making anymore? How to draw the boundaries of legitimate debate, while guarding against domination by unelected experts and technocrats? While the main problematic was already formulated in debates in the 1920s, it has become more and more topical over time, and the boundaries of the debate have expanded from the narrow focus of social scientists and philosophers to involve politicians, social movements and the public at large. Increasingly, it has been discussed as the "politics of expertise."[13]

Let me summarize what I see as the common pattern uniting these different cases. If talk about expertise is symptomatic, it is symptomatic not of the rise of post-industrial "knowledge society," but of its *crisis*. Clearly, the common pattern is one of uncertainty about who the experts are: could administrative agencies of the government be considered experts, or is their claim to expertise bogus? How to tell whether witnesses are true experts whose opinion constitutes legitimate testimony or not? Can computers be experts? When professionals work for the government, are they speaking as experts or as ideologues? The common pattern is that discussions of expertise developed against the background of increasing instability and doubt regarding the established professions, regulatory science and similar authorities. I am afraid, therefore, that just as we cannot appeal to "the facts" or to "science," we cannot appeal to "expertise" – contributory or interactional – to serve as our guide out of the current impasse. "Expertise" cannot be the standard to which we appeal in order to sort out legitimate from illegitimate interventions in public affairs, because the word comes to us congenitally infected with the perplexity surrounding these matters. "Expertise," as was evident in the New Deal debate, is an "essentially contested" concept.[14] Different definitions or theories of expertise apportion social worth to certain actors, entities, statements and performances, and withhold it from others. Consequently, the very nature of expertise, what it is and what the term should mean is a matter of struggle and disagreement. This should suffice to explain why I will refrain in this book from providing a straightforward and unambiguous definition of expertise.

Put differently, considered historically and from the point of view of pragmatics, expertise is not a thing, not a set of skills possessed by an individual or even by a group, but *a historically specific way of talking*. It is a way of talking occasioned by a situation in which the number of contenders for expert status has increased, the bases for their claims have become more heterogeneous and uncertain, and the struggles between them have become more intense. It is a way of talking necessitated when the mechanisms of gate-keeping and adjudication between claims have become weaker and more uncertain, and yet the institutional demand for expert discourse is ever-increasing. Talking in terms of "expertise" communicates the new and urgent need to find accepted ways of adjudicating whose claim is legitimate, when the old definitions and exclusions no longer work. It is a way of talking, finally, *about the intersection, articulation and friction between science and technology on the one hand, and law and democratic politics on the other.* It points us at the problem, but it is no Ariadne's thread to lead us out of the maze of their entanglements.

   To say that expertise is not a thing but a historically specific way of talking, however, does not exempt me from trying to clarify this way of talking and thereby reshape it for current purposes. There is an entire school of thought that insists that we must treat expertise in realist fashion, as a real set of accumulated experiences, abilities, skills, and knowhow. If they are correct, then I have muddied the waters considerably, perhaps even opened the floodgates by creating the impression that expertise is "nothing but" a way of talking, merely "socially constructed." I must deal with these objections before I proceed.

2

The Debate about Expertise

At first sight, the meaning of expertise appears straightforward. Expertise is defined by *The Oxford Dictionary* as "expert skill or knowledge in a particular field." So it is a skill, an ability or knowhow that certain people, called "experts," have, while other people don't. Etymologically, "expertise" derives from the Latin *experiri*, "to try," and *expertus*, "tried," "experienced." The word "expert" first appeared in the English language in the fourteenth century as an adjective or participle meaning indeed that somebody was "tried" or "experienced." It only became a noun denoting a specific type of person in the early nineteenth century. So, etymologically, "expertise" identifies practical knowhow possessed by an individual by virtue of experience and long practice, rather than scholastic knowledge and credentials. Whenever we pick up the phone to call a plumber; whenever we bring our car to the mechanic or our laptop to the technician, we express our faith (supported by experience) that expertise is real; that some people have it in their heads and hands, and others (especially ourselves) do not. A "historically specific way of talking" won't fix my car. When the plumber is called away, expertise has left the building with him, and no amount of "articulation" is going to fix the pipes.[1]

This seems straightforward, but it is not. One difficulty has to do with the fact that in any given situation there is often more than one type of expert offering to deal with a given problem. I could have called another plumber, who might have offered a different solution. I could have watched a YouTube video by an amateur handyman, who would have explained how to diagnose and resolve the issue on my own. Remember, this was one of the objections raised by the critics in the New Deal debate. How do we decide, "when we are faced with the dilemma of choosing between two experts?" Typically, we cannot directly compare the *performances* of the competing experts (I do not want to fix my pipes twice!). We resort, therefore, to comparing *claims* to expertise by means of socially recognized signs. This means that the victors, the recognized experts, may prevail for reasons other than their actual skills. Sociologists have argued convincingly that many different groups and individuals lay claim to be recognized as experts, but that such recognition goes to only a few due to their capacity to win "jurisdictional struggles," namely struggles over who actually has control over a set of tasks. In this sense, expertise is a quality *attributed* to the experts by audiences, rather than a quality they possess on their own. The realist approach has it backwards, these sociologists would say. It is not the expertise possessed by certain people that sets them apart as experts, but being recognized as experts qualifies what they do as "expertise." I called the plumber because he is "certified" and "licensed," namely, he belongs to some sort of trade association and thus possesses some legal guarantee of his skills issued by a licensing board. He came, mucked around a little bit, put in a new pipe and left. My pipes are still leaking and I am not at all certain he knew what he was doing.[2]

An opposite difficulty has to do with the implication that only that which is socially rare counts as expertise. This too was a point originally made in the New Deal debate – if the knowledge involved was "possessed by the ordinary run of men," it couldn't count as expertise. Yet, as phenomenologists have shown, ubiquitous competencies such as speaking a natural language or "passing" as a normatively gendered person, things that most of us do as a matter of course, require the acquisition of quite complicated skills and enormous amounts of background knowledge. If you doubt this argument, think about what computers – even with all the recent fundamental breakthroughs in AI – can and cannot do well. When it comes to specialized performances, such as playing Chess or Go, computers easily outdo the best human experts, but they still cannot carry a natural conversation in idiomatic English, something that every kindergartener does without giving it a second thought. Harry Collins and his collaborators, therefore, are absolutely right that from a realist perspective expertise does not have to be a specialized sort of knowledge. It could be downright practical, everyday sort of knowledge. I knew that I had to call a plumber. I knew how to find one and how to persuade him to come to my home. I could tell he was a licensed one without looking at his papers. I could also tell he was shifty and did not know what he was doing. All of this is practical knowhow, developed through experience and "training" (socialization). It is expertise, but a ubiquitous, rather than specialist one.[3]

These two difficulties are clearly at cross-purposes. One brackets the content of expertise (the knowhow, skills and competencies involved) in order to understand how the experts are set apart from the lay. The other doubles down on realism. In order to understand expertise, it says, it is immaterial whether its possessors are recognized as experts or not. There is an additional difficulty that does not fit neatly into this divide. Acquired by virtue of experience and long practice, expertise is typically understood as practical, tacit knowhow. On one level, this is entirely convincing. When selecting a surgeon (or a plumber), we all look for one who has performed the relevant procedure multiple times. We recognize that book knowledge (or YouTube knowledge), knowledge of the general rules, is the mark of the novice. True expertise, by contrast, consists of a "feel" for the relevant details in a complex whole, a feel that could only be acquired through experience and cannot be fully verbalized. This accords with the etymology of "expertise," as noted earlier. Yet, if tacit knowledge is the mark of true experts, how can we be confident of the soundness of their advice? If expertise involves "an understanding of rules that cannot be expressed," shouldn't we be legitimately suspicious? When I ask the plumber how he knows that the pipe needs to be replaced, he mutters something about how in three out of four cases it is always the pipe that needs to be replaced, and how the pipe "sounds" cracked. He invites me to listen.

I hear nothing alarming, but he gives me a look that plainly says, "Keep to what you know best, Professor, and leave the pipes to me." This, too, bothered the critics in the New Deal debate, who demanded that for somebody to be considered expert, their knowledge "must be knowledge in a substantial sense," it must contain "some reasonably objective standard of certainty." "Absent this, there is, of course, no way in the world of knowing whether the expert has any idea what he is talking about." Astrologists, too, can claim that their reading of the stars, the tea leaves or what have you, involves "an understanding of the rules that cannot be expressed."[4]

Tacit knowledge is, in fact, the norm. As a condition of going about our everyday business, we do not make explicit the background knowledge upon which we draw. Arguably, it is impossible to make explicit many of the ubiquitous forms of expertise. Ask an English speaker to explain to you how to speak English, or how to ride a bike. The real riddle, as Harry Collins argues convincingly, is not tacit knowledge, but how some forms of knowledge are made explicit. Yet, we expect of our experts that they would be able to explicate and defend their diagnoses and decisions. An English speaker does not need to explicate her knowledge of speaking English. Her speaking is evidence enough. But experts inhabit multiple forums where such explication is mandatory. Think of giving expert opinion testimony in court, or sitting on an advisory expert committee. Indeed, what experts often do is give advice and opinion, that is, they explicate. In these forums, and in jurisdictional struggles more generally, for claims to expertise to possess prima facie plausibility, it *must be possible* to formulate and express the rules.[5]

A final, related difficulty, discussion of which I need to postpone for later in this book (Chapter 4), is: as noted above, much of what is meant by "expertise" is not captured by the plumber example because it involves the giving of advice, opinion, assessment, and "technical assistance." In these situations, the expert is typically called upon to speak not about what she routinely does and knows best, but about a new problem, only one aspect of which is germane to her area of expertise.

A good example is the case of radioactive contamination of the Cumbrian Fells, studied by Brian Wynne. The Chernobyl nuclear accident in 1986 released a radioactive cloud, which passed over the UK and rained radiocaesium deposits over upland areas. Sheep grazing in these areas began to show elevated levels of radiocaesium, which led to a ban on slaughtering the sheep and selling the meat. The nuclear scientists consulted by the government predicted confidently that the contamination would not last longer than three weeks, so there was no need for compensation or a relocation plan. The sheep farmers, whose livelihoods were at stake, were not convinced and predicted a much longer, perhaps indefinite contamination. They turned out to be correct, and the nuclear scientists spectacularly wrong, with some of the sheep showing elevated levels even six years later. The scientists were wrong because, while they knew a lot about the behavior of radioactive materials, they knew very little about other aspects of the problem, namely the type of soil in the hill areas; the behavior of caesium in this soil; the local vegetation; what sheep ate and where they typically grazed. At least some of these aspects were things about which the sheep farmers knew a lot more. To arrive at a correct assessment of contamination risk, it was necessary to know what the scientists knew, plus what the sheep farmers knew, plus a great deal more that was not yet known. So, the scientists' advice and assessments were wrong, until they began to listen to the sheep farmers. By this time, however, their credibility was damaged.[6]

This is why Niklas Luhmann says, as quoted in the epigraph to this book, that "an expert is a specialist to whom one can put questions that he is unable to answer." Less cynically, the point is that we often speak of expertise in a promissory mode, not as something that exists but as something that needs to be developed. The rapid pace of scientific and technological development creates numerous new problems that law and policy must address, in regard to which nobody is expert, yet expertise is the only legitimate way to address them.[7]

These difficulties explain why the meaning of expertise is not altogether straightforward and why there are different theories of expertise. These can be organized in a neat two-by-two table, on the basis of two disputes: first, is expertise inside or outside individuals? Second, is it practical, tacit, embodied, situational knowledge, or is it a body of general,

Table 1 Typology of Theories of Expertise

		What makes expert knowledge different from lay knowledge?	
		Explicit, abstract knowledge ("theory")	Tacit, practical knowledge
Where is expertise?	Inside individuals	Early AI and expert systems research	Phenomenology, critique of AI (Hubert Dreyfus)
	Outside individuals	Sociology of professions	Distributed cognition, ANT

explicit rules formulated at a high level of abstraction (AKA "theory")?

The two-by-two table in Table 1 represents in static, frozen fashion, what was in fact a dynamic process of debate, struggle and position-taking. Beginning from the top left-hand box, early artificial intelligence and expert systems research represented expertise as a set of general, abstract rules that, when applied to specific facts, generated a specific diagnosis or a decision with a high degree of confidence. Drawing on research in cognitive psychology that suggested "that experts reason at a more abstract or principled level than novices," computer scientists interviewed experts to elicit rules that would be encoded in an algorithm. This process came to be known as "knowledge acquisition," or "knowledge elicitation." The very imagery of "elicitation" implied that expertise resides inside experts, in the form of increasingly abstract and generalized representations developed as a result of experience, practice, and trial-and-error. The knowledge elicited was used to build decision-support systems for other experts. The first such expert system was MYCIN, a computer program designed to assist doctors in selecting antibiotics for patients with severe infections. The program presumably aggregated all knowledge about infectious diseases and their treatment in the form of 500 rules. The rules took the conditional and branching form of a decision tree. For example, "(i) if the infection is meningitis and (ii) organisms were not seen in the stain of the culture and (iii) the type of infection may be bacterial and (iv) the patient has been seriously burned, then there is suggestive evidence that *Pseudomonas aeruginosa* is one of the organisms that might be causing the infection."[8]

Two things are noteworthy about this early effort to build expert systems. First, despite the connection with research in cognitive psychology, this conception of expertise as a set of explicit, abstract, general rules was much less descriptive than *prescriptive*. It was not necessarily intended as a description of what expertise "really" is, how human experts actually think. Early AI researchers and designers of expert systems were aware that expert knowledge is often tacit. They knew, from the research of cognitive psychologists, as well as from the frustrating task of "knowledge elicitation," that experts find it difficult to verbalize rules that apply across contexts (though they can explicate their thought processes regarding specific tasks). But they thought that these were limitations that should be overcome. They thought that expert knowledge could be improved by encoding it in a computer program, because in this way it would become "explicit and public": "Indeed, one of the most important results of this enterprise may be the development of ways to express formally, and to record systematically, knowledge that is usually unexpressed and unrecorded." This is tantamount to saying what expertise should be – public, explicit, objective – rather than what it is. Put differently, when you scrape the thin coating of description and definition, what you discover underneath is something much more fundamental and solid – *a normative, indeed political, vision of the role that expertise should play in society, and a prescription of how to generate trust in expertise.*[9]

The second noteworthy point is that early expert systems provided the initial impetus for theories of expertise. It was the gambit from which the whole debate unfolded. Especially the theories in the top right-hand box were developed as explicit rebuttal of the claims of early AI and expert systems developers. This is in line with the point I made earlier: talking about expertise, asking what it is, only began when a difficulty was introduced: could computers be considered experts? Could they replace human experts or just support them? Would their addition improve upon human experts and require them to change (for example, because computers make the basis for expert decisions explicit, generalizable, objective, and thus more trustworthy)?

Moving to the top right-hand box, thinking about expertise as practical, embodied, tacit knowledge possessed by experts has roots in phenomenology, but it was first formulated as a critique of early AI and expert systems. The critics wielded Wittgenstein's famous demonstration of the impossibility of "following a rule" as a cudgel, with which they proceeded to destroy the obviousness of codifying expertise in general abstract rules. As is known to anyone who has tried to put together a piece of furniture from IKEA, in order to "follow a rule," one needs to make multiple little decisions. When the instructions are to connect the handle to the pre-drilled holes on the "left," does this mean left when viewed from the front or when viewed from the back? And which is the front, anyway? I search the diagram for orientational clues that would indicate which is the right way, and I also draw on my experience with putting together furniture (the numerous mistakes I've made in the past, the wobbly chair that stares at me reproachfully as a reminder). The difficulty is that, inescapably, the rule is composed of indexical expressions ("here," "now," "this"), that is, expressions whose meaning depends on the situation (who's saying what to whom? When? From what angle, side or perspective? Pointing at what?) If we were to write down a set of rules about how to interpret these indexical expressions, the exercise would quickly ramify to infinity. If we were to try to write a completely trans-contextual rule without any indexical expressions, no one would know how to follow it. Put differently, each rule comes with a *ceteris paribus* ("other things being equal ...") clause. If you open the clause and look inside, you will be staring down the abyss of infinite regress.

And yet, we do appear to follow rules. We speak fairly grammatically correct English, most of the time at least. I do put together IKEA furniture – however long it takes and at whatever emotional toll to me and my loved ones. The "condition of possibility of all rule-like activity," phenomenologists argue, is a "background of practices." I *just know* how to fit the handle in the right way, because I have done this many times (and learned from my errors); because one particular way "feels right" as I try it out different ways; because normally you would expect instructions to orient you from the front, unless explicitly told to turn the damn thing around (though "do it yourself" kits that come from other countries, with instructions written by members of a different culture, can often prove baffling precisely because these expectations prove incorrect). This means standing on its head the venerable tradition according to which learning is a process of abstraction: you start with specific cases and gradually abstract and interiorize more universal rules. For someone like Hubert Dreyfus, the process of acquiring expertise is exactly the opposite. You start with abstract rules and end with particular cases. While novices begin by learning a set of rules, what differentiates the true expert from the novice is the embodied and tacit mastery of the practices that the rules attempt imperfectly to codify. Put differently, when people or computers attempt to follow rules, they act like novices, and they fumble. Expertise, on the other hand, consists of a vast stock of knowledge of specific situations and the honed, embodied, emotionally involved intuition that allows the expert immediately to "see" which situational *details* are important, what needs to be done and how to get there.[10]

A couple of notes about the phenomenological approach, AI, and their entanglements, before continuing to the next box in the table: though formulated as a critique of AI and expert systems, it could also be seen as *fieldwork* for it. Computer scientists, as we saw, were not strongly attached to a description of what expertise is, but to what it should be. The frustrations of knowledge elicitation and the poor performance of first-generation AI were enough to convince them that the critics had a point. AI engineers discovered that they had to read Dreyfus, ethnomethodology, sociology, and social studies of science, learning from them about the context-bound nature of expertise. And they began adapting the procedures of knowledge elicitation in accordance with what they've learned. So, what appears at first sight as being an irreconcilable clash of perspectives could become, over time, productive collaboration through a shared perspective. By the same token, once the task of knowledge elicitation is accomplished, expertise is no longer inside the expert, but distributed in an expert system consisting, at a minimum, of the machines, the experts whose knowledge is used to formulate the algorithm, the algorithm itself, the technicians or users who digitize the input, and the experts or users who interpret and repair the output. So, the opposition I will detail below can also become attenuated and reconciled over time.[11]

Going diagonally now to the bottom left-hand box, the understanding of expertise in the sociology of professions developed independently of the debate about AI and expert systems, yet it constituted a stark challenge to both sides. Once you begin thinking about professions and why they are organized the way they are, it is no longer obvious that expertise is "inside" the expert. It is rather an external quality attributed to them by others and residing in the disciplinary "knowledge system" belonging to the corporate professional group. Social recognition conferred by relevant and authoritative audiences (clients, state agencies, universities, other experts, the media) is what qualifies one as a professional, not the knowhow and skills that one possesses. As in the Judgment of Paris, there is often little connection between the real merits of the contestants and who ends up with the prize. Obtaining such social recognition requires that the corporate group of professionals exercise some control over the *supply* of expertise (control over the training and certification of experts; control over the distribution of expert knowledge and skills), and over the *demand* for it (the capacity to define clients' needs and the aims of expert action; the ability to require that organizations employ certified professionals in order to be accredited). Experts organize themselves in corporate groups to exercise these forms of control, and ultimately to obtain and defend sole *jurisdiction* over certain tasks.[12]

From this point of view, the phenomenologists' equation of expertise with tacit, embodied knowledge seems suspicious. It echoes centuries-old arguments that guilds and crafts mobilized to protect their monopoly over certain tasks and work processes. It can be plausibly read as a defense of the jurisdiction of certain professions against encroachments by computer scientists and engineers. Moreover, from this point of view what distinguishes modern experts from older crafts and guilds is precisely the degree of abstraction of their knowledge. Abstraction is a much more potent weapon in jurisdictional struggles, as compared with practical mastery, because it allows much greater flexibility in defining a jurisdiction. As Andrew Abbott argues: "Only a knowledge system governed by abstractions can redefine its problems and tasks, defend them from interlopers and seize new problems." If one's expertise is tied to certain specific techniques, work processes or contexts (Abbott's example is the long-since defunct occupation of railway surgeons), one is liable to become obsolete when techniques change, new technologies are introduced, or other experts deploy abstractions to redefine what one does as merely one instance of a larger category of which they are in control. Expertise, thus, is doubly external to the expert. It is a quality attributed by others, and it resides in the disciplinary knowledge system composed of abstractions and general rules.[13]

Finally, if expertise is not located within individuals, but in the relationships between them, it would seem unduly narrow to conceive of these relations only as claims and attributions, relevant only to how experts secure recognition and protect their jurisdiction. Why not consider also the experts' practical skills and tacit knowhow from a relational perspective? In the bottom right-hand box, we find those anthropologists and cognitive psychologists who have developed concepts of "distributed cognition," as well as the philosophers and sociologists who practice Actor-Network Theory (ANT). The task of flying a commercial airliner, for example, is performed not by a pilot *per se*, but by a "distributed socio-technical system" composed of two pilots and the cockpit's instrumentation (and one could add also the control tower, and other factors). A small part of this instrumentation are the speed cards and "speed bugs" used by the pilots to accomplish the task of coordinating airspeeds with wing configurations at different weights. Speed bugs are not "memory aids." They do not enhance the pilot's memory. What they do is transform the pilot's task from remembering critical speeds to making judgments of spatial proximity (how close is the dial hand to the bug). Remembering is no longer something that the pilot does, but the cockpit instruments. Originally lodged in the expert, the cognitive competence of memory has been redistributed to a constellation of humans and instrumentation. This is not de-skilling, but redistribution of expertise. Embodied skill is still necessary, but it has been reorganized by the instrumentation, into which are codified certain rules and procedures.[14]

By the same token, however, the instruments and tools become extensions of the expert's body. Some anesthesiologists, for example, prefer to continue to use manual ventilators (even when mechanical ones are available) because the tactile feedback from the ventilation bag enables them to judge the depth of the narcosis. Essentially, they use the anesthetic bag as a diagnostic instrument, like a stethoscope. The manual ventilator or the stethoscope become "ready-to-hand" or "ready-to-ear." They "withdraw" in use to become incorporated as an extension of the skilled expert's body. This line of thinking can be traced back to Heidegger and Merleau-Ponty, or, perhaps more surprisingly, to Dewey's critique of the dualism of individual and society: "A collective unity may be taken *either* distributively *or* collectively, but when taken collectively it is the union of its distributive constituents, and when taken distributively, it is a distribution of and within the collectivity. It makes nonsense to set up an antithesis between the distributive phase and the collective."[15]

Two-by-two tables are wonderful tools for organizing one's thoughts. The moment, however, that all the boxes are filled, they become an obstacle to thinking. They are static, and by definition divide reality into neat little boxes sealed from one another. Luckily, there is a simple solution. Remove the outer line enclosing the grid and you get, instead of a table, the diagram of an open field crisscrossed by opposing forces pushing and pulling in different directions. On this open space it is possible to begin to think in terms of continua, variables, ranges, movements from one point to another, "resting points" where the opposing forces temporarily balance, and counter-movements which upset the balance.

On this field, as represented in Figure 2, we no longer need to keep the distributed cognition and/or actor-network theories tucked in the lower, right-hand corner. After all, they think in terms of assemblages or socio-technical systems composed of *both* human experts and instruments. To paraphrase Dewey, they think in terms of a distributed phase and an assembled phase, between which "it makes nonsense to set up an antithesis." They also show how the speed cards and speed bugs encode explicit rules and abstract formulae into the embodied practices of the pilot. ANT completes the mediation between abstract and practical knowledge by demonstrating how embodied practices are transcribed into abstractions. An abstraction is what Latour calls "an immutable and combinable mobile," that is, something that can move from context to context without changing. Latour's example is the map. You can take it with you anywhere, compare it to your surroundings, and use it to find your way. Yet, the map you hold in your hand is the product of a long chain of transcriptions (naval expeditions along the coast, land surveying, measuring, satellite imagery, and so on), each consisting of entirely practical devices and concrete forms of reasoning. Each transcription causes the new inscription to lose certain qualities possessed before and endows it with new ones, until it gradually becomes mobile, combinable and "liquid."[16]

On this field it becomes possible to represent a second round, as it were, of the debate. Each "pure" theory gives rise to a modified and nuanced version of its former self. While it may still accentuate certain distinctions, the modified version ultimately incorporates some of the insights of its

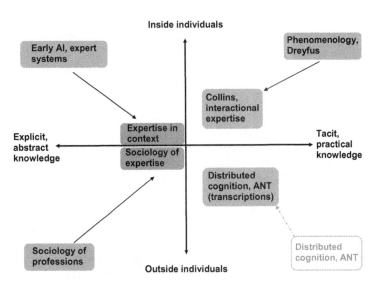

Figure 2   The debate about expertise

antagonists and thus draws closer to them coming to cohabit a common zone at the center. AI and expert systems researchers are, perhaps, the most explicit and honest about needing to modify their original position and learn from others. They have found out the hard way, they report, that knowledge, and especially expert knowledge, cannot always be written down in rules and, therefore, that what computers or expert systems do cannot be treated as a veridical simulation of how human experts think or work. They realized that experts actually have no use for highly abstract, extremely general rules. "Their preferred level for processing is actually a 'moderately abstract level' of representation." Seeking a more realistic model of human expertise, they have turned to sociology, phenomenology, ethnomethodology, and cognitive psychology, from which they have learned that expertise is socially attributed, embodied, situated in ecological niches, and distributed. They sum this up by saying that "though individuals' expertise is indeed in their heads, the meaning of the expertise does not reside in the individuals, but rather arises in a dynamic interaction matrix involving the individual and his physical/cultural domain. Thus, when studying expertise, the minimum unit of analysis is the 'expert in context'."[17]

A similar move towards the center has been undertaken by Harry Collins and Robert Evans' program for "studies of expertise and experience," specifically by their introduction of the idea of "interactional expertise." Unlike "contributory experts," the possessors of interactional expertise lack practical competence in a given specialist domain. They do not know how to run the experiments. They couldn't fix the pipe themselves. You shouldn't give them the keys to the cockpit. What they can do, however, is *converse* about this specialist knowledge in a fully competent and interesting way. Competence means that they can pass a Turing test. They have achieved a level of fluency in the special linguistic dialect of the domain that is indistinguishable from that of a contributory expert. They can converse about pipes, drains, wrenches, and clogged toilets at a level of detail such that even a trained and experienced plumber would not be able to tell that they are amateurs. Indeed, the plumber would enjoy the conversation and might even learn something – this is what is meant by "interesting."[18]

Interactional experts have acquired this competence by having undergone "enculturation within a linguistic community," that is, something less than full immersion in the form of life of the contributory experts, but more than merely textbook knowledge. They have not undergone practical training as airline pilots or gravitational wave physicists but, like ethnographers, project managers, or science journalists, they have logged countless hours of talking with them, in detail, and observing how they go about their work. The concept of interactional expertise thus relaxes the opposition between practical, tacit knowledge and explicit, abstract, rule-like knowledge. It moves leftward into the intermediate common zone at the center. Yet, it also moves downward, relaxing the opposition between inside and outside. Even though Collins and Evans insist that expertise is a real and substantive possession (rather than a mere attribution) of experts, the necessity of enculturation clarifies that expertise is possessed by individuals only by virtue of being members of a specialist group. Here, too, the expert is an embodied or distributed phase, not to be set up against the collected phase. Expertise is acquired in a social process of "socialization into the practices of an expert group," and an individual may lose expertise if he or she is disconnected from the group of experts. By the same token, if expertise did not exist primarily as a group phenomenon (though inscribed within individuals) there could be no "interactional expertise." Given that Collins also includes machines within these collectives, with human actors digitizing their input and repairing their output, expertise moves even further out of the individual and into the coordinated activities of these collectives.[19]

Finally, once the sociology of professions encountered the phenomenon of "lay expertise," that is, non-professionals who, despite their lack of credentials, come to play a crucial role in the performance of professional tasks, it began drifting as well towards the center. It became clear that even as professions hold formal jurisdiction over certain tasks, actually to accomplish these tasks requires the cooperation of multiple actors, many of whom possess practical, hands-on knowledge of concrete contexts. Too much abstraction is detrimental to the control of jurisdiction or to coordinating with other actors. Expertise consists in an "optimal level of abstraction" (similar to the computer scientists' "moderately abstract level" of representation). Ultimately, it became possible for sociologists to move beyond the limited conceptualization of expertise as attributed quality, and to consider the realist meaning of expertise as *capabilities*, but in a relational way. Capability is an underlying property that is observed by means of the actions that it makes possible. Expertise, specifically, stands for the capacity to carry out certain specialized tasks that are either impossible to carry out in its absence, or that are performed better, faster and with greater certainty of desired outcomes in its presence. Logically speaking, there is no reason why an account of capability should stop at the boundary of the expert's body. A full description of the conditions necessary in order to fly a jetliner, as we saw, would include the instrumentation (including speed cards and speed bugs), the actions and communications of other actors (the second pilot, air traffic controllers), the conceptual system (including maps) by means of which communication and coordination takes place, and so on and so forth. In short, to account for the capability underlying expert statements and performances it is necessary to posit a network of expertise composed of other actors, devices and instruments, concepts, and institutional and spatial arrangements, distributed in multiple loci yet assembled into a coherent collective agency. This network reaches all the way to interactions with the audiences and the clients, whose cooperation (and not only recognition) is essential to performing the task.[20]

If there is so much agreement, why all the heat? Why the acrimonious debate and accusations flying back and forth? The answer is that the debate is about something else altogether. It is not about what expertise *is*, but about what it *should be*. Work on expert systems, as we saw, was driven less by a clear understanding of the nature of expertise, than by a political vision which demanded that for expertise to play its proper role it must be explicit, public, and objective. Similarly, Collins and Evans say that their goal is to come up with "prescriptive ... statements about the role of expertise in the public sphere." The statements they come up with privilege experience and specialization as key to addressing technical matters of public concern. On the left-hand, lower side, the research on "lay expertise" saw itself as championing the ignored voices of patients, parents, sheep farmers, and activists, leading to a more inclusive vision of expertise. And on the right-hand lower side, ANT has been elaborating its own version of the "politics of things": a technical or "object oriented" democracy, wherein "hybrid forums" composed of experts and lay stakeholders assemble to equip themselves with expertise as a socio-technical prosthesis. These hybrid forums represent an enriched "democracy that can pick up the challenges of the sciences and technologies."[21]

What we need to do is to magnify the center of Figure 2 and ignore its periphery. When we do so, what appeared before as minute nuances and hairsplitting, the much ridiculed scholasticism of academics, emerges in sharp focus as a debate about the relations between technical knowledge and democracy, the role of expertise in the public sphere. The disagreements are, in fact, so sharp, Figure 3 seems almost like a two-by-two table once again.

The vertical axis represents what Collins and Evans called "the problem of extension." Namely, in a world where science no longer enjoys automatic credibility, and where competing claims to expertise clash, how far to extend the boundaries

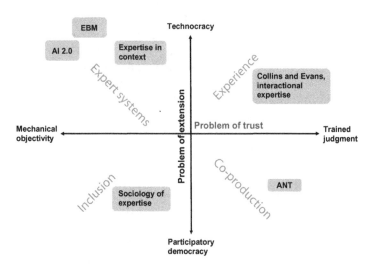

Figure 3 The debate about expertise in the public sphere

of participation in debate about technical matters of public concern? Is there a relatively objective way of deciding whose advice we should heed? To put it bluntly, in the matter of global warming, should all opinions enjoy equal weight? Or, viewed from the other side, not unlike Lippmann and Dewey in their time, how should ordinary citizens be involved in decisions about technical matters? In a world where it is no longer acceptable to limit debate and decision only to "the scientists," how should we educate, support, and/or equip ordinary members of the public so they may have an informed view on the matter? This is one of the fundamental dilemmas of our times. The polar positions – technocracy and participatory democracy – are irreconcilable, unstable, and, consequently, are not embraced wholeheartedly by anybody. Yet they exercise their forces of attraction and repulsion on intermediate positions.[22]

The horizontal axis represents what may be called "the problem of trust" (or credibility, or legitimation, or reputation – the relative merits of these terms will be discussed in coming chapters). Every debate about technical matters of public concern is bound to expose, unfurl, the extent to which the normal goings of social life, from routine everyday actions to policy decisions, are embedded in complex socio-technical systems run by experts. Not only is it difficult for ordinary individuals to grasp the complex details of one such system, it is virtually impossible for one individual to do so with respect to *all* such systems, and it is *necessarily impossible* as a condition of going about one's daily affairs. Some form and measure of trust in far-flung, complex systems and the experts who design and run them is, therefore, an inescapable dimension of the modern condition. When my daughter is complaining of not feeling well, I take her temperature and give her a Motrin (an over-the-counter fever reducer). I may be vaguely aware of the existence of regulatory bodies and procedures to guarantee standard measures for temperature, reliability of thermometers, the safety and efficacy of medications, but I give these no serious consideration at the moment. I simply trust that the thermometer and the pill are and do what they purport to do by virtue of the operation of these systems, of which I have only the vaguest notion. Yet, if something goes awry, I may wonder what exactly has inspired my trust and whether it was justified. A debate about technical matters of public concern would force a reflexive interrogation of the bases of such trust – should we place our trust in the systems or in the experts who run them? Should we design the systems to operate on the basis of explicit, transparent procedures, free as much as possible from human judgment and biases, or do we place our trust instead in the reasoned judgment of experts (whether credentialed or experience-based) equipped with a disciplinary stock of knowledge? Do we "trust in numbers" or do we "trust in experts"? When deciding whether new medications are effective and safe, or whether annual mammograms are necessary for women under fifty, do we rely on the judgment of the best experts in the field, or do we rely on randomized controlled trials, epidemiological evidence, and standard decision rules? Once again, the polar positions are untenable, but the dilemma is real.[23]

The two dilemmas are orthogonal to one another. Being in favor of certain limits on public participation does not prejudge whether one trusts in experts or in numbers and procedures. Collins and Evans want to limit decision-making mostly to a core-set of experts (including the non-credentialed), whose experienced judgment they consider to be the best available. Yet, a professional movement like Evidence-Based Medicine (EBM) tilts the balance in favor of explicit, standardized procedures and objective, numerical decision rules, while not necessarily increasing public participation in the setting of these rules. On one side, the prototypical image is of *expert systems*; on the other, it is of core-sets of *experienced* experts.[24]

Similarly, privileging expert judgment does not pre-judge whether one seeks to limit or increase participation. The assemblages of affected individuals and experts envisioned by ANT are definitely tilted in favor of greater participation, but ANT displays no particular love of objective measurement and procedures. In the best example of this approach – the French Muscular Dystrophy Association (AFM) – parents and activists participate in research, indeed they control its direction. For years they were told by the relevant scientists that nothing could be done for their children because the mechanisms and causes of the condition were not yet understood. Yet, the parents knew that there was a lot that *could* be done – maybe not to cure their children, but to prolong their lives, to improve their quality of life, and to lessen the burden on the families. One should conduct fundamental research on the genes involved, no doubt, but there should be also research on factors and technologies that prolong and improve life as it is. And when fundamental research shows promise, even if it is still tentative, there should be serious effort dedicated to developing applications. So, the parents took matters into their own hands. They formed an association wherein the scientists and experts, organized in an advisory scientific council, were subordinated to the lay Board, composed of parents who have become "lay experts." The Board controlled the direction of research, as well as when it was time to move from pure research to application, whatever uncertainties still remained. The judgment of these lay experts (in dialogue with the scientific experts), not objective procedure, was the key factor. Research remained subordinated to the overall "strategic table" of proximate and longer-term objectives dictated by the parents. The two sides, parents and scientists, engaged each other in a process of *co-production*, that is, "discovery" a-la-Dewey. Neither the goals (research objectives), nor the means (the relevant expertise), were known in advance, before the two sides began speaking to one another. Hence, the laypersons and the scientists engaged in a truly meaningful dialogue, out of which both sides emerge changed.[25]

Collins and Evans' approach, in comparison, is definitely tilted in favor of limiting participation. They separate the political and technical as two different phases of decision making about technical matters of public concern. Stakeholders are limited to the political phase, and are not permitted to trespass into the technical phase, which is ruled by *experience*. Moreover, the terms they establish for conversation between scientists and members of the public seem one-sided because interactional expertise is distinctly "less" than contributory expertise. Interactional expertise is like passing a Turing test, a test where one side possesses all the relevant knowledge and the other side seeks to produce a convincing imitation. Put differently, the goals may not be known, but the means are.[26]

Finally, being in favor of increased participation fits quite conveniently with an emphasis on standardization, objective procedures, and transparency. Here is where standardization of expert knowledge meets with standardized procedures for representation and *inclusion* as, for example, in the mandatory representation of stakeholders (patients, parents, activists) in advisory bodies formulating medical guidelines. The goals are known, but the means must be discovered.

I have come, therefore, full circle, though not without profit. By delving into the descriptive debate about what is expertise, I have arrived back at where Chapter 1 ended, namely the political debate about the relations between technical knowledge and democracy. The word "expertise" has evolved in order to chart the changes taking place in these relations, the emergence of new claims and new contenders, the transformations of trust and credibility, the changes in the conduits through which knowledge flows into the public sphere. It records the tensions to which they give rise, but it does not contain any secret core, any formula for sorting them out. Nonetheless, the discovery of a common zone at the center of Figure 2 is useful. The disagreement about what *is* expertise has not proven as robust as the disagreement about what it *should be*. To account for expertise as a capability would require an analytical framework that brings together conditions internal to the expert – training, tacit knowledge, embodied skills – and that are the product of socialization into a group of experts. But the analytical framework would also include conditions external to the expert – the socio-technical system of which the expert is but one part, the chains of transcriptions by which abstractions are generated, the disciplinary body of knowledge composed of such abstractions, the audiences who ratify, amplify, and redistribute expert statements and performances. These sets of conditions can be taken distributively, in terms of their multiple locations and implications, or they can be taken collectively, in terms of their assembly into a coherent agency.

This chapter began with the realist meaning of expertise, because I felt that I needed to deal directly with the argument that it could anchor a normative approach to the contemporary crisis. A good grasp of what is expertise, it was suggested, would allow – in the manner long ago suggested by Lippmann – to draw the line where increased participation in public debate about technical matters was no longer advisable.

Crucially, it would provide a reasoned account of in whom and under what circumstances we should place our trust. Yet, behind the realist meaning of expertise I discovered no such touchstone. Instead, I discovered a distributed set of actors, conditions and operations, only temporarily and provisionally assembled and embodied by an expert. I discovered a built-in dilemma of trust, not an answer as to whom and what we should trust. The next task, therefore, is unavoidable: before we ask whom and what we *should* trust, we need to ask what *is* trust? Under what conditions do people trust in experts or expertise and under what conditions and for what reasons they do not?

3

Trust

Talking about trust is the inverse, the mirror image, of talking about expertise. "If we only knew what expertise is," one says, "we would know whom to trust." "If we only knew what trust is," its mirror image counters, "we would know how to communicate and signal expertise." In expertise, one seeks an objective criterion that separates the credible from the untrustworthy. With trust research, the promise is that we could build upon the subjective, psychological mechanisms of attributing credibility. The realist theory of expertise focuses our attention on *mistrust*. Why do people mistrust experts, it asks, given experts' real skills and all the tangible benefits that reliance on expertise has provided? For those who conduct research on "trust in science," however, the real question is not why do people mistrust experts, but why would they ever trust them to begin with? This is a valuable insight. Mistrust is not the puzzle. Trust, the "leap of faith," is. By bemoaning the "assault on science" and the loss of trust in experts, we may be underestimating the problem of securing and keeping this trust to begin with.

The image of the scientist as a virtuous, self-denying, lonely seeker after the truth is long gone, and has been replaced by the "moral equivalence of the scientist," namely by the awareness that scientists are after the same things as other humans – power, fame, income. More importantly, decades of sociological research have shown that "the very things which give academic science its strength," namely trust among scientists and reliance on trained judgment, "are the characteristics which make it suspect in practical circumstances," especially with respect to regulatory science.[1]

A great deal of "normal science" depends on trust between scientists. Scientists cannot check for themselves each and every detail within another's work upon which they may be building. If they did, the pace of scientific advance would grind to a halt. They rely on informed trust, on reputation, on collective assessments of the skills, meticulousness, and integrity of other scientists within their "core-set." This is called "virtual witnessing," because the gentlemanly code of conduct of science seems to imply that testimony by another (virtuous) scientist is as good as seeing for oneself. But internal trust does not translate to external trust, quite the contrary. In the public eye, and especially in adversarial contexts (courtrooms, commissions of inquiry) this can easily appear as collusion, or at best as negligence, not doing one's due diligence.[2]

And the public would not be altogether wrong. When a scientist who is judged to be trustworthy by his peers reports a finding, typically nobody is going to bother to replicate it, especially since journals are not interested in publishing "mere replications." When the Reproducibility Project actually went through the painstaking task of replicating one hundred well-regarded psychology studies, it found a significant result in only 36 percent of replications and even in these the effect size was typically much smaller than in the original study. The problem is not limited to psychology. John Ioannidis and his colleagues have modeled the effects of small sample sizes, reliance on small effect sizes, confirmation bias, non-replication, and conflict of interests, compounded by the perverse incentives of "publish and perish," to conclude that "most reported research findings are false," or at least overblown. Their demonstration and results – relevant for all research that employs statistical methods and reports p-values, but especially for medical research, including genetics – are sobering.[3]

Similarly, trained judgment is inevitable in scientific work. The results of experiments and observational studies do not "speak for themselves," but require expertise, honed by experience, to interpret and transform. At multiple points, trained judgment is called upon to make decisions about how the data needs to be corrected, missing values included or not, curves smoothed and weights applied. This expertise is often tacit, or relies on conventions shared by those practicing "normal science" in the particular field of research. But if this means that the scientist cannot fully explicate the grounds for her judgment or explain why another scientist arrived at a different, though equally legitimate, judgment, the scientist can easily be made to look biased and arbitrary. Scientists aware of these weaknesses usually fall back on the defense of "long-termism," namely that while all of this is true, in the long run "it all comes out in the wash" and "the truth will out." Not only is this not quite reassuring, it simply makes no sense with respect to regulatory science and policy expertise, where research is geared towards informing a decision about how to act in the here and now, and where the demand for "more science" can be a stalling device (as with second-hand cigarette smoke or climate change). If my anti-diabetes drug is poisoning me, I am not likely to be heartened by the thought that sometime after my demise the "truth will out" and the mistakes in judgment or the undue trust will be corrected. I am far more likely to demand action now and to suspect the scientists of self-serving motives.[4]

And a body of recent research would support my suspicions as not far off the mark. About 70 percent of 500 recent trials of top-selling drugs for cancer and heart disease were industry sponsored and/or their authors had financial ties to drug companies. There is strong evidence that sponsorship and financial ties lead to bias. For example, of fifty studies of arthritis drugs, not a single one found evidence against the drug of their sponsors. In 2007, a review of almost two hundred trials comparing cholesterol lowering drugs found that a study reporting a positive result for a particular drug was twenty times more likely to have been funded by the drug's maker than by the manufacturer of the comparison drug. Similar results were found with respect to studies of anti-diabetes drugs. Studies with unfavorable results are simply not published, as was recently shown with respect to antidepressants. All of this has led the former editor and Chief Executive of the British Medical Journal Publishing Group to conclude that "medical journals are an extension of the marketing arm of pharmaceutical companies."[5]

In view of this, long-termism can feel a little bit like the Churchillian defense of democracy: "science is the worst form of organized inquiry, apart from all the others that have been tried." The present, however cruddy, is better than the past, and in the future things would likely improve. Not a ringing endorsement. It is not a given, therefore, that people should trust science. Laypeople may not understand how arthritis drugs work, but they know how to interpret the finding that no study is published that finds evidence against the drug of its sponsor. In view of this, it is pertinent to ask whether people trust science or not? What kinds of science? Even when they trust science, do they also trust scientists and experts? What kinds of experts? Under what conditions do people change their minds regarding their trust of science and scientists? These are real questions. Given the above, one cannot approach them assuming that people obviously would and should trust science, thus treating any deviation from this baseline as indicating the irrationality of ordinary people, their ignorance and resentment, or their manipulation by interested politicians, corporations, and charlatans. But how to study this slippery and subjective phenomenon – trust?

A small cottage industry of survey research is dedicated to measuring the public's levels of trust in science. In the US, general attitudes regarding science, measures of scientific literacy, and questions about confidence in the leadership of the "scientific community" or in the results of specific disciplines, are included in the General Social Survey (GSS), the National Science Board's *Science and Engineering Indicators*, and surveys conducted by the Pew Research Center. Roughly comparable questions are included in the European Commission's (EC) *Eurobarometer*, the German *Wissenschaftsbarometer*, the UK's Wellcome Trust Monitor and the Swedish *VA Barometer*.

With remarkable consistency across countries and time periods, these surveys find that the "public holds a rather positive and optimistic view about Science in general." In 2017, 76 percent of respondents in the Pew Survey said that they have a "great deal" or a "fair amount" of "trust in scientists to act in the best interests of the public." The Pew Research Center framed these results as demonstrating that "public confidence in scientists tends to be high." Since 1973, the percentage of respondents to the GSS who say that they have "a great deal" of confidence in the leaders of the scientific community has remained stable, increasing slightly from 37 to 40 percent in 2016 (though confidence in the leaders of *medicine* has plummeted over the same period of time from 55 to 36 percent). The fraction of Americans who believe that the benefits of science outweigh the costs has been stable at about 70 percent from 1979 to 2008. Contrary to jeremiads about Americans' lack of scientific literacy, anti-intellectualism, hostility towards experts, and so on, on all these measures the US ranks either equal to or higher than the countries of the European Union or the Asian Tigers (China, Japan, South Korea, and Taiwan). Yet there is no evidence that in any of these countries trust in science, at least measured in this way, is particularly low. 82 percent of Europeans think that scientists working at a university behave responsibly toward society and show proper regard for the impact their activities may have. 83 percent of Britons agree that scientists want to make life better for the average person, and 90 percent think scientists working at a university can be trusted to follow the rules regulating their research.[6]

Case closed? Not really. I would urge the reader not to trust these results (pun intended). In view of all the problems with scientific research noted above, it would be a miracle indeed if people were really so sanguine. There are many reasons to doubt these reassurances that trust in science is robust and stable. First, as the reader surely had noticed, it is not altogether clear what to make of the finding that 37 to 40 percent say that they have "a great deal of confidence" in the leaders of the scientific community. Stable it is, but what is *it*? Is it trust or mistrust? The same result could be framed as "a large and stable majority of US adults, around 60 percent, do not have a great deal of confidence in the leaders of the scientific community." A larger group, 48 to 50 percent, say that they have "only some" confidence, which does not sound reassuring at all. Similarly, the aforementioned 76 percent of US adults trusting in scientists were composed of 21 percent expressing a "great deal" of trust and 55 percent who opted for a "fair amount of trust." So the same results could be read as saying that 79 percent of US adults do not have a "great deal" of confidence in scientists – which sounds down-right alarming. The Pew researchers, therefore, hedge their bets with an adjectival sleight of hand. Their initial assessment that "public confidence in scientists tends to be high," they qualify by calling this confidence "soft" – whatever this means; presumably, not the sort of confidence that you could rely upon in a pinch; that is, an untrustworthy trust, a confidence about which you cannot be confident.[7]

Not only is the meaning of the results ambiguous and dependent on framing, but there are also holes in the assurance that things have not changed. It depends, first, on the time frame. From 1979 to 2008, roughly 70 percent of Americans agreed with the statement that the benefits of science outweigh the costs, but when the question was first asked, in 1957, the proportion was 83 percent. Something clearly happened during the 1960s and 1970s to dampen public enthusiasm about science.[8]

It also depends on *whom* you are asking. There is clear evidence that at least one group – US conservatives – has lost its confidence in the leaders of the scientific community. In the early 1970s, Americans self-identifying as "conservative" were more likely than "moderates" or "liberals" to answer that they had "a great deal" of confidence in science. By 2010, however, they were the least likely, due to a precipitous decline of about 12 percent. When you control for other variables, there is a small but significant negative effect of time, constituting evidence of a "general downward trend in public trust in science." This decline was especially pronounced among educated conservatives, with college or graduate degrees.[9]

These findings, however, are unique to the US, where the matter of trust in science has become one of those "litmus tests" of ideological purity. It is not that conservatives *have* less trust in science, but that being an American conservative is now *defined by, attested to* by, doubting science (essentially rejecting the long-termist or Churchillian pleasantries). Indeed, over the same period of time, the proportions of Republicans and Democrats professing "a great deal" of trust in science exactly flipped from 41 and 35 to 35 and 42 percent respectively. In contrast, a cross-national survey of attitudes towards science in 47 countries at varying levels of development found overall that people on the political right in these countries were *more likely* than people on the left to express confidence in the positive impact of science on society. Studies in European countries found – instead of the American litmus test – that the relationship between political views and trust in science depended on the specific topic in question. People on the left are distrustful of scientists working on GMOs or pesticides, for example, while people on the right are distrustful of climate scientists.[10]

If trust in science is measured by asking people, it clearly matters how the question is worded, what choices respondents are given and which responses are counted. The same year that 76 percent of respondents told the Pew Research Center Survey that they have a "great deal" or a "fair amount" of "trust in scientists to act in the best interests of the public," only 50 percent of respondents told the German *Wissenschaftsbarometer* that they "trust science and research" either "completely" or "somewhat." 37 percent of them, however, said they were "undecided." Are Germans more mistrustful of scientists than Americans? More unable to make up their minds? Perhaps, but I think it matters that the Pew Survey constrained respondents who felt they had less than a "fair amount" of trust in scientists to choose either "not too much confidence" or "no confidence at all." My guess is that if American respondents were given the "undecided" option, the Pew results would not have been all that different from the German ones.[11]

Moreover, if you present people with a more specific (and indeed, more realistic) way of expressing their distrust without forcing them to appear as backward "science deniers," many more join the skeptical side. From 2001 to 2010, anywhere between 48 and 59 percent of American respondents agreed that "scientific research has created as many problems for society as it has solutions," allowing the Virginia Commonwealth University (VCU) Life Sciences Survey researchers to declare that there is a "consistent near even divide in US public opinion about science." Asked if the "best available scientific evidence influences the research findings of scientists working on GM foods," only 30 percent say it does so "most of the time," which means that 70 percent of respondents do not think that these scientists are trustworthy. As noted above, upwards of 80 percent of Americans, Europeans, and Britons think that academic scientists are socially responsible, can be trusted to follow the rules regulating their research, and are working to improve life for ordinary persons. Yet, if they are asked the same questions about "scientists working at private company laboratories," these percentages decline as far down as 35 percent (regarding social responsibility) or hover around 60 percent. Now just imagine what would happen if the question was worded – in line with the results reported above – to ask about "scientists whose research is sponsored by industry" or "scientists who have financial ties to industry" (which is true for the vast majority of *academic* medical researchers)? Asked if scientists adjust their findings to get the answers they want, equal proportions of Britons agree or disagree (35 and 34 percent respectively) – the "wisdom of crowds" happens to accord with Ioannidis' analyses.[12]

The levels of trust also vary greatly when respondents are asked not about general, vague topics, which I too would find bewildering, but about specific topics about which they make daily decisions or hear often. While 62 percent of US adults think that science has a positive effect on "food," only 37 and 28 percent agree that it is safe to eat GMO food or food grown with pesticides respectively. Only 50 percent of US adults agree that climate change is due to human activity, but this is not some American peculiarity. Statements regarding climate change are trusted by only 37 percent of Germans. In short, if you ask people about specific topics; if you specify the context and referent of their trust; if you do not constrain their responses into a binary litmus test; what you discover is that their confidence in science is not "hard" or "soft," nor is it unchanging. Their trust is not blind, but conditional and qualified, a sort of "vigilant trust," suspicious of all the problems noted earlier of conflict of interests, confirmation bias, research misconduct, and lack of reproducibility. This vigilance – whether justified or not – seems to have increased over time and can easily flip into outright mistrust of science and scientists.[13]

This vigilance is especially marked regarding regulatory science. As we saw, when people are asked whether they trust scientists working for private companies, their answers differ substantially from their answers regarding the vague notion of "scientists" or leaders of "the scientific community." What about the scientific research conducted by government agencies? Unsurprisingly, it inspires much less trust and, more importantly, things here have changed considerably over the last few decades. Confidence in the FDA, for example, has been declining steadily in opinion polls from upwards of 80 percent in the 1970s to 61 percent in 2000 to an abysmal low of 36 percent in 2006. By 2015 it has sunk well below confidence in many other government agencies, with 43 percent of respondents saying that the FDA does a "poor" or at best a "fair" job.[14]

Respondents typically express a lot more confidence in agencies that they do not readily connect with regulatory science – US Mint, NASA, and NOAA (National Oceanic and Atmospheric Administration) – than agencies where such research is highly visible (EPA, USDA). Predictably, trust in the research conducted by government agencies is strongly influenced by one's political ideology, with conservatives expressing the least confidence in the most visible agencies of regulatory research – another one of those American political litmus tests.[15]

Yet, the mistrust of "government science" is by no means unique to the US. When, in 1998, Monsanto wanted to assess the British public's attitudes towards GMO foods, it discovered a delicious, though unsettling paradox: if simply told about a GMO food product, British consumers made more or less reasonable estimates of its safety, "but when told that the British government had stated that it was satisfied that the product was safe, the levels of confidence in the safety of that product fell sharply." Coming in the wake of the "mad cow" scandal, this was perhaps to be expected. Nonetheless, it indicates that trust in science is not a thing unto itself. Not only is it extremely sensitive to recent events or to how a question is formulated, but it simply cannot be neatly separated from trust in other institutions (government, industry, organized medicine, the media, etc.) As Hans Harbers puts it, "trust" is a de-differentiating concept. It links science and technology with politics, culture, consumption, medicine, ethics, and the law. Moreover, it blends together inextricably what people think about "a science-related topic of interest," how they evaluate the individuals and institutions involved, and their overall level of "default trust in science." The result is that "trust in Science develops and changes in light of the public's views about specific scientific topics." It is a moving target shifting with the winds: You ask people whether they trust scientists, and they answer you about their perceptions of risk concerning GMOs. You ask people about GMOs or vaccines and they answer you about their mistrust of the government. You ask people whether they trust the FDA, and they answer you about what they've heard about pharmaceuticals and how they woo scientists with research funds and other perks.[16]

Yet, perhaps the most striking finding regarding trust in the research conducted by government agencies is that respondents *simply do not know what these agencies do*. When asked whether they trusted the scientific research conducted at eleven named agencies, the percentage of respondents indicating that they did not have an opinion ranged from 45 percent (regarding the NSF) to 18 percent (regarding the CDC) with the average being about 28 percent. The less educated and less affluent, the more likely they were to have no opinion. Moreover, less education and lower income were also predictors of expressing lower levels of trust. If they were to make up their minds and have an opinion, therefore, it is far more likely that these respondents would indicate that they do not have trust in regulatory scientific research, though clearly they would do so without knowing very much about it.[17]

We are obliged to pause before these results and wonder what exactly is being measured when respondents are asked if they have confidence in scientists or in scientific research, especially since the question is vague and the respondents' familiarity with the subject matter is minimal. Consider the following observation: trust in the FDA is low and plummeting, we are told. Yet, it is a safe bet that most of the people who gave the FDA such a poor grade do not think twice when, three times a day, they take their FDA-approved medicine; or when they consult the insert in the pill bottle, mandated and checked by the FDA; or when they check food packaging for the "best used by" date, based on FDA inspections, regulations, and research. Which is more revealing of their level of "trust"? What they say or what they do? Is trust better understood as an explicit attitude or as "tacit acceptance of circumstances in which other alternatives are largely foreclosed"? Which is a better measure of the extent to which Americans trust in the FDA: the artificial situation in which they are asked to pretend that they are judges giving the FDA a grade for "job performance," while knowing very little about how the job is carried out (though obviously aware of some spectacular failures – the low numbers in 2006 no doubt reflect the Vioxx debacle of 2004), or the multiple real-life situations in which their actions rely on the underlying sense that the FDA is doing its job reasonably well for them to proceed?[18]

The problem with the measurement of "public trust in science" is thus even more fundamental than the wording of questions or the framing of results. Who can blame the respondents if they seem inconsistent? Not only can they be easily forced into a particular position by the question's wording or the choices it offers, not only are they prompted to respond in pre-specified ways by "litmus test" questions, but they are being asked to make explicit what often exists only as a tacit implication of conduct ("trust") – thereby transforming its very significance – towards something ("science") that either does not exist, or of which they have no firsthand experience and no real way of separating from other things (government, corporations, etc.). No law of large numbers, no random sampling, nor even a longitudinal panel study, can overcome this congenital deformity.

Perhaps the main thing to be learned from the literature about public trust in science is not to be found in any of its reported results, but merely in the simple fact of its recent existence. If there wasn't a palpable sense, indeed anxiety, about the public's mistrust of experts and science, this literature would not have existed. You do not measure what you are not worried about. The rise of "trust talk" signals concern about lack of trust.

Indeed, the research on "trust in science" can be traced back to the British Royal Society's 1985 influential *Bodmer* report. The report was commissioned in response to the sense that public attitudes toward science have turned negative. The main recommendation was to improve science literacy and promote the public's understanding of science. This came to be known later critically as the "deficit model" – people have negative attitudes towards science because they do not understand it. A new journal – *Public Understanding of Science* – was founded a few years later. Institutes and programs in "risk communication" were endowed. A whole academic-governmental-non-profit apparatus was geared into action on both sides of the Atlantic. Yet, disillusionment with the top-down nature of this apparatus and with the deficit model came quickly. This led researchers and institutions, beginning in the mid 1990s, to focus instead on *trust* and to devise various "science barometers" to measure the public's levels of trust in science. The research on trust, therefore, was motivated by the same concerns regarding negative attitudes towards science, but it aimed for a bottom-up approach, one which sought to understand the public's expectations from science and the reasons for their mistrust.[19]

The enterprise of measuring trust in science is failing because the question whether people trust science or not is too simplistic, unable to contend with how quickly trust can become mistrust; how context-bound it is; how it cuts across and links various spheres; and how it can be manifested in both explicit and tacit ways that can contradict one another. It presumes, for example, that trust and mistrust can be easily distinguished from one another as opposites. By marking "how much" you trust on a 5-point Likert rating scale, you also indicate how little you mistrust, and vice versa. Yet, as Anthony Giddens argues, trust and mistrust are not strict opposites. A certain element of mistrust is necessarily included in any trust relationship: "for trust is only demanded where there is ignorance – either of the knowledge claims of technical experts or of the thoughts and intentions of intimates upon whom a person relies. Yet ignorance always provides grounds for skepticism or at least caution." In short, some mistrust of whomever or whatever you trust is in fact the norm; trust and mistrust come packaged together. This ambiguity is at the core of all trust relations, accounting for the speed with which the attitude – trust – can flip into its opposite. Everybody knows how dubious the injunction "trust me!" sounds. The moment you hear it, doubt and mistrust creep into your heart.[20]

It gets more complicated. This coupling of trust with mistrust extends also to the moral dimension. To place one's trust in somebody or something means to direct the arrow of responsibility at them. The trustee is saddled with the moral responsibility of guarding the interests of the trusting party as if they were her own. Yet, like a weathervane, the arrow of responsibility can swing back with every passing wind. If trust placed has been abused, the blame rests not only with the trustee but also with the trusting party. "How could they have trusted him?" would be the retrospective reproach. And it would echo and resonate with the trusting party's own feelings: "how could I have been so lazy and beguiled?" This self-reproach indicates that at any given moment, even when trust had not been abused, responsibility is also with the trusting party to trust responsibly. Trust presumes ignorance, but ignorance could easily be framed as moral fault – "I should have checked," "don't believe everything they tell you!" – which goes to the very core of one's character.

This is why Giddens says that at stake in basic trust is the stability of one's own self-identity. This sense of an almost existential dread – which is the true opposite of trust – is clearly evident in research on vaccination uptake. In the early 2000s, trust in vaccination was shaken by two reports. First, in 1998, British doctor and researcher Andrew Wakefield published in the *Lancet* – the most respected British medical journal – the results of research indicating a link between the MMR (Measles, Mumps, and Rubella) vaccine and autism. Then, in 2001, a group of parents in the US published a study in *Medical Hypotheses*, claiming that the mercury-based preservative thimerosal, present in most vaccines, caused autism in some children. They called autism a form of "mercury poisoning." Both reports were quickly and decisively refuted by follow-up research, and Wakefield was shown to have committed fraud and lost his medical license in consequence. Nonetheless, fears and mistrust of vaccination did not abate, vaccination rates have declined, and measles seems to have returned with a vengeance to places as varied as Italy and Disneyland. At the height of the fears stirred by these reports, British sociologists Julie Brownlie and Alexandra Howson conducted interviews and focus groups with British parents whose children were of vaccination age. Parents who expressed fears of vaccination, indeed even refused to vaccinate their children, Brownlie and Howson found, were not irresponsible anti-vaxxers. They were at a loss as to what would it mean to trust responsibly. They did not act upon unfounded fears, but articulated a sense that the foundations for prudent action have collapsed: "Although it might be a very, very small percentage risk, it's your child and if it gets that, you have to

deal with that for the rest of your life, I mean would you ever
forgive yourself? To feel that you were responsible and that
you could have prevented that?"[21]

The relationship between trust and mistrust here is non-
linear. A "very small percentage risk" should have meant a
lot of trust and a little mistrust, but instead we find the arrow
of responsibility swinging wildly, and the curve diving down
precipitously to zero trust. Yet, as the example of vaccination
brings home, under modern conditions it is not at all clear
how or what would it mean to trust responsibly. We are asked
to trust not simply other people, but far-flung expert systems,
the workings of which are often obscure even to their own
staff. We are asked to trust these not occasionally, but continuously. We wouldn't know how to take the next step, if
we didn't trust the workings of these systems. This seems to
set the stage for wild swings in which trust gives way to
mistrust and blame.[22]

The very enterprise of asking people about trust is contra-
dicted, as I have already noted, by the fact that trust often exists
as a tacit and habitual premise of everyday action. When I get
into the car for my morning commute, my actions bespeak
trust in car makers, engineers, mechanics, other drivers, the
municipality and numerous other government agencies, of
which – if asked – I would have expressed various levels of
misgivings. To reveal this trust, what you need to do is not to
ask people about it, but to provoke them, to perform one of
Harold Garfinkel's naughty little breaching experiments (go
to the supermarket, pick a random item off the shelf, bring
it to the cashier, and when she scans it, begin to haggle ...).[23]

This sort of tacit, habitual trust is what fascinates the major
theorists of trust – Niklas Luhmann and Anthony Giddens.
They consider it an essential medium of modern social relations,
without which – like oxygen – everything would immediately
grind to a halt. How could I drive to work without trusting
that the overpass won't collapse under my wheels, or that the
combustible material in my tank won't erupt into flames? This
seems to set up a conundrum. Trust – including in science and
expert systems – is inevitable, yet it is rooted in ignorance.
I have no idea why the overpass doesn't collapse or the fuel
tank doesn't explode; I just trust that they won't and that
in principle, if I inquired, there are precise calculations that

can be made to back up this trust. If you asked me about it, I would probably report high levels of trust (I'll mark 5 on the Likert scale), but if you provided me with news stories about collapsed overpasses (like the one in Florida that killed a few people) or about how automakers fudge safety tests (why not? We know that they fudged emissions tests), my reported trust would correspondingly decline. For this reason, all the major theorists of trust distinguish between two types or components of trust: confidence and trust (Luhmann), trust and basic trust (Giddens), default trust and vigilant trust (Origgi). The list could be extended, but they all hark back to Georg Simmel's original observation that while there is an element of "weak form of inductive knowledge" in trust, at its core trust entails something altogether different, a sort of "quasi-religious faith."[24]

The reference to "religious faith," however, is unhelpful. It is tantamount to throwing one's hands up in the air and saying that we cannot understand and explain trust (unless it is of the weak inductive kind). It should be clear that what appears as "quasi-religious faith" is a fairly reasonable assumption, to the extent that it is embedded in experiences, routines, familiar scripts. Put differently, trust thrives when certain social arrangements are in place. These arrangements are robust, which explains the pervasiveness of trust. At the same time, trust also depends – as I will argue below – not on mystical faith, but on framing operations that strike a delicate balance between contradictory social forces. This is why trust can so easily flip into its opposite, when this balance is upset. To understand trust in science and in experts; to explain how and why this trust collapses; is to study these social arrangements and the forces impinging on them, not the mysteries of "social psychological quasi-religious faith."

Why do the theorists resort to two different terms to describe trust? Why is trust composed of these two opposing sides – faith and knowledge, default and vigilance? It seems to me conditioned by the fact that either side of the opposition, when stretched too far, ceases to be trust and becomes something else. The other side serves, therefore, as a counter-balance. To trust in science could mean, in the first iteration, to explicitly assess the evidence, whether the source providing us with information is trustworthy. In this regard, the literature has

not advanced an iota beyond Aristotle and his trio of practical
intelligence (now "ability"), virtuous character ("integrity"),
and good will ("benevolence"). This is a ubiquitous form of
expertise. We all know how to do it, what to look for. But if
we do it too much, too often, too insistently, it is no longer
trust, but mistrust. If we ask to see documentation of ability;
if we periodically ask for assurances of good will; if we repeat-
edly search for counter-evidence to refute the presumption of
integrity; if we keep the trustee in our view at all times to
continuously assess her integrity; if we cite the "replicability
crisis" to demand that all data will be publicly accessible (as
did Scott Pruitt, the EPA's now deposed anti-Director); then
our vigilant trust is no longer trust but mistrust. As Giddens
says: "trust is related to absence in time and space. There
would be no need to trust anyone whose activities were con-
tinually visible and whose thought processes were transparent,
or to trust any system whose workings were wholly known
and understood."[25]

Hence, in a second iteration, the assessment of trust collapses upon itself into a single, originary, infinitesimally brief
moment of a "leap of faith." To trust in vaccination means
that "you just go and do it." One moment you are on one
side, teetering on the precipice of existential dread; the next
moment you are on the other side, having restored the world
into its familiar shape by simply trusting that contingencies
will not happen and that everything will turn out for the
best. Yet, parents bringing their children to be vaccinated
are not Abraham taking a leap into the complete unknown
in the face of a cruel, inscrutable paradox. Theirs is not a
trust beyond what is humanly reasonable to trust. If it were
so, if they knew nothing at all about vaccination, have never
encountered it in their life, yet immediately, without hesita-
tion, offered their infants to the needle, we would call this
blind faith, not trust.[26]

Abraham's leap of faith meant that he dared to hope beyond
all rational hope. Parents bringing their children to be vaccinated have fairly good reasons for hope. Their trust is embedded in networks, scripts, and biographical experiences,
supported by the arrangement of the scene and the attitudes
of the actors involved (as evidenced by what happens to their
trust if the doctor and the nurse seem shifty and unresponsive),

not by some "quasi-religious faith." It is precisely this embeddedness, the length of time that produced it, that allows them
to "just go and do it" seemingly immediately and with no
thought. Put differently, just as trust is necessary only where
knowledge is incomplete and full of gaps; so, it can only
subsist where ignorance, too, is incomplete.[27]

Discussions of trust that seek to peg it *either* as a "leap of
faith" *or* as explicit assessment of trustworthiness suffer from
the same scholasticism that Pierre Bourdieu detects in discussions of the gift. We all know that gifts need to be returned in
some way, that they will be returned and predictably so; that
not returning a gift is a breach. This does not mean, however,
that one could simply treat gifts as economic exchange, as some
theories do. We all know that if we were to take the rational
exchange theory as a guide to action, and respond to a gift with
an immediate counter-gift (which we conveniently wrapped
ahead of time and placed at the ready), we would destroy the
whole delicate dance of gift exchange. We would most likely
insult the giver by seeming to negate her act of generosity. Yet,
this does not mean either that one could treat gifts as pure
altruism, as acts of generosity with no concern for reciprocity,
as other theorists might do, looking for the "pure gift." We
all know that if we were to take the pure altruism theory as a
guide to action, and fail to respond with a counter-gift at the
proper time and occasion (or if we refuse to accept a well-timed
counter-gift), we would once again insult the giver and incur
their ill will. The "two-fold truth" of the gift, says Bourdieu,
depends on observing the correct *interval*, neither too short
nor too long, between gift and counter-gift, and on observing
the correct formulas of giving and receiving, which avert the
glance from the character of the act as exchange (though one
remains aware of it and on other occasions could even rail
against "its constraining and costly character"). It depends,
in short, on a "practical sense" that is mostly about a feel for
the correct *timing*, skillful observance and manipulation of
form, and on *frames* which organize what is foregrounded
and what is left outside the frame in a situation.[28]

Trust, too, has a "two-fold truth." It is, in fact, a modern
gift relationship, the cement of modern, liberal societies. The
one who trusts gives to the trustee the gift of personal faith,
hoping to be rewarded in return by trustworthy stewardship

of her interests. Yet, she can neither give too readily, nor can she give too grudgingly. As Guido Mollering emphasizes, trusting involves a skillful suspension of doubt, bracketing, an "extremely sophisticated methodology of practical consciousness" through which people "manage to live with the fact that there are gaps and missing pieces." We all know that we should not trust blindly, that we should have some basis for giving our trust, some basis for the expectation that it will be reciprocated. In fact, too quick a "leap of faith," without any reasonable basis for it, could insult the trustee or at the very least reflect badly on the trusting party's moral character. Given too readily, it is not trust, not a skillful suspension of doubt, but blind faith and pious hope (an unserious gift, given without much thought or consideration for the obligations it imposes on the giver and the receiver). The same considerations apply to the trustee – "trust me!" is either cavalier, making light of the solemn responsibility placed in one's hands (the gift one has been given), or is downright dubious.

By the same token, however, if we foreground our search for the bases of trust, if we take too long scrutinizing the trustee, we run the risk of destroying the delicate dance, turning trust into mistrust, just as an immediate counter-gift insults the giver. The trustee runs the same risk the longer they take exhibiting their credentials and providing assurances. In short, the successful accomplishment of a trust relationship depends, like the gift, on a feel for correct timing, skill, observance of proper form, and on frames that organize what is foregrounded and what is bracketed.

Both the gift and trust involve forms of organized, collective self-deception. The self-deception made possible by the interval between gift and counter-gift is about the logic of exchange, which guarantees that the gift will be returned. The self-deception made possible by trust frames is about the logic of "advance payment," as Luhmann puts it, namely the absence of guarantees that trust is justified. A setting which provides for long and intensive scrutiny of credentials, or which on the contrary requires an immediate leap in the dark, foregrounds this absence of guarantees instead of keeping it in the background as something which is not in good form to mention – though we all know it, and may acknowledge it in forms of dark humor.

The framing operation is thus not only about timing. No less importantly, it is about information: how much information is provided or sought, when and by whom? Keeping mum is clearly untrustworthy. "Trust me!" with no information given is not likely to elicit trust. But the opposite, flooding the trusting party with information, giving too many assurances, can backfire and appear suspicious – which is why the call for "transparency" is not necessarily always the right antidote for the problem of mistrust in science. Health visitors in the UK, tasked with countering public fears about vaccination post-Wakefield, report that their ability to build trust was compromised by the very public relations effort meant to provide information about the MMR vaccine. The government's transparency blitz caused parents to feel "that they were being channeled down an avenue that they really didn't want to take and their personal choice was being ignored." Put differently, trust, the skillful suspension of doubt, was their gift to give, but the government's information campaign implied that there could be no doubt in the matter, thus no need for their gift. Sequence, timing, and responsiveness are important too. A transparency blitz coming after a long period of being relatively opaque does not inspire trust. The provision of information as part of routine interactions, responding with openness when the trusting party wants to know more, does inspire trust.[29]

The settings and framings which generate and sustain trust bracket the logic of advance payment, while foregrounding familiarity, predictability, and responsiveness. When it comes to trust in science, medicine, and expert systems more generally, it is the experience at "access points," as Giddens calls them, which matters most: the vaccination is included as part of a routine well-visit with a familiar pediatrician. The pediatrician displays the photos of her own children prominently on her desk, and is willing to talk about her own considerations when vaccinating her children. Previous vaccinations are noted in a yellow card that records also other "milestones" of development, which parents compare proudly while in the waiting room. The nurse examines the baby while chatting amiably about her own children. Most importantly, nothing in the scene implies that there is a decision to be made, risks to be weighed against benefits; nothing calls attention to uncertainties, judgment calls, or alternatives. Yet, if prompted, the staff is open and responsive to discussing these. There is a division between frontstage and backstage, and strict control over the passage between them – because the procedure needs to be prepared in advance; because experts, too, make mistakes sometimes; because there is an element of uncertainty – yet accompanied by a willingness to open the curtain (this is not a magic act) at the right moment. This sort of setting generates trust. By the same token, access points are places where science, medicine, and expert systems are vulnerable. If the interaction is botched, if the setting is not well-prepared, if the framing operation fails, if the staff is surly or cagey, people will mistrust vaccination.[30]

Simmel said that in trust there was an "additional element which is hard to describe: It is most clearly embodied in religious faith … the feeling that there exists between our idea of a being and the being itself a definite connection and unity, a certain consistency in our conception of it, an assurance and lack of resistance in the surrender of the Ego to this conception, which may rest upon particular reasons, but is not explained by them." But he was wrong. It *is* explained by them. The sense of "definite connection and unity," which can be so elemental as to appear as "quasi-religious faith," *is the product* of a working trust relationship, not its underlying cause. It *is* explained by all the framing mechanisms and skillful acts, which foreground what is familiar about bringing one's child to be vaccinated, and which bracket what is uncanny and uncertain about it. Similarly, trust in science and experts is not an attitude measured by surveys. It is a byproduct of institutional mechanisms, their output, so to speak.[31]

To understand why this trust currently seems to be failing in multiple domains, I need to look more carefully at how the reputation and credibility of scientific institutions, experts, expert systems, and government agencies are generated, reproduced, and challenged. Yet, Simmel's phenomenology of trust as "definite connection and unity," the "lack of resistance in the surrender of the Ego," is extremely valuable in one important respect. It serves to remind us of the symbolic significance we attach to the expression "breach of trust." A breach of trust is much more than a breach of contract, much more than a mere reneging on a contractual obligation. It is experienced as a betrayal, an assault upon the self, indeed even as *pollution*, since to trust is – as Simmel says – to feel a certain unity with the person or thing trusted, a certain "surrender of the ego," as if extending one's body boundaries to include the trustee within them. When trust framings fail, the trustee is likely to appear as a contaminated and contaminating agent, just as the mistrusted vaccination suddenly became "poisoning our children." This explains a peculiarity of trust that others have noted, namely that it is asymmetrical: "It is typically created rather slowly, but it can be destroyed in an instant – by a single mishap or mistake." This quality of trust is exactly parallel with how Durkheim describes the arrangements and framings that create the sacred: It is built up by elaborate rituals that separate the sacred from the profane and sanctify it, yet it can be destroyed, profaned, by the smallest contamination, the fleetest touch of the unwashed. Simmel was right then: in every relationship of trust there is an element of the sacred (if by this we understand, with Durkheim and Douglas, a purely relational quality created by the ritual frame). To complain about a breach of trust is to level an accusation of pollution, that is, to express a general view of the social and natural order and their interrelations, a cosmology. I need to examine, next, the context in which most of these pollution accusations have been leveled in recent decades, namely the debate about *risk*.[32]

4

Risk

"There is no expert on risk."

Ulrich Beck, *Risk Society*

What happened in the 1960s and 1970s to trigger a "general downward trend in public trust in science" or more precisely to set in motion the accelerating seesaw of alternating trust and mistrust? There is a ready answer. *Risk* happened. As can be seen in Figure 4 below, the frequency of appearance of the word "risk" in books and articles began to increase in the mid 1960s, and took off in exponential fashion in the following decades. This intensifying scrutiny given to risk has been roughly parallel to the increased talk about expertise (in terms of when it began and how fast it increased), to the raging debate about the relations between science and politics encoded by this term. The fortunes of these two words seem to be intertwined, and it's a safe bet that the purposes for which they are used are intimately related to one another.

Correlation, of course, is far from conclusive evidence of causation, but in the case of "risk" there are good reasons to think that its prominence in public debate indexes processes that have destabilized, perhaps even polluted, the authority of the regulatory and policy sciences, generating a crisis of endemic mistrust. These reasons are beautifully captured by Ulrich Beck's enigmatic and succinct formulation, bearing the

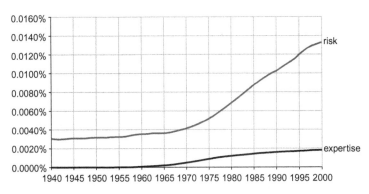

Figure 4 Frequency of appearance of "expertise" and "risk" in *Google Books* from 1800 to 2000[1]

~~force of a~~ Heraclitean paradox, that "there is no expert on risk."[2]

First, there is no expert on risk because there are too many experts ~~on risk~~. We hear often about "risk analysts" – as in financial risk analysts, who failed in ~~their task~~ prior to the great recession; or political risk analysts, whose job is to advise governments and corporations – one would think that there is such a profession, to which is entrusted jurisdiction over a clearly demarcated task. This is not the case. Political risk analysts are recruited from among area specialists, former diplomats or intelligence officers, political scientists, and suchlike. Many financial risk analysts have some training in economics, but undergraduate degrees or coursework in accounting, math, statistics, or business are also typical. Toxicologists once had sole jurisdiction over many forms of risk assessment regarding environmental pollution, medications, and chemicals in consumer products, yet over time they were forced to share the scene with many other experts – pharmacologists, epidemiologists, microbiologists, statisticians, food analytical chemists – as the task of analyzing and countering risks extended also to prevention, to balancing safety with efficacy considerations, and to post-marketing surveillance of adverse events.[3]

There is no single, well-demarcated expertise pertaining to risk analysis. The assessment and management of risk is an interdisciplinary or multidisciplinary affair, conducted by a "multi-professional" group of academic and commercially employed scientists, state and transnational regulators, who have moved away from their original disciplinary research to become specialists in evaluative tasks. From its inception in 1980, the membership of the Society for Risk Analysis, for example, included biological and health scientists (especially toxicologists), engineers, physicists, mathematicians, economists, sociologists, and psychologists. The largest contingent of members came from government agencies, with universities and industry supplying the rest. This heterogeneity of expertise reflected the complexity of the problems involved, and the need for "cooperation across the trenches of disciplines, citizens' groups, factories, administration and politics." But it also made it difficult to determine who has the relevant expertise regarding a given set of risks.[4]

The difficulty was exacerbated because risk controversies – which revolve around the collateral effects of scientific and technological developments – pitted one group of experts against another, each questioning the quality and integrity of the other's research, as well as its relevance to the problem at hand. Clearly, this is why the two terms correlate on *ngram*. Risk controversies are one of the contexts in which the question of expertise – namely, what makes somebody an expert about this slippery and multi-sided topic? What body of knowledge qualifies as expert knowledge about risk? – was raised, because there were too many contenders to the title. This was evidenced, as I noted in Chapter 2, by the difficulty courts faced in trying to apply the *Frye* criterion of "general acceptability in the particular field." Which, to begin with, is the relevant field, within which the expert witness or the method enjoy "general acceptability"? Nobody would dispute Freeman Dyson's general acceptability as a theoretical physicist, nor the soundness of his mathematical methods, but does his expertise in this field qualify him to evaluate the models and predictions of climate scientists (about which he is famously, notoriously, skeptical)?

Second, there is no expert on risk because there is no one with expertise exactly relevant to the problem at hand. If Dyson's expertise is dismissed as irrelevant or tangential to the problem of climate change, he might argue in retort that the same is true for the expertise of climate scientists, since their models "do a very poor job of describing the clouds, the dust, the chemistry and the biology of fields and farms and forests." Surely, many readers would have liked to say something similar about financial risk analysts in 2007. Their models did a very poor job of describing some of the most relevant parameters, if they included them at all. Health advocates focusing on the accumulated "body burden," created by exposure to many different pollutants over one's lifetime, feel the same way about toxicological expertise.[5]

I do not have enough knowledge to evaluate the substance of Dyson's claim, but I think it illustrates the more general point that I began discussing in Chapter 3. This point is made, in fact, by Beck himself; by Luhmann's cynical quip about experts being unable to answer the questions put to them; by Michel Callon and his collaborators' guide to *Acting in an Uncertain World*; or by Brian Wynne's analysis of the relations between risk, uncertainty, ignorance, and indeterminacy: the problems dealt with under the general rubric of "risk" – climate change, hazardous waste disposal, industrial pollution, industrial accidents, nuclear radiation, adverse reactions to medications and vaccines, the vulnerability of the financial system ("systemic risk"), earthquake preparedness, etc. – "overflow" the specialism of any specific group of experts. That is why there are too many experts on risk. These problems typically overflow the current state of knowledge, leaving large margins of uncertainty into which many different groups may enter with claims to expertise.[6]

As noted earlier, in the case of radioactive contamination of the Cumbrian Fells, the nuclear scientists called in as experts had no expertise in some of the most important parameters of the problem – the type of soil in the Fells, the chemical mobility of Caesium in different types of soil, the uptake of nutrients by local plants, the behavior of sheep. They could not even recognize that these were relevant parameters, until their perspective was changed by the controversy caused by evidence of the overflows. Nobody – neither the scientists, nor the sheep farmers – had expertise in the specific question of whether nuclear fallout will contaminate the sheep. We should not conclude from this example that the problem is simply solved by combining different types of expertise, by making the scientists listen to the local residents, to lay experts or "experience-based experts." This is certainly essential, but is not a panacea. Some of the necessary expertise may be found lying around, but much of it will have to be developed for the first time. This is why Callon and his collaborators say that the concept of risk is a "false friend," because it implies that the danger is well-identified, and the experts know how to calculate its odds; that they have compiled an exhaustive list of alternatives open to us and the odds of these alternatives are also calculable; and it implies that the experts understand the system of interactions for each alternative well-enough to anticipate outcomes, side-effects, and so on. This is hardly ever the case. It was not the case on the Cumbrian Fells, not even after the scientists and the sheep farmers had begun talking to one another in earnest. It was not the case before the financial crisis, nor, unfortunately, is it the case a decade later.[7]

Instead, the problems are shot through with profound *uncertainties, ignorance and indeterminacies*. Uncertainties differ from risks in that the probability distributions of the relevant parameters are not known in advance, and hence the odds are not calculable, unless with the aid of various assumptions, heuristics, and boundary conditions. These are the bread-and-butter of risk analysis, part and parcel of the trained judgment of risk experts, how they transform the gaps in knowledge and uncertainties into putatively calculable risks. The assumptions are almost always influenced by particular epistemic cultures and normative values. They are therefore disputable, and in fact often disputed.[8]

There are some, relatively rare, cases where these assumptions and heuristics are so well accepted and widely distributed that they stabilize the situation. They are shared widely by all relevant participants and are embedded in institutional routines and regulatory standards, maybe even hard-wired into existing technology. Most importantly, it is possible to govern the actions of all relevant parties (by means of surveillance, incentives, standardization, bench-marking, or what have you) so they do not deviate significantly from what the assumptions anticipate. In these cases, it is probably proper to speak of risks rather than uncertainties.

Insurance is the best example of a technology and institutional framework that has transformed uncertainty into risk.

But even in this exceptional case, the transformation only works if participants are convinced that the risks of future harms have been fairly distributed, which depends on the soundness of experts' assumptions and heuristics, the procedures by which they may be amended, their degree of transparency, and the overall viability of the political strategy of which they are a part. To put it in terms that anticipate the next chapter, even insurance is not self-legitimating but depends on the *defensibility* of expert judgment and procedures.[9]

Moreover, in most cases other than insurance, the assumptions, heuristics and boundary conditions necessary to reduce and tame uncertainties produce, as their inescapable price, ignorance (which means that we do not even know that we do not know) about what was left outside the boundary conditions, as well as genuine indeterminacy (because whether the assumptions hold or not depends on the future behavior of relevant agents). This has been demonstrated a thousand times by now regarding the regulatory concept of "acceptable levels." It is important to recognize that this concept works on the basis of an analogy with insurance. "Acceptable levels" are like the premiums we all must pay so that our individual uncertainty is transformed into collectivized risk, fairly distributed among all. Yet, being averages of single chemicals, calculated on the basis of animal studies, with the testing pipeline extremely slow and literally thousands of chemicals as of yet untested, "acceptable levels" produce ignorance regarding the actual level of exposure, accumulated body burden and true impact on any given individual. The same can be said for the complex probabilistic tools used to transform uncertainty about borrowers' default into capitalizable risks. No wonder, then, that something like the financial crisis appears to strike "out of the blue." It emerges out of – and is no doubt exacerbated by – the ignorance actively created by the very attempt to tame uncertainty. The experts purportedly designated to assess and manage risks become complicit in their proliferation.[10]

This is true not just for the financial crisis. *It is inescapably true whenever risk is involved.* By definition, risk cannot be eliminated. It is always potential, which means that when disaster strikes – however tiny were the initial odds – the procedures for minimizing and managing risk appear to be complicit in the result. Homeowners in Houston, who were told that their houses were in a "100-years flood zone," and yet found them under water after Hurricane Harvey, now doubt the competence of the experts and their models, or worse, they suspect venality and collusion with real-estate developers. That's why something like a sense of *broken trust* accompanies almost all the problems enumerated above, symbolic pollution superimposed upon and exacerbating the indignation caused by actual pollution.

Yet, given the complexity of the problems, the uncertainty and indeterminacy of their parameters, the reality is that everybody's specific expertise is somewhat to the side, so to speak, touching only on this or that limited aspect, carefully hedged by the boundary conditions of her specialism. Risk expertise can only be spoken of in a promissory mode, as something that needs to be developed, which means that risk expertise *always* comes after the fact. It is worth quoting Beck at length here: "Science's rationality claim to be able to investigate objectively the hazardousness of a risk permanently refutes itself .... No matter how benevolently one looks at it, the whole affair remains a very complicated, verbose and number-intensive way of saying: we do not know either. Just wait. Practice will show us." There are no experts on risk, therefore, because "risk" is more a promise and a pious hope than a solid object of knowledge and regulation.[11]

Third, there is no expert on risk because (like trust) it is a de-differentiating concept, which transgresses the stable boundaries between disciplines and professions, ultimately the very boundaries between experts and laypeople. This quality is not intrinsic to the concept, not an essence. It is a quality acquired during the course of jurisdictional struggles between disciplines and professions. Risk is the disastrous – because at first seemingly so unstoppable – "Winter Campaign" of the hard-nosed wing of the regulatory and policy sciences. At first, they sallied forth wielding "risk" as an objective probability. In response to public fears and resistance to nuclear reactors, they never tired of pointing out that the objective probability of accidents was exceedingly small (of course, this was before Chernobyl and Fukushima), and that people were already tolerating a much higher level of fatalities associated with other, non-controversial technologies, such as cars. People were simply being irrational, focusing on extremely unlikely events and tiny probabilities. The engineers championing risk analysis thought they could devise a method relying on "revealed preferences" (i.e. the historical rates of accidents associated with accepted technologies) to calculate the exact level of acceptable risk for new technologies. The question, they said, is "how safe is safe enough?" for which risk analysis will provide a clear-cut answer. Risk analysis would thus convert the interests, fears and concerns of affected citizens into quantitative inputs into its calculations, just as insurance does.[12]

This imperialism of risk analysis did not stop with the laity, but extended also to the experts themselves. Risk analysis means that you can measure and compare – on the flat surface of a balance sheet – not only the interests and concerns of ordinary citizens, but also the substantively heterogeneous knowledge and expertise of different professions and disciplines. They can be captured, so to speak, and subordinated to the "intellectual jurisdiction" of the risk analysts. As the "new penology" took over American prisons in the 1980s, for example, the claim of the "helping professions" (psychiatry, psychology, counselling, social work) to rehabilitate prisoners became merely one factor among many in a probabilistic calculation of risk profiles. Their claim to in-depth knowledge of individual psyches was transcribed into a surface "actuarial language of probabilistic calculations and statistical distributions," in which you could compare the "outcomes" of this many weekly hours of group therapy against the "yield" of, let's say, a more stringent parole policy or a surveillance camera placed in the cafeteria. Similarly, reforms in the healthcare sector – from Evidence-Based Medicine (EBM) to the introduction of Electronic Healthcare Records (EHR) – sought to subordinate the decisions of doctors and psychiatrists to the actuarial calculations of administrators, regulators, and risk managers.[13]

But, just as the risk analysis juggernaut seemed unstoppable, its wheels got stuck in the Bayesian mud, so to speak. The more the hard-nosed faction contrasted expert "risk assessments, characterized as objective, analytic, wise, and rational – based on the *real* risks," with the public's "*perceptions of risk* that are subjective, often hypothetical, emotional, foolish, and irrational," the more exposed they became to the counter-argument that, regarding risk, the opposition between real and perceived makes no sense: "Risk is inherently subjective ... [It] does not exist 'out there,' independent of our minds and cultures, ready to be measured." Expert risk analysis is subjective through and through because it relies on value-laden assumptions and judgments. Even such a seemingly straightforward task as estimating the probability of human fatalities due to certain hazards depends crucially on the value-laden choice of how to measure fatalities (as actual deaths or loss of life expectancy? Over the whole population, or only within a certain radius from the source of exposure? By tons of chemical produced or by what people actually absorbed?). By the same token, non-experts are not irrational. They simply place more weight in their risk assessment "models" on factors that the experts tend to discount – the catastrophic potential of low probability events (nuclear accidents rank high here), the high uncertainty regarding unknown risks that may be delayed in their impact and unobservable (carcinogens of all kinds rank high here), their consequent lack of control over these imposed risks. Low probability, non-observability and involuntariness mean that harm comes from what you tended to trust, the doubling of physical pollution with symbolic pollution increasing the "weight" of these factors in laypeople's calculus. Naturally, laypeople also tend to understand risk from an ego-centered perspective, as the probability of harm to themselves and their loved ones, rather than as distributed over a population, where they themselves can be sources of risk to others – as in the concept of "herd immunity."[11]

With these arguments, psychologists contested the terrain captured by the engineers and toxicologists for whom risk was "a technical problem with technical solutions." Over time, psychologists increased their representation on the Executive Committee of the Society for Risk Analysis, reflecting the fact that their ideas "captured the limelight." By redefining risk from objective hazard to a problem of contrasting subjective percep-tions, psychologists captured intellectual jurisdiction (now the calculations of risk analysts were merely one perception among many), while expanding the whole realm of risk by inventing new tasks under their own jurisdiction – surveying and assess-ing "risk perception," designing "risk communication" tools, and so on. Of course, the hard-nosed faction could recontest jurisdiction – and it did – by incorporating the public's risk perceptions, as measured by psychometric tools, as discrete inputs into a seemingly objective procedure of decision-making. Yet, the overall effect of jurisdictional struggles was to underscore the impression that "science does not speak with one voice ... the illusion of apolitical expertise collapses ... leading to an overall loss of credibility," and to the replacement of narrow technical definitions of risk with frames incorporating the judgments of lay people and social movements. The psychologists' foray profoundly blurred the boundaries between experts and laypeople. Paul Slovic, who served as the President of the Society for Risk Analysis in the late 1980s, summarized the moral of psychological research on risk perception thus: "Perhaps the most important message from this research is that there is wisdom as well as error in public attitudes and perceptions. Lay people sometimes lack certain information about hazards. However, their basic conceptualization of risk is much richer than that of the experts and reflects legitimate concerns that are typically omitted from expert risk assessments. As a result, risk communication and risk management efforts are destined to fail unless they are structured as a two-way process. Each side, expert and public, has something valid to contribute. Each side must respect the insights and intelligence of the other." There is no expert on risk, therefore, only different stakeholders with different perceptions.[15]

Into the breach created by the psychologists, now swarmed also the cultural theorists. Why do people – including experts – they asked, focus on certain risks rather than others, accord more or less significance to different aspects of risk, perceive more or less urgency in preventing or reacting to this risk and not the other? These differences are dictated by their embrace of different "myths of nature" (whether it is self-correcting or fragile) and their trust in institutions, itself conditioned by their social position. The most alarmists are the members of sect-like groups, like environmental advocacy organizations, where the strong boundary between inside and outside leads to suspicion of industry and government, and to a perception of nature as fragile. The least alarmed are the entrepreneurs and market actors, who trust the "hidden hand" to correct any deviations from natural equilibrium. In this analysis, once again, there is no expert on risk because the experts are just as conditioned by their social position as are all the other parties.[16]

Finally, and perhaps most importantly, there is no expert on risk because risk analysis is ethics and politics camouflaged by numbers. If you are a little bit tired of the sociologists and the critics and find their denunciations of risk analysis a little bit too shrill (and Beck does get shrill every now and then), just look at what the *judges* made of risk analysis.

American legal doctrine regarding the admissibility of expert testimony is punctuated by two Court decisions that gradually transformed the judge from "a passive umpire who watches over the rules of the game ... [to] an active gatekeeper charged with the responsibility of screening unreliable scientific evidence": the *Frye* decision of 1923 and the *Daubert* decision of 1994. While Anglo-American jurisprudence has been grappling with the problem of scientific expert testimony for more than two centuries, since Lord Mansfield's decision in *Folkes v. Chadd* (1783), only twice did the US Supreme Court find that the difficulties presented to it required rethinking the doctrine of admissibility.[17]

What provoked these two episodes of rethinking? It was not the general difficulty of permitting testimony about opinion that potentially carries the weight of testimony about facts (which is the general and enduring problem of scientific expert testimony in Anglo-American jurisprudence). Nor was it the problem of experts being "guns for hire," the accusations of "junk science," and a moral panic about scientific misconduct. While judges often complained about the unseemly spectacle of experts contradicting one another and impugning each other's credibility, they were used to it. Nor was the rethinking occasioned by the overall effects of "weaponizing" expert testimony in terms of prolonging the proceedings, increasing costs and confounding the issues, however loudly judges decried it. It is very clear from Tal Golan's superb history of scientific expert testimony that these problems and the attention paid to them were not new, not unique to the 1920s or the 1970s. They were present from the very beginning and throughout the history of scientific expert testimony – often bemoaned and often dealt with pragmatically. "The Common Liar, the Damned Liar, and the Scientific Expert" were a constant of this history.[18]

The *Frye* opinion was provoked by something else, a much
more fundamental threat regarding which the Court could no
longer maintain its "traditional neutral approach towards the
processes of scientific proof." The *Frye* case was about the
attempt to introduce the *lie detector* technology as part of
expert testimony. Experimental psychology presented itself
as a form of expertise relevant not to this or that truth the
court needed to establish, but to the court's "own central
processes of fact-finding, persuasion, proof and worst of all,
judgment." What provoked *Frye* was not a struggle for jurisdiction between experts, conducted on legal turf, but a challenge to the court's *own* jurisdiction, specifically to the jury's
jurisdiction over deciding who is a credible witness to be
believed, and the judge's jurisdiction over advising the jury in
this task.[19]

Lest I be misunderstood, let me emphasize that what provoked *Frye* was a challenge not merely to the narrow professional interests of judges. The jury system, and the procedures
of fact-finding organized around it, may seem antiquated and
arbitrary to Continental observers. Max Weber was certainly
perplexed by it. Yet, they are crucial to the *legitimacy* of
Anglo-American law. Just imagine a future where black-boxed
AI technology replaces the jury system because it is able to
predict with greater accuracy who is telling the truth (a *Google*
lie-detector, a twenty-first-century ordeal-by-algorithm). In the
aggregate, its results may be statistically superior, but the
defensibility of any individual decision would be extraordinar-
ily *frail* in comparison with the defensibility afforded by the
unanimous opinion of twelve of one's peers, before whom
both sides laid their best arguments and evidence in adversarial
fashion. In choosing to strengthen the judge's gatekeeping
role, the Supreme Court was also protecting science from
itself. Forensic science was pushing its nose too far, into the
truly nether regions where the *hocus pocus* of modern democratic legitimacy is performed, and it was risking a ferocious
counter-reaction. With *Frye*, the judges for the first time
"became ... active participants in the development of scientific
proof," in collaboration – as Golan makes clear – with the
new professional associations with whose interests and "new
pragmatic epistemology" the criterion of general acceptability
"resonated admirably." Together they worked to ensure that

the interface between these two truth-producing practices –
science and law – so crucial to modern democratic legitimacy,
worked as smoothly as possible.[20]

Similarly, I would argue that the *Daubert* opinion was also
provoked by something more fundamental than the concerns
about scientific misconduct, experts for hire, and accusations
of "junk science" circulating in the 1970s and 1980s. The
context for *Daubert* was litigation connected to "accidents,
technological breakdowns, dangerous drugs, industrial defects,
environmental pollutants, and other toxic substances" ... where
"the central legal questions were those of risk and causation."
When judges tried to resolve these questions by applying the
Frye criterion of "general acceptability" they ran into the
problems noted above: too many groups of experts contending
for jurisdiction; the problem itself requiring input from multiple domains of inquiry, some of which were still in their
infancy. Hence, there was genuine uncertainty about how to
draw the boundaries within which "general acceptability"
was to be assessed. The professional associations no longer
were of any help because risk problems, as we have already
seen, cut right through professional jurisdictions and disciplinary domains.[21]

The key issue, however, was that just like the lie detector, risk analysis and risk management potentially infringed
upon the court's own processes of judgment. The challenge
they posed and continue to pose is not to this or that truth
produced by law, but to its very mechanisms for producing
truth. Risk knowledge is not knowledge of *actual* dangers or
harm, but of *potential* harm. The question about risk is not
how to eliminate or reverse it (as in restitution for harm), but
how much of it is acceptable, given the opportunity costs of
risk reduction measures (up to and including precautionary
prohibitions). Not only is this a question in which facts and
values are inextricably entangled – a matter for "trans-science,"
as Alvin Weinberg, the Director of the Oak Ridge National
Laboratory put it as early as 1972 – but it is part and parcel
of what it means to be an American judge, part and parcel
of the pragmatist judge's tool kit: judges make decisions on
the basis of some analysis of probable, systemic, long-term,
institutional consequences, often balancing several different
consequences one against the other, employing "tests" to

evaluate their costs and benefits. Risk analysis, if it attempts to present itself as a unified science dealing with objective probabilities, or as specialized regulatory expertise into which judges need not inquire, challenges the jurisdiction of the judge at its very core. Risk analysis is consequentialist ethics camouflaged by numbers. No wonder, then, that *Daubert* reasserted the judge's gatekeeping function and empowered her to look beyond "general acceptability" into the testability of the theory or technique in question; whether it was peer-reviewed or not; its known and potential error rate; and whether standards existed to control its operation.[22]

As in *Frye*, the judges "created a new degree of freedom for the judicial scrutiny of scientific expert testimony," not simply to protect their own domain. They ventured into the processes of scientific validation to protect regulatory science from itself. They knew that when it came to balancing alternative costs and benefits, determining winners and losers, the legitimacy of decisions depends on all the framing devices that experts and scientists deem extraneous, but which judges and courts employ: the pomp and circumstance of the proceedings; their transparency and publicity; the *time* taken for deliberation; most importantly, the adversarial frame, the duel, between the champions of opposing interests. There is no expert on risk, therefore, because there is an obstinate and fearsome gatekeeper guarding the door through which risk analysis was meant to pass back and forth seamlessly.

There is a sense in which a crisis of trust would seem inevitably to accompany risk analysis. If we go back to the origins of risk analysis, namely insurance, it is clear that its capacity to transform individual uncertainty into collectivized (and capitalized) risk depends on the principle of *no-fault liability*. No employer would pay premiums for work accidents insurance if every accident investigation led to criminal proceedings. Insurance, to adopt Mary Douglas' terminology, is a system by which we hold each other accountable, by agreeing not to blame each other. The ambition of risk management is to dispense with blame altogether. By the same token, we no longer need to trust each other. If the employer is negligent, premiums will go up, literally calling him to account. Yet, this means that we must place enormous amounts of trust in

the workings of the system and in whoever ultimately guarantees its smooth and fair functioning. Risk management,
therefore, does not truly dispense with blame but ultimately
displaces it onto itself, or more precisely onto those in authority, those running the system – the government, corporations,
experts. I do not blame my neighbor for his tailpipe emissions,
or for the chemicals in the weedkiller he sprays. I blame the
manufacturers of these instruments of pollution; the regulators
who did not impose more stringent limits; the experts whose
research is cited in support of the regulations. I blame them
all for abusing my trust. It seems almost inevitable, in a risk
society, that blame and mistrust will be directed at the experts.
As Douglas argued, risk is better understood as a "forensic
resource" used to hold others, especially those in power,
accountable. The rise in risk talk, stripped of its "pretension
of precise calculation," is equivalent to the eruption of pollution accusations in a tribal society, a way of working through
threats to the moral order, with the crucial modification that
the sources of pollution are no longer other individuals but
the government and its experts.[23]

Nothing demonstrates these dynamics better than the inter-
play of vaccination and anti-vaccination. Vaccination is equivalent to insurance. It is a way of transforming individual
uncertainty and blame – my fear that I will become ill because
of *you*, because you will infect me – into collectivized risk.
We all agree to pay a small price – the pain of the pinprick,
the aching shoulder, the minuscule risk of more serious side-
effects, these are the "premiums" we all pay – to create the
collectivized funds that would protect us in the future, namely
"herd immunity." No-fault liability is institutionalized by a
specialized "vaccine court," which limits the exposure of
vaccine manufacturers to malpractice suits and damages. Yet,
the other side of vaccination – as is true for insurance as well
– is that it *individualizes*. The pooled resources – herd immunity – recede into the background and what is foregrounded
is the individual's faultlessness, her autonomy in taking protective measures, the trust placed in the system. At this point,
blame can return with a vengeance, when the vaccination
itself is experienced as an infringement of the very same individual autonomy it afforded. Pollution accusations, drawing
on a symbolic opposition between "natural" and "chemical,"

will be directed at the manufacturers of vaccines, at the authorities and experts mandating vaccination.[24]

These dynamics, however, are not inevitable. The proliferation of insurance plans and prudential government during the first half of the twentieth century was not accompanied by a crisis of trust. The deployment of risk analysis does not, in and of itself, displace blame onto the experts. The missing ingredient in this account is a broader crisis of legitimacy, which engulfed risk analysis within it:

> Appealing to degrees of risk, assessed by accredited experts, is appealing to an external arbiter, an independent, objective judge of the rights and wrongs of the case. Normally the appeal to professional experts to settle questions of accountability works when their methods and their results are backed by authority. There has to be a Solomon to judge; the evidence does not provide the judgment by itself. In the present circumstances the appeal to science is made because of the absence of respect for any adjudicator. Solomon's role is not acceptable. The very idea that there could be a technical solution to a disagreement about goals and purposes shows that political reconciliation is rejected. The predictable consequence of using science in politics is that both sides consult their own scientific experts. ... When science is used to arbitrate in these conditions, it eventually loses its independent status, and like other high priests who mix politics with ritual, finally disqualifies itself.[25]

At first glance, the most conspicuous fact about the contemporary risk debate is how the tables have been turned. Forty years ago, in the first round of the debate, the target of the radicals was the "massive denials" of self-satisfied scientists who, they felt, collaborated with industry to downplay the seriousness of the risks involved. Conservatives defended the scientific establishment's good sense in taking the warnings of environmentalists with a grain of salt. The whole enterprise of risk assessment had begun because the scientists and engineers – especially those building nuclear reactors and hazardous materials disposal sites – felt that the public's perceptions of risk were irrational, and their appetite for safety was unrealistic. The most sophisticated cultural critique coming from the right essentially replicated this argument. Transported to the present, the leading protagonists would have been astounded to find how their roles and alliances shifted. The scientific elite is attacked not from the left, but from the right; not for denialism, but for alarmism. The long-haired environmentalists, now turned into sober bourgeois, find themselves in lockstep with the scientific establishment, defending not only its dire predictions about global warming, but also its dismissal of irrational public fears about vaccination. Conservatives, for their part, seem to find great wisdom and secret meaning in this popular risk consciousness they abhorred in the past. The world of risk, it seems, is topsy-turvy.[26]

On a closer look, however, the upheaval seems less impressive than the enduring dilemma, on the horns of which we still find ourselves, as did our predecessors. On the one hand is the mirage of risk analysis, which presents itself as an objective calculation of known, identifiable events that can be exhaustively described in all their manifold paths and interactions, then balanced against one another to reach a rational decision. Since, as we saw, in most real-world situations the conditions necessary for such analysis do not obtain, risk analysis can only proceed by means of a double boundary. It draws a boundary around its assumptions, its methods and heuristics of extrapolation, weighting, standardizing, averaging, using surrogate and composite variables, outside of which are new uncertainties, outright ignorance, and genuine indeterminacy. At the same time, it also draws a boundary around risk experts, outside of which is the irrational public or mere "risk perception." When it fails, as inevitably it must, it is left with no additional resources with which to defend its decisions, since it purported to dispense with "a Solomon to judge" and since it has excluded the public from its deliberations. Democratic institutions are threatened, as Alvin Weinberg said long ago, when the public is excluded from "trans-scientific" debate.[27]

The countervailing response has been, therefore, to abandon this notion of risk, this "false friend," and to remove the double boundary. The closed circles of official risk experts are replaced by "hybrid forums" composed of experts and laypersons, wherein uncertainties are recognized, embraced, and renegotiated. The overflows and the normative dimension of risk assessments are to be tamed by opening up and multiplying the stakeholders involved. Immediately, we are faced with the worrying prospect that uncertainty equals indecision and inaction, and that to expose the uncertainties left hidden by risk analysis would lead to systemic paralysis: "The insistence that connections are not established may look good for a scientist and be praiseworthy in general. When dealing with risks, the contrary is the case for the victims: they multiply the risks ... To put it bluntly, insisting on the purity of the scientific analysis leads to the pollution and contamination of air ..." This reproof was originally written to shake the scientific establishment out of its complacency, but it can now be directed – word for word – at the champions of participatory science who, like Michel Callon and his collaborators, insist on the virtue of controversy, as open as possible, taking time "to explore conceivable options before deciding" and who see "no reason to halt" the "socio-technical spiral": "The only reasons for halting it are bad ones." On the other side of the dilemma we find, therefore, "inclusion friction": research slowed down, forced to go down blind alleys and waste resources, energy, and precious time as it is engulfed by myriad controversies opened up by the inclusion of "stakeholders," "lay experts," and the "concerned public." Or worse. On this side of the dilemma we may find Weinberg's countervailing worry that the procedures for opening up debate and decision-making will be abused. We find the specter of agnotology, the social construction of ignorance by means of injecting uncertainty and doubt, indeed precisely by pointing out the questionable assumptions, the humdrum heuristics, the pragmatic conventions of which risk analysis is made. This too represents a threat to the interrelations between democratic institutions, regulatory science and expertise, of which democratic legitimacy is made.[28]

5

Crisis, Take 2

Narratives of crisis emplot events to create a meaningful sequence. The way they construct this sequence is prior to and entails the choice of explanatory mechanisms and the fingering of guilty parties. To speak about "post-truth," declining trust in science, and/or the "death of expertise" is to sketch the faint outlines of a sequence, a set of slots into which the usual suspects will slip naturally and self-evidently. The sequence of events is linear, leading to a break: a long-term process of decline that ultimately leads to a "collapse of the relationship between experts and citizens," a breakdown of trust that threatens to send "democracy itself [into...] a death spiral." Sketched in this way, the linear sequence implies a culprit: the "foundation of all these problems," the "soil in which all the other dysfunctions have taken root and prospered," is the "abysmal literacy, both political and general, of the ... public." The public is worse than a phantom; it is willfully ignorant. Enter the Great Multiplier – the internet and social media – and the secular trend combusts into a full-fledged crisis: "a google-fueled, wikipedia-based, blog-sodden collapse of any division between professionals and laypeople." The internet allows the ignorant to believe that they have real knowledge at their fingertips, and they feel themselves equal to the experts, allowing confirmation bias to run rampant. Political polarization means that they feel free to ignore or even impugn the motives of experts who bring bad news to their side.[1]

I wholeheartedly disagree with this diagnosis. The multiplier effects are real enough, but the narrative sequence is wrong. What we are witnessing is not a secular process leading to an unprecedented "post" or "death of." We've been here before. The process is recursive, the crisis is systemic and protracted. To understand the current impasse we need a different narrative emplotment, not linear but "dialectical," sensitive to contradictions and tensions, to the combined action of opposing forces and their unintended consequences as they pull once this way, then push in the other.[2]

One way to see this – loosely analogous to Marx's third thesis on Feuerbach – is to try to imagine what could arrest the linear decline; what could avert the crisis? The relationship between experts and laypeople has collapsed. How could it be made to work? In a working relationship between laypeople and experts, the former judge the performance of the latter. To do so, laypeople "must familiarize themselves with the issues at hand ... Voters have a responsibility to learn." Yet, if they learn and familiarize themselves, wouldn't they be even more likely to challenge the experts? Wouldn't they be even more likely to reject any "assertion of expertise from an actual expert ... [as] fallacious 'appeals to authority' ... an obvious effort to use credentials to stifle the dialogue required by a 'real' democracy"?[3]

When the medicine is also the poison, we know that we are in the presence of an *antinomy*. For the rational authority of experts to be recognized, citizens need to be educated. Yet, to be educated, they first have to recognize the authority of the educators. And once they are educated, they no longer accept "appeals to authority" and they criticize the experts. Or put differently, in terms that disrupt the linear narrative sequence: is the collapse of trust between experts and laypeople the result of the "abysmal [il]literacy" of the public or, on the contrary, of their having "familiarize[d] themselves with the issues at hand" so now they can see the gaps and uncertainties in expert assurances? The antinomy goes to the heart of the matter: can there be rational recognition of an appeal to authority? Since the authority of rational commands is based on their "discursive redeemability," that is, on the supposition that they *could*, *if necessary*, be justified and defended against critique, is it permissible to say that right now, here, for this purpose, it is *not necessary* to produce the full defense; that instead it should be accepted on the authority of the expert? The antinomy shows that we need a different emplotment, a different narrative sequence and a different analytical focus. The *pushmi-pullyu*, whereby trust and reliance on science constantly alternate with mistrust and skepticism, whereby recognition of expert authority alternates with refusal of "appeals to authority," cannot be explained by some linear factor that moves the needle on an imaginary "trust dial." Moreover, the explanation needs to be sensitive to the core issue, the heart of the matter, the dynamics of legitimation and justification of rational authority. The crisis is not about knowledge and ignorance, not even about manufactured ignorance (agnotology), but about authority, legitimacy, credibility, and reputation.[4]

I'd like to be decidedly old-fashioned and resurrect the mid twentieth-century concept of "legitimation crisis," though refurbished for twenty-first-century purposes. Unlike the original concept, which likened the crisis to a chronic deficit, I will describe a recursive, tangled process, where every attempt to check the vicious spiral ends up lending it momentum, yet the attacks designed to accelerate it often strangely land flat and have the opposite effect. It is a strange crisis that feeds off the attempts to prevent or fight it, yet its recursive spiral often ends up sapping its own strength. I grew up in Israel, not far from the Mediterranean coast. As kids, going to the beach, we were warned by the adults about those hidden vortices that sometimes formed not far off the shore. We were told that if we happened to be swept up into one of these, the surest way to drown is to attempt to fight one's way and swim out. You couldn't do it, the adults said, and you would quickly expend all your strength and would no longer be able to keep your head above water. The adults told us that our best bet was not to fight the vortex but try to "ride" it, so to speak, until it spit you out or somebody came to help you. Whether this was true or not, I do not know, having been fortunate enough never to be swept by one of these vortices. Perhaps, however, it can serve as an apt metaphor for being in the midst of the current legitimation crisis. The various responses to it – as I will try to show below – often backfire and tend to amplify the crisis. Our best bet may be to find a way to "ride" it.

Before I develop this argument, however, I need first to explain how I am using this term – legitimacy. This is a notoriously difficult and ambiguous concept. Max Weber offers it as an answer of sorts to the basic question of his sociology of domination: why do people obey commands? Why, for example, do I wait at the red light even though the intersection is empty? There may be many reasons for doing so – people may obey "from simple habituation," or they may be afraid of punishment (there might be cameras at the intersection!), or they may be calculating that their obedience will be rewarded – yet none of these reasons is enough to guarantee the stability of a system of domination. Weber's peculiar, unsentimental approach to systems of government, including democracy, was to treat them as "techniques, like any other machinery." By this he meant that the most important thing about them is not whether they are just or not (legitimacy is not justice), but whether they *work* in the sense that *most* of the time, *most* of the people, obey *most* of the commands, without too much friction gumming up the works. Not *all* the commands are obeyed, mind you – some people do deliberately drive through the red light because they calculate that there will be no repercussions. Obedience is a probabilistic, aggregate, machine output, measured by its efficiency, namely minimization of "rejects." The system can certainly tolerate a few people driving through red lights. Sooner or later they will be caught. There will be summons, points, fines, and a strong incentive to obey traffic lights the next time around. But if *enough* people do not obey traffic lights too many times, it becomes possible, indeed necessary, for everybody else to ignore them as well. Chaos ensues, and the system of rule collapses.[5]

Whenever the machine is working well, says Weber, whenever most commands are obeyed by most people most of the time, this is evidence for the presence of an extra ingredient, over and above all the other motives for obedience, namely "belief in legitimacy ... which every such system attempts to establish and to cultivate." I wait patiently at the red light because it is the right thing to do, because I believe that the

lights provide a fair and convenient means of organizing competing claims to expediency, which it would be imprudent
and inefficient to attempt to weigh one against the other in
terms of "justice." Yet, Weber immediately cautions against
treating this belief in legitimacy purely psychologically: "it is
by no means true that every case of submissiveness to persons
in positions of power is primarily (or even at all) oriented to
this belief." None of these thoughts enter my mind as I wait
at the red light. I simply wait "from simple habituation." So,
what is this "belief in legitimacy"? This extra ingredient that
is absolutely essential, yet never truly present? Weber leaves
us dangling, but adds a crucial parting shot: whatever motives
play a role in any individual act of obedience, they are "not
decisive ... What is important is the fact that in a given case
the particular claim to legitimacy is to a significant degree
and according to its type treated as 'valid.'"[6]

So everything hangs on how we understand what is meant
by "valid." My suggestion is that we think of validity as
defensibility, and that we keep this term intentionally ambiguous, gesturing as it does in one direction to strength, fortifica-
tion, and struggle – etymologically, the Latin *validus* means
"strong, effective," the verb *valere* is "to be strong" – and in
the other direction to truth and logic; the ambiguity summed
up in the expression "force of the better argument." If you
bring up arguments against obeying – that the red light is
unnecessary at this intersection, because most of the traffic
comes from only one direction – you are met with stronger
and more convincing arguments, themselves embedded in a
forceful chain of reasoning, in institutionalized procedures,
formal rules, and substantive findings – the decision to place
the light at this intersection has been made by the democrati-
cally elected city council; a traffic study by credentialed civil
engineers was commissioned prior to the decision and followed
the administrative rules guiding such study; the study's findings, plans, drawings and calculations are deposited at the
city archive and could be consulted – all of which serve as
fortifications for the command, repelling the attack and channeling it, so to speak, to an "obligatory point of passage"
where it could be decisively demolished. Validity – hence
legitimacy – is a well-woven web of arguments, procedures,
measurements, and institutions, all supporting one another.[7]

I have knowingly entered here a terrain of high-stakes debate between two formidable thinkers. I'd like to extricate myself quickly, before I get caught in the crossfire. All I need is just a little bit of *time*. In many respects, the whole of Jürgen Habermas' oeuvre is encapsulated in his interpretation of the expression "belief in legitimacy." If the belief is a purely empirical phenomenon, he says, then it is a very shaky basis upon which to establish the stability of a system of government. If a demagogue, a good orator, persuades you and other drivers that it is not wrong to drive through the red light, the whole edifice comes tumbling down. If, on the other hand, the belief is *valid*, in the sense of having an immanent relationship to truth, then the grounds for the command – as Weber says: "the position of the persons claiming authority ... the choice of means of its exercise" – can be tested and criticized independently of the temporary psychological impact of the orator's rhetoric. You may have been persuaded by the orator, but now as you set out to persuade other drivers, the very enterprise opens you up to counter-arguments. Other people cite the results of the traffic study. They report bringing up similar objections at the Town Hall meeting and what the engineers said in response. They pointedly ask you what right do you have to ignore a decision that was discussed, debated and ultimately voted upon in accordance with the rules.[8]

This testing of the grounds for the command, says Habermas, is embedded in the very structure of reasoned discussion. Whenever we engage in discourse, "we unavoidably presuppose an ideal speech situation ... whose structure assures us ... that no force except that of the better argument is exercised; and that, as a result, all motives except that of the cooperative search for truth are excluded." Empirically speaking, of course, this is not always what happens. A "persuasive" argument may be built on a veiled threat, or people are swept by the emotional force of an orator's charisma. Habermas thinks, nonetheless, that the "fundamental norms of rational speech" continue to exert a regulative force even in these situations, leaving them open to dissent and critique.[9]

For Habermas' chief antagonist, Niklas Luhmann, however, the idea that you can "probe behind the factual belief in legitimacy and the validity claims of norms for criticizable grounds of validity" is a "functionally necessary deception."

The regulative ideal has no teeth. Its main function is to "absorb uncertainty," to reassure people that if they would bother to check, they would find that the particular decision was rationally taken and justified, so no need to bother! In reality, however, many different, and sometimes opposite, decisions can follow from the same premises, rules and findings. You pointedly ask your critics whether they were really able to check for themselves the engineers' calculations at the Town Hall meeting; whether they were able to propose alternative traffic arrangements and obtain comparative calculations; and if not, wasn't the whole "discussion" a charade whose results were known in advance?[10]

The dispute between Habermas and Luhmann can be boiled down to the question of how to reconcile the supposition – necessary for legitimacy – that the command could, if necessary, be justified and defended against critique (i.e. that it is "valid" or "true"), with the fact that in nine cases out of ten no such defense is needed, and when it is offered, it is never quite complete. At one point or another the debate must be brought to an end by appealing to "what we all know," or to what "we all hold as self-evident," or to the authority and reputation of the experts (or even more tellingly, by appealing to the ticking clock and the need to reach a decision). Passé Habermas, we never get all the way down to the "ground," it is *never necessary or possible* to produce the full defense.

For Luhmann, this means that legitimacy is a "deception," while for Habermas it is a "regulative ideal" exerting its force from without, so to speak. What appears as an irreconcilable dispute complete with name-calling – "deception," "decisionism" – seems eerily similar to the disputes about the gift or trust, and like them can be resolved or at least advanced by attending to the crucial dimension of *time*. For Luhmann, the defensibility of the command is a deception – just as for the economist, the gift giver's altruism is a self-deception – because he assumes the breathless, here-and-now, *irreversible* time of a *decision*. As the gavel comes down at the town meeting, you are left with many more objections, many more questions that can no longer be answered. You feel deceived.

For Habermas, on the other hand, the defensibility of the command has an "immanent relationship to truth," because he assumes a theoricist, *reversible* time of interminable discussion.

When he says that the very act of engaging in discourse "unavoidably presuppose[s] an ideal speech situation," this is the
same as the economist saying that the very act of gift-giving
presupposes the gift's return and can therefore be modeled as
rational, self-interested exchange. Game theory as the gift's
"regulative ideal." Any arbitrary ending to the debate, any
appeal to authority, can in principle be challenged in the next
round. In the next Town Hall meeting you appear equipped
with calculations and drawings under your arm, secured by
a "freedom of information" request, and you make a special
motion to reopen the debate about the traffic lights. While
you feel the hate stares at the back of your neck, the formal
rules guarantee that your opponents must meet you on the
same terrain of rational debate, and provide stronger arguments and better evidence if they wish to prevail.

If this opposition between decision and interminable discussion seems similar to the metaphor of the three-lane highway
with which I began, this is because the work of legitimacy,
the work of defensibility, takes place in the middle lane (in
fact, in multiple middle lanes, of which regulatory science is
but one). Defensibility takes time and it takes *repetition*, but
it cannot tolerate a fully reversible temporality. This is why
the ideal speech situation is "ideal," because nobody could
take the time necessary for an exhaustive attack and defense
that leaves no stone unturned; that reverses time so as to
delve all the way down to the "ground" the next time around.
Luhmann is partially right to call defensibility a deception.
At the end of the day not everything is up for debate, not all
grounds can be criticized, because "we ain't got all day." As
science studies have shown time and again, even in the more
rarefied realm of basic science, controversies must be brought
to an end by some means other than "the force of the better
argument." Even more so in the sweaty, heated, urgent debate
at the town hall. When it comes to regulatory debates, there
is typically, as we saw regarding risk analysis, a substratum
of assumptions, heuristics, stylized facts, experimental para-
digms, and tools, that facilitate standardization, commensuration, and comparison, etc., that are shared, of necessity,
by all participants to rational debate because they serve as
the very infrastructure for debate, the means that render the
disputed reality legible. One or two of these "typifications"

may be disputed at any given point, but not all at the same time.[11]

Yet, Habermas too is partially right to treat defensibility seriously. If controversies are closed too quickly, if dialogue is short-circuited ("because I told you so!"), the deception is exposed and the command loses its legitimacy. They are both wrong, however, because neither treats temporality practically, as an artful, skilled accomplishment. The time of legitimacy is neither reversible, nor irreversible. It is a time of *finite repetition*. Legitimacy depends not just on taking time, but on crafting temporal frames that foreground discussion, indeed cermonialize the time it takes; that offer a glimpse into an horizon where reasoned discussion may continue even as it is brought to a temporary halt ("we can pick it up again next time"); while relegating to the background the points at which discussion will necessarily end, for example by burying them in long manuals replete with complex calculations that are distributed to all participants minutes before the Town Hall meeting. Legitimacy operates through the mechanisms that bring a debate to an end while keeping its potential continuation in sight. These mechanisms are indeed discursive, but in the Foucauldian sense, which includes not just logical statements, but also tools, charts, formulas, instrumentation. Getting people to follow commands depends on an *art of persuasion*, namely *rhetoric*, understood in the broadest terms to include not only metaphors and symbols, but also institutional routines and spatial arrangements, instrumentation, quantitative measurements, tests and demonstrations, even appeals to authority and implied threats.[12]

The logic of legitimacy, therefore, is not always linear. It can be circular, self-referential, defensibility operating like a catch-22. Finally, defensibility does not only take time and repetition. It works by taxing the time resources of your opponents, by giving your opponent the *runaround*, foregrounding the futility of wasting precious time and channeling her towards an apparently reasonable shortcut offered by reputation, credibility and an appeal to authority. *Kafka*, ultimately, will be our guide to legitimacy, not Habermas and Luhmann:

> Before the Law stands a doorkeeper. To this doorkeeper there comes a man from the country who begs for admittance to

the Law. But the doorkeeper says that he cannot admit the man at the moment. The man, on reflection, asks if he will be allowed, then, to enter later. "It is possible," answers the doorkeeper, "but not at this moment." Since the door leading into the Law stands open as usual and the doorkeeper steps to one side, the man bends down to peer through the entrance. When the doorkeeper sees that he laughs and says: "If you are so strongly tempted, try to get in without my permission. But note that I am powerful. And I am only the lowest doorkeeper. From hall to hall, keepers stand at every door, one more powerful than the other. And the sight of the third man is already more than even I can stand."[13]

Defensibility means that you lead your opponent into a maze, where all the road signs point towards the conclusion at which you'd like her to arrive, and all the other turns lead into blind allies, exits guarded by fearsome doorkeepers, long corridors where all the doors are closed, and interminable waiting rooms. And all the while the clock is ticking. Having tried her hand at some of these confrontations; exhausted herself in some of these runarounds; wasted time in the cul-de-sacs; having tried "enough" times; she ultimately follows the signposts and arrives at the appointed exit acknowledging that the conclusion is "valid." The maze has no center. There is no Ur-source in which the capacity to persuade is stored. There are only walls and the cunning intelligence that built them.[14]

A final observation by Weber will complete this understanding of legitimacy. Every system of domination, he says: "requires a staff ... a special group which can normally be trusted to execute the general policy as well as the specific commands." The motives that lead the staff to obey commands are not quite the same as the motives of the rank-and-file. While ordinary people may obey a command "from individual weakness and helplessness," that is, the limiting case of belief in legitimacy is the purely negative belief that "there is no acceptable alternative," the staff's "ideal [value-rational] motives" for obedience "largely determine the type of domination." In short, when it comes to the rank-and-file, a system of domination can sometimes "afford to drop even the pretense of a claim to legitimacy" (i.e. it becomes equivalent to pure deception, without any defenses at the rear), but it cannot do so with the staff. The officials and experts who transmit a command, a regulation or a ruling, who issue, enforce and supervise it, must believe that it is valid, rationally defensible, since they are the ones who will conduct the defense, who will lead the opponents into the maze and guard its exits.[15]

Ultimately, they must believe in the legitimacy of the system of rule not only because they are its relays and conveyer belts, not only because they draw their livelihood from it, but also because they are *repeat players*. In fact, the status of "staff" should be extended to all repeat players in a system, even if they are ostensibly "on the other side" – defense lawyers, lobbyists, compliance officers, union negotiators, or non-profit watchdogs. Their temporality is neither the irreversible, singular command that descends like fate on the lowly rank-and-file, nor the fully reversible, limitless horizon of the "ideal speech situation." It is a temporality of finite, cumulative, repetition, where precedent matters, where debate doesn't begin from a blank slate, but is picked up somewhere well above the "grounds," and must also be brought to an end at a certain point. Without positive belief on the part of the staff, without defensibility being their "regulative ideal," the system collapses. I wish to drive through the red light. I can see no other cars and no reason not to do so. But the patrolman sits there on his motorcycle and shakes his head. I quietly curse the fools who put the traffic light here, but I obey the patrolman's nod because I do not have an acceptable alternative. But the patrolman who supervises the intersection must feel that there are good reasons for the command communicated by the traffic lights, even if he doesn't quite know these reasons, or even if the reason is simply the vague and general idea that obedience to a correctly issued command is an important value in and of itself. If the patrolman no longer believes any of these things, and ignores the drivers who openly flout the law, or waves one through but stops the other arbitrarily, then the system of rule no longer appears legitimate.

And all the while, a system of domination must also contend with the dynamics of symbolic pollution. The staff are personally invested in the system of rule and its legitimacy, not only because they draw their livelihood from it, but also because they inhabit the fuzzy temporal boundary where the "force of the better argument" shades into force plain and simple, where logic and correct procedure shade into bias and summary judgment. One moment they are the executors of rational and fair procedures; in the next moment, however, as they bring debate to an end, they run the risk of appearing as the agents of arbitrary and capricious power. When they bring debate to a halt, they must believe that if it were to proceed, the command would be found to have been correctly issued, and fair and rational. Otherwise, they become tainted, even in their own eyes, with the attributes of deception, cynicism, and scandal, the well-known trope of the "crooked cop." Moreover, symbolic pollution is "sticky." It cannot be reversed, unless by a costly ceremony of cleansing and purging. Just like precedent, it accumulates and solidifies through repetition. Once tainted, the very attributes of rationality and fairness – slow deliberation, expert opinion, studied neutrality – begin to appear, like the crooked cop's badge, as the façade behind which sinister and illegitimate forces operate.[16]

The take-home point from this all-too-hasty foray into the debate between Habermas and Luhmann is that a crisis of legitimacy is neither the flash moment at which citizens see through the deceptions, nor a protracted questioning in the course of which the "normative force of counterfactual validity claims" is exhausted, but a crisis of the institutional frames and mechanisms that organize deliberation, and especially of the temporal frames that separate, in time, technical problem-solving from political decisions, facts from values, natural necessity from political bias, force (of the better argument) from force (of "appeal to authority"). This crisis is perceived by, and weighs most heavily upon, the staff, the repeat players, who find themselves at an ever-increasing frequency in compromising and uncomfortable situations. It is a crisis of boundary mechanisms in which the rhetoric of pollution plays a crucial role. That's why the crisis is recursive, because the accusation of pollution reinforces, by its very direction, the position of those entrusted with maintaining correct partitioning, yet their response, in the form of renewed separation and purification, must be carefully calibrated. It depends on ingenuity, delicacy, sense of correct timing, patience, and constant adjustment, without which the frames collapse again. This is also why the great multiplier – the internet – exacerbates the crisis. Its main pernicious effect is not the proliferation of fake news and unreliable information, but the incredible *speeding-up* it imposes. Defensibility, as I said, takes time, has its own rhythm and tempo. Its frames and boundary mechanisms no longer function if they are forced to operate nearly instantaneously.

The mid twentieth-century concept of legitimation crisis referred to the problems of state-regulated capitalism. When the hidden hand of the market is replaced by the "visible hand" of the state, inequalities, economic crises, disasters, and epidemics no longer appear as a natural fate but can be traced to political decisions. Responsibility for the financial crisis can be laid at the door of the lawmakers who repealed Glass-Steagall, the regulators who looked the other way, and the politicians who encouraged "irrational exuberance." Responsibility for the "mad cow" scare can be laid at the door of government officials, who were too cozy with their industry clients. The result is a "universal pressure for legitimation" impinging on the state – politicians, legislatures, state administrative agencies, even the judiciary. They respond by presenting their decisions as foregone conclusions, forced upon them either by formal legal rules or by technical considerations. And they seek to further integrate natural, social, and psychological environments into the workings of the state, to render them legible, so as to better predict, control, justify, or obscure the redistributive consequences of political decisions.[17]

In this context, the post-war recruitment of scientists and experts into state agencies served to harness science and technology as auxiliary means of legitimation and control. Take, for example, the institutionalization of the system of National Accounting, developed by economists at the National Bureau of Economic Research (NBER). The initial impetus for this effort was a directive by the US Senate to the Department of Commerce to estimate the impact of the Great Depression. The Senate wanted to know how great the loss was, but nobody knew how to calculate the answer. To do so, NBER economists led by Simon Kuznets introduced business accounting methods into economics to construct aggregate measures of national economic activity as a set of inter-related "controlling accounts" (national income produced, national income paid out, etc.), in the same way that a firm, for example, would estimate its profit and loss. The measures developed by Kuznets became the basis for calculating the GDP (Gross Domestic Product). The system of national accounting, as a set of systematically inter-related measures incorporating the GDP and its different components as well as the Consumer Price Index (CPI – developed earlier) and various indicators of aggregate productivity, came together in the course of World War II and its immediate aftermath. It was developed in order to answer a set of urgent policy questions: How to pay for the war effort? How to determine the correct balance between defense and civilian spending ("guns or butter tradeoff")? How to avoid spiraling inflation at the end of war? What would be the effect of demobilization on employment? How to determine the correct split between profits and wages and thereby avoid industrial conflict? In the 1950s, finally, the system of national accounting was adopted by the United Nations as a universal standard (though it took a while until the Soviet Bloc joined).[18]

The crucial point is that this system of national accounting rendered something like the "national economy" seeable, legible, and therefore governable. "The economy" became the joint object of state intervention and economic expertise. It anchored a mutually beneficial alliance between the economics profession and the liberal state. The compilation and calculation of the various indicators was a massive jobs program for the economics profession, both inside and outside the state. Moreover, the indicators and aggregate accounts provided the variables to plug into the general equilibrium models devised by economists. By the same token, however, the system of national accounting bolstered the legitimacy of national economic planning. Political decisions with profound redistributive consequences were now not merely justified by reference to the theories of economists. *They were taken and formulated within a world that the economists constructed.* Value choices and ideological assumptions – for example, the exclusion of unpaid domestic labor from the GDP or the idea that the wages of laborers were rewards for increases in productivity – were baked into the very means of "seeing the economy" and rendering it legible. The very technologies of quantification and representation, not just the ideas of economists, functioned, as Habermas argued, as ideology legitimating unequal redistributive decisions. The system of national accounts formed a permanent interface, a "port," so to speak, into the body of the Leviathan, through which economists, economic expertise, models, concepts, and standards flow back and forth; through which the state was rationalized and "governmentalized," to use Foucault's term, and the economics profession was "officialized."[19]

Compared with this fundamental entanglement of economics and the state, with this permanent port into the body of the Leviathan, the much-bemoaned (or celebrated, depending on one's preferences) eclipse of Keynesianism and its replacement with neo-liberalism, monetarism, or what have you, appear as mere ripples on the surface of a deep and unchanging pond. No doubt it was motivated, at least in part, by wanting to undo this entanglement, to pull the state away from its involvement in the economy, and by the same token to disinfect economics from the pollution it suffered (see below). Hence the deregulatory agenda, massive privatization, the critique of all forms of economic planning, the near-blind faith in the rationality of the market, as well as the subjection of state agencies and auxiliary units to a permanent audit in the form of New Public Management (NPM). These measures, identified as "neo-liberalism," were extremely consequential, often quite harmful. The "efficient market hypothesis," formulated by economist Eugene Fama, stating that stocks always trade at their fair value, their prices incorporating all available information, certainly played a role in legitimating the irrational deregulatory exuberance that brought us the Great Recession of 2008. Yet, the by now extensive research on neo-liberalism does not document any reversal in the role that economic expertise plays in governing the economy and legitimating state action. If anything, we inhabit now a world that is even more economized, even more seen through and organized by the categories of economic expertise.[20]

While post-war critics like Habermas were much exercised by the danger of technocratic rule by experts, or by the capacity of science and technology to provide objective, seemingly neutral, justification for political decisions, they mostly missed the obverse and much more consequential effect of this mobilization. Science itself – or more precisely the regulatory and policy sciences – has become polluted, infected, by the very same problems and suspicions it was called upon to assuage.

Michael Gove, as the reader surely remembers, pointed to economists' complicity in the financial crisis to justify his claim that "people in this country have had enough of experts." This is true for all branches of regulatory and policy science. When administrative decisions redistribute pollution risks and prevention costs in a particular way, the research mobilized to support these decisions itself becomes suspect, its uncertainties and sleights of hand exposed to the glaring light of public criticism. In response, state agencies take it upon themselves to rescue their rescuers – since their fortunes are now entwined – either by organizing scientific consensus, or, on the contrary, by increasing participation and transparency, or by replacing expert judgment with explicit, objective procedures and tests, or by subcontracting regulation to quasi-independent bodies, held at arm's length. When these measures and framing devices work, they shore up the credibility of the experts and thereby the legitimacy of redistributive decisions. Yet, the inevitable result of these measures, indeed their intended result, is to set up politico-administrative-scientific hybrids. These are vulnerable to attacks that expose them as abominable transgressions, illegitimate mixtures of facts and values, where rational debate is brought to a premature end because of a hidden political agenda, pure bureaucratic formalities or the interests of researchers.

No less importantly, these measures fragment "science" further still. They create new policy sciences and regulatory disciplines – from risk assessment to "pharmacovigilance" – thereby exacerbating the other engine of legitimation crisis, namely jurisdictional struggles, mutual criticisms and mutual undermining among experts. The surge of interest in "expertise," as we saw, is a response to the increased uncertainty about who are the legitimate experts and about these hybrid institutions and disciplines. There is, in short, a sort of recursive process of mutual support, mutual shoring up, but also mutual pollution and collateral damage, between state agencies and scientific institutions. The "scientization of politics" inadvertently causes the "politicization of science," and the two processes reinforce and entangle one another in an unstable, crisis-prone mixture.[21]

In the first round, science and technology were mobilized in response to the legitimation problems of the liberal state.

The wager was that if political decisions could be construed as technical problem-solving, then their unequal distributive consequences would be perceived as legitimate. They would be "naturalized" as necessitated by objective constraints, rather than biased, interested decisions giving one group undue preference over another. The validity of commands could be defended, and debate brought to an end, by reference to scientifically established facts. Scientific advisory councils and expert advisory committees were set up to provide politicians with technical analysis of the means by which problems could be addressed. The sciences of "risk" evolved to replace the uncertainties and judgment calls attendant on these decisions with an ostensibly objective calculation of probabilities. They determined "acceptable levels" of pollution and thus a specific distribution of the costs between corporations and the affected population. If one wanted to challenge this distribution, one had to contend with the formidable array of studies, calculations, and stock-of-trade conventions employed by chemists and toxicologists.[22]

In other cases, regulative decisions were entrusted to an objective and transparent procedure, overseen by scientific experts. The Kefauver–Harris amendments of 1962, named after the Senator and Congressman who introduced them with the support of the Kennedy Administration, empowered the FDA to require that any "new molecular entity," vying to become a marketable drug, will be subjected to multiple rounds of clinical trials to determine its safety and efficacy. The amendments, long in the works and building on regulations that the FDA has already issued in previous years, were given a crucial boost when news broke out that Frances Kelsey, an FDA pharmacologist, has singlehandedly prevented the marketing of Thalidomide in the United States. Thalidomide was marketed in Europe beginning in 1957 as an anti-morning sickness drug for pregnant women. In early 1961 it was taken off the market after it was found to cause horrific birth defects. More than 10,000 newborns were affected, 2,000 of whom died. One year earlier, the American distributor of the drug, Richardson-Merrell, applied for approval to market the drug in the US. Kelsey examined the evidence and rejected the application. Merrell applied again, and were again rebuffed by Kelsey. In all, she has refused approval six separate times. As a result, very few American newborns were affected. The episode was leveraged by the legislation supporters – Kelsey was given the Distinguished Civilian Service Award by President Kennedy in a White House ceremony – to pass the amendments solidifying the FDA's oversight and gatekeeping powers.[23]

The Amendments required that all new drugs will be subjected to a careful sequence of clinical trials, culminating in randomized, double-blind, controlled trial (RCTs) to determine whether they were safe and effective. RCTs are a form of "mechanical objectivity." They promise to arrive at a determination by means of an objective procedure, a simple comparison between an experimental and a control group, which requires as little as possible reliance on subjective judgment (even the judgment of experts), and therefore minimizes potential "bias" – whether the bias is introduced by industry pressures, or by the expert's own unexamined assumptions, ideological convictions, and unconscious cognitive habits. Thus, the objectivity of clinical trials was mobilized to generate trust, to reassure the public that the FDA will protect it from the dangers of unbridled competition in the pharmaceuticals market. At the same time, the objectivity of clinical trials was also mobilized to respond to the legitimacy problems of the liberal state. For years, the FDA's attempts to claim *de jure* jurisdiction over evaluating and regulating not only the safety of drugs, but also their efficacy, were thwarted by the Courts, corporations, and conservative politicians, who argued that it would be tantamount to letting the State pick winners and losers in competition among manufacturers. Only the hidden hand of the market, they argued – namely, sovereign consumers, advised by their knowledgeable and trustworthy physicians, freely choosing between available products – could do so fairly and legitimately. So powerful was this legitimation concern that West Germany, in contrast, remained committed to self-regulation by manufacturers in collaboration with the Federal Chamber of Physicians even after the Thalidomide tragedy. With the 1962 legislation in the US, however, the jurisdiction over "calling winners and losers in the market" and over determining a fair distribution of the costs of protection between producers and consumers, was delegated to RCTs. Their objectivity would guarantee the fairness of the procedure. No less importantly, the careful orchestration of the process – with pharmaceuticals submitting a study protocol identifying hypotheses and measures prior to their being tested in phase I, II, and III trials; and with a period of review, consultation, and hearings preceding the final decision – served as a temporal frame that foregrounds technical deliberation and bounds it from the exercise of gate-keeping power.[24]

Or, in yet other cases, the experience and judgment of experts – "disciplinary objectivity" – were pooled together to support bureaucratic decision-making. A good example is the British Industrial Injuries Advisory Council (IIAC). It is composed of medical experts and entrusted with compiling a list of occupational diseases entitling specific groups of workers (but not others) to compensation for injuries sustained and illnesses acquired on the job. If you were a British worker suffering from ill-effects that you attributed to hazards in your workplace, but your ailment was not on the schedule of occupational diseases created by the IIAC, good luck to you! If you tried to dispute the decision, you were referred to the fact that most members of the Council were eminent medical experts, thus presumably neutral with respect to the conflict of interests between employers and unions, and representing the prevailing medical consensus. You were also told that the experts themselves did not make the decision in your case. They considered the existing scientific evidence, engaging in a wide-ranging and continuous debate, to determine the schedule of recognized occupational diseases. The decision to deny your petition was made by bureaucrats in the relevant Ministry or at National Insurance, who took the schedule into account as a way of disciplining their decision-making and guaranteeing that it would be fair and reasonable. This framing mechanism carefully separated means and ends; facts and values; knowledge and power; the repeatable time of expert weighing of the evidence from the clear-cut, irreversible time of a decision; to guarantee that each did not infect the other. While your case may now be closed, petition denied, the Council's experts will continue to review the evidence as it emerges. The debate will continue, and perhaps in the future the Council will revise the schedule to include your ailment as a bona fide occupational disease.[25]

In the second round, however, science and technology themselves became infected with the very pollution they were meant to cleanse. It became clear, for example, that the determination of "acceptable levels" was based on tests that measured the impact of one chemical at a time, instead of considering the far more realistic question of the synergistic effect of multiple chemicals present at once. A disciplinary convention meant to guarantee the comparability, reliability, and reproducibility of laboratory experiments now appeared as the worst kind of "cheating tactic," a license to pollute designed to shield regulators and manufactures from the true (human) costs of their decisions. For Ulrich Beck, this was damning "enough to call for the public prosecutor."[26]

In the UK, critics from among the former staff of the IIAC pointed out that despite the promise of unbiased and open-ended weighing of the evidence, the panel of experts was extremely reluctant to include any new occupational diseases in its schedule, or to remove diseases from it. Worried about making a mistake and opening the floodgates to new claims (or to protests), it hid behind a combination of evidentiary and procedural arguments, a hybrid epidemiological-administrative calculus, to effectively freeze the schedule and thus arbitrarily favor some groups of workers and employers (those already in) over others. Moreover, by failing to take action on revising the schedule, the IIAC was essentially making the decision to deny new claims. The framing mechanism that separated expert review from administrative decision, repeatable time from irreversible time, became strained.[27]

This immobility was not some peculiarity of British medical conservatism or bureaucratic sclerosis. In the US as well, the agencies involved in carcinogen regulation were faced with a dilemma: anticipating judicial review, they needed to bring scientific debate to an end and lay down clear-cut, transparent, procedurally fair decision rules. But this meant that they could not keep up with the scientific evidence, appeared overly inflexible and ultimately (when cutting-edge research was mobilized by petitioners) arbitrary. New, more flexible guidelines allowed them to modify their substantive determinations of carcinogen risk in accordance with new evidence, "but in doing so [they] virtually invited case-by-case attempts by manufacturers to rebut the presumption of risk." The case-by-case litigation increased the chances that agencies' decision-making will appear, at least in some cases, arbitrary and biased, adulterating the scientific evidence with administrative considerations, or conversely, leaving decision-making in the hands of unelected scientists. As Demortain says: "Scientists shape risk regulation more than they would care to admit."[28]

The "stickiness" of symbolic pollution guarantees that these cases, where the agency's decision-making is exposed as biased or overly technocratic, would have a disproportionate effect on the reputation of the agency. Paradoxically, therefore, the very recourse to expertise increases uncertainty and threatens legitimacy because now the public is witness to controversies between scientists, conducted in the open and often descending to *ad hominem* attacks. The result is, as we saw in Chapter 4, that the whole huge domain of risk – of risk discourse, risk disciplines, risk litigation – becomes thoroughly politicized, and the authority of experts destabilized. The pernicious consequences of the decisions legitimated by risk experts – the resulting inequalities, the actual pollution and environmental degradation, the hidden triage of population health – were laid at their doorstep. Instead of politics becoming technical problem-solving, science became politicized. Patients' groups, environmentalists, anti-nuclear activists, NIMBY groups, all combined in demonstrating the biases, hidden assumptions, value choices, and interests that underlay seemingly technical measurements and determinations of facts. They demanded transparency and a seat at the table. They equipped themselves with their own science, their own experts, which meant that the various regulatory and policy sciences became arenas of conflict between competing expert groups, lay experts, social movements and think tanks.[29]

Even the FDA, which for a long time withstood attacks on its reputation better than most other agencies, did not escape becoming tainted. In the course of Congressional hearings about oral contraception in 1970 and 1974, FDA career officials testified about numerous infractions, including extensive undocumented consultations with drug companies, and the overriding of drug reviews without documentation or justification. The short-circuiting of temporal frames meant to separate technical review from administrative decision seemed to have caused the staff itself to question the rationality and impartiality of regulation. The taint of "industry bias," in its turn, left the agency more vulnerable to political attacks from both sides, including libertarian complaints about the "drug lag," the overly lengthy process of approving new drugs. Reforms meant to expedite drug review had the predictable effect of increasing the suspicions from the left of industry bias and of demoralizing the staff.[30]

Hence, in a third round, the state must intervene to rescue its rescuers; it, or a third party, must organize regulatory science in a way that minimizes its exposure to potentially fatal criticisms. It is possible to distinguish at least four types of approaches seeking to defuse the crisis. I summarize them in Table 2, which is meant as a visual representation of the following hypothesis: the social scientific debate about expertise outlined in Chapter 2 mirrors the competition and struggle between the different responses to the legitimation crisis. Each distinct position in the debate parallels one way in which state authorities, scientific institutions and groups of stakeholders seek to reorganize regulatory science so as to avoid the recursive dynamic by which the "scientization of politics" and the "politicization of science" continuously infect and entangle one another. Unfortunately, the mechanisms discussed in the next chapter, just like the theoretical positions discussed in Chapter 2, are unstable, shot through with tensions and contradictions, and dependent on careful, continuous calibration of framing devices. They also contradict one another, each constituting an implicit, and often explicit, criticism of the other, thereby combining into a tension-ridden, crisis-prone mixture.

Table 2   Typology of Responses to the Legitimation Crisis

		Problem of Trust	
		Trust in transparent, objective, public procedures	Trust in trained judgment of experts
Problem of Extension	Technocratic decision-making	Objectivity	Exclusion
	Participatory decision-making	Inclusion	Outsourcing

6

Inside the Vortex

The crisis of expertise is a strange crisis that feeds off and derives energy and momentum from the strategies devised to prevent or to fight it. The responses to the crisis become indistinguishable from its dynamics, incorporated into its swirling vortex. In what follows, I discuss the four responses detailed in Table 2 – exclusion, inclusion, objectivity, and outsourcing – noting especially their limitations, weak points, and vulnerabilities, the unintended ways in which they add fuel to the fire, rather than put it out. Before I begin, however, I would like briefly to clarify the sense in which I call them "strategies" or "responses" to the crisis of expertise. More often than not, they are a "strategy without a strategist." There is no master planner behind them, nobody who has grasped the full depth and dimensions of the crisis, and has set out to devise an appropriate response. There are, however, myriad local actors whose perceptions of difficulties, failures, and challenges, and their consequent lines of action, initially diverge but gradually become aligned and orchestrated into a coherent strategy by the *engines* of the crisis: the ever-closer entanglement and blurring of boundaries represented by regulatory and policy science; the intensifying of jurisdictional struggles, exacerbating the uncertainty as to who are the relevant experts for the problems at hand; and the constant dynamic of "overflowing" by which technical or organizational solutions to existing problems generate a new set of unforeseen problems and create new publics composed of stakeholders and lay experts.[1]

Strategy I: Exclusion, or boundary-work to generate trust in technocratic expert judgment

Perhaps the most common response is for state agencies to double down on their efforts to organize scientific consensus by a variety of gate-keeping mechanisms designed to maintain an artificial scarcity of expertise. These are – typically – quasi-governmental bodies composed of the most trusted experts, consecrated as the mouthpieces of scientific consensus – science courts, advisory committees, scientific boards, consensus panels, and so on. These are precisely all those "organizations with acronyms," about which Gove complained: the National Academy of Sciences (NAS), the National Research Council (NRC), the Institute of Medicine (IOM) and the National Academy of Engineering (NAE) in the US, the Superior Health Council (HGR) in Belgium, the Dutch Health Council – the *Gezondheidsraad* – to name but a few.[2]

Or the state agency compiles a list of approved experts and sets out the criteria, career ladder, and probationary period one must fulfil in order to become an expert, as the FDA does with chemists (including those working for pharmaceuticals) and with monitors of pre-clinical studies. With its emphasis on gatekeeping and selecting the correct experts, this solution is clearly analogous to Collins and Evans' position in the debate about expertise, who would limit technical advising and decision-making to a core-set of experts with genuine contributory expertise in the matter.[3]

In order to organize scientific consensus, these agencies typically isolate the experts and their deliberations from public scrutiny. To the extent possible, they work under principles of confidentiality and consensus, avoiding as much as possible public scrutiny of their deliberations and the surfacing of controversies onto the public sphere. Finally, the separation of facts from values, science from politics, is organized by the frame of "consultation." The Dutch Health Ministry, for example, is supposed to initiate the process by posing a

question or defining a problem; the *Gezondheidsraad* is supposed to research the matter and come back to the Ministry
with a report. The Ministry, seemingly, drives the process,
defines the ends, and then merely consults the experts about
the facts. This is, however, an institutional *frame*, almost a
ritual, geared to generate legitimacy by clearly separating the
moments of decision and consultation, fact-finding and choice
between values. Underneath the frame, however, a different
reality obtains. To prevent tensions, misunderstandings and
controversies, the *Gezondheidsraad*'s staff meets regularly with
the Ministry's officials, prior to the moment when the official
question is posed, to work out together the definition of problems and the wording of the questions that will be put to the
Gezondheidsraad.[4]

In an odd case of "going native," the sociologists of science
who were contracted to conduct a study of the *Gezondheidsraad*, abruptly jettisoned their usual support for transparency and public participation, and instead reaffirmed the
Health Council's exclusionary organization as their "normative
conclusion." They thus succinctly formulated the logic of
exclusion as a strategy for dealing with the crisis of legitimacy.
Independent scientific advice, they said, can only "be acquired
from institutions in which scientists can deliberate, disagree,
and argue in relative seclusion without the weight of interests
and representation. Thus, we will argue against the 'democratization' of such advisory bodies, if this democratization
would mean that their deliberations will all be public, and
that their members will be selected as representatives of various
social, economic or scientific interests."[5]

The obvious weakness of this strategy is that the very procedures meant to select and shield the experts can appear as
stacking the deck; as being non-transparent and cutting off
debate prematurely. To a skeptical observer they can appear
as an arrangement in which the political and scientific estab-
lishments band together and close ranks against renegade,
iconoclastic scientists or lay experts, an argument used to
great effect by Andrew Wakefield and his supporters in the
controversy about the purported link between autism and
the MMR vaccine. It only requires relatively small "bugs"
or oversights in the selection procedures to destabilize the
whole mechanism, shatter the protective frame, and introduce

skepticism and suspicion. Or, if the delicate negotiations preceding the consultative frame are foregrounded by critics; if the public learns that the experts routinely collaborate with the authorities to predefine what questions can and cannot be put to them, trust will quickly flip into mistrust. Once tainted, the stickiness of symbolic pollution greatly reduces the effectiveness of this strategy. In fact, it can exacerbate the crisis of legitimacy, rather than forestall it.

Hence the decided emphasis, increasing over time, on communicating public guarantees of the *neutrality* of the experts, a greater attention to the public relations aspect of how the experts are selected, and to the framing devices necessary to maintain their legitimacy. This tendency, however, inevitably works against the principle of selecting on the basis of contributory expertise; it introduces a tension between searching for the experts that best represent disciplinary consensus and the experts who appear most trustworthy.

This tension is especially evident in the selection procedure employed by the judge in the highly contentious Silicone Breast Implants litigation analyzed by Sheila Jasanoff. In the absence of established knowledge about the implants' potential adverse effects; with dueling experts for the two sides arriving at diametrically opposed conclusions; and with the certain prospect of continuing litigation even after he rendered his decision, the judge sought to "create a body of authoritative scientific opinion for use in future trials." He appointed a National Science Panel composed of four experts in related fields to assist him in the most contested evidentiary issues. What made the report of this panel credible, given that they did not conduct their own research on the problem at hand, that is, they did not possess contributory expertise in research about silicone implants? The key was the public dramatization of neutrality. The judge worked very hard to devise a procedure that would guarantee no apparent bias in the selection and functioning of the experts. First, he selected a provisional panel of experts, whose job was to make nominations to the National Science Panel. The judge was, as Jasanoff says: "building walls within walls"; that is, he was building the labyrinth within which potential challengers would lose their way. Nominees were questioned by the two sides' representatives. Nobody with connection to the manufacturers could be selected. Nobody who was ever involved in implants' litigation could be selected. *In effect, nobody who was actually conducting research on the matter could be selected.* In other words, the selection procedure was geared to communicate objectivity by minimizing as much as possible potential bias, while sacrificing the degree to which experts possessed first-hand, substantive knowledge of the matter at hand. Interactional expertise sufficed. Once constituted, panel members were shielded from intrusion. All communications with the panel went through an attorney appointed to represent it.[6]

These carefully constructed frames and boundaries, these "walls within walls," were meant to empower the expert panel to bring the debate to an end, without appearing arbitrary or unduly biased. The judge directed the panel to consider whether other experts in the field would consider dissent from their report a "legitimate and responsible disagreement within your profession." As Jasanoff says, this instruction turned the prevailing standard for evaluation of expert testimony – the *Frye* standard – on its head. Instead of asking whether a particular expert's testimony enjoyed general acceptance in the field, whether it represented disciplinary consensus, the judge was in effect asking the National Science Panel to "manufacture a consensus that would function as general acceptance." The panel members were uncomfortable with the directive, but ultimately gave the judge a mostly "case closed" statement, finding that silicone implants were not linked to any disease and that "a large majority of scientists in our respective disciplines would find merit in our reviews and analyses." In short, the extraordinary efforts taken to rarefy the pool of experts, while preserving the image of neutrality, were intended to pay off in the form of the ability to bring debate to an end in a legitimate manner.[7]

The most consistent and far-reaching project – though, probably for this very reason, never realized – to rebuild legitimacy via the exclusionary strategy is Supreme Court Justice Stephen Breyer's proposal to create a new centralized Federal agency composed of elite professionals, modeled upon the Office of Management and Budget (OMB), entrusted with jurisdiction over all matters relating to the regulation of risks in the Federal Government. Scientific consensus panels, in Breyer's view, no longer shore up the legitimacy of regulatory agencies. However carefully selected to communicate neutrality, the assumptions they make in order to arrive at risk estimates are deconstructed by the adversarial process and become a lightning rod for contending political forces. He is similarly skeptical about the strategy, discussed below, of increased participation and transparency. Openness leads to increased public pressure on regulatory agencies, and in an "age of political distrust" merely leads to increased controversy. Breyer puts his trust, therefore, in mechanisms – especially a dedicated career track within the civil service – that would insulate the new agency from political pressures, while guaranteeing that its staff are politically savvy, experienced in legislative and administrative affairs, and have "the ability to communicate in a sophisticated way with experts in all [relevant ...] fields ... and to determine which insights of the underlying discipline can be transformed into workable administrative practices." Their neutrality will be reinforced also by the "long time horizon" informing the work of the Agency, "rather than responding in extreme fashion to the latest health risk." The Agency's prestige, professionalism and demonstrated neutrality will allow the staff to develop strategies for bringing debate to an end, methods to determine a "natural regulatory stopping place ... which does not depend upon the regulator's subjective reaction to the facts of an individual case." I am very sympathetic to Breyer's proposal. Like him, I do not think that the bad rap civil servants get is justified. The ideals of professionalism, studied neutrality, and commitment to the public weal characteristic of a strong civil service are one of the prize assets of liberal democracies. But even Breyer himself can provide no realistic account as to how or why Congress will support his proposal. It is extremely unlikely that legislators would be interested in empowering experts and career civil servants to have final say on the highly politicized matter of risk, while they themselves would endure the electoral consequences of such decisions. Needless to say, Breyer's proposal never got off the ground.[8]

To put the preceding considerations in the most general, admittedly abstract, way: in the exclusionary strategy, legitimacy is produced by organizing scientific consensus by means of various gate-keeping mechanisms, namely by what sociologists call "boundary work": the rhetorical strategies and organizational arrangements by means of which scientists and their allies distinguish "science" from "non-science," experts from laypeople, facts from opinions. Retracting Wakefield's article and revoking his medical license is an obvious example of boundary work, even if one thinks that it was fully justified and necessary. The frame of consultation, mentioned earlier, is another such device. Politics is on one side, posing a question; science is on the other, providing an answer. These strategies present science as neutral and disinterested, while everything outside the boundary is deemed political and partial. What the sociologists of boundary work have never stopped to ask themselves is: *where is boundary work itself located?* It can't possibly be on the "science" side of the boundary, since it is clearly rhetorical, political, interested action. Yet, it cannot be on the other side either, because those who draw the rhetorical boundaries attempt to encircle themselves and leave the impure others out. So where is it? The only possible answer is that it takes place *within* the boundary itself, which must be understood not as a fine line, but as a thick zone of interface, a zone of hybridity where science and non-science are entangled; the zone, finally, of expertise. This means, essentially, that in order to draw the boundary, one must transgress it. In order to preserve the frame of consultation, staff members from both sides must meet and negotiate in the interface. To expel charlatans, ultimately requires not just rebutting their arguments and evidence, but also the exercise of administrative power. Boundary work, by itself, can never succeed in defending science because by its very operation it becomes public, interested action on the part of scientists and their allies. It takes place in op-eds, press conferences, well-publicized consensus documents, etc., as well as in the semi-bureaucratic zone of interface between experts and decision-makers.[9]

Recall, moreover, that the judge in the silicone implants case did not pick any scientists who actually researched the topic. This is because none of them was neutral anymore, precisely by virtue of their research. *Politics was already inside science*, already present at the laboratory bench, before the judge set out to construct an intermediary, interface zone of interactional expertise that could be defended as neutral. Similarly, when the *Gezondheidsraad* needed to formulate policy advice regarding dyslexia, it carefully avoided the professionals working with dyslectic children because disciplinary affiliation almost invariably predicted a particular position in the societal debate about dyslexia. Once again, politics were already inside the professional division of labor, and special measures were necessary to construct a "balanced" committee that would be perceived as neutral by outsiders. What this critique of the concept of "boundary work" means is that legitimacy is secured not by boundary work, exclusion and gatekeeping, but by those additional "walls within walls," these auxiliary mechanisms of framing and balancing. Yet, these mechanisms themselves are inside the volume of the boundary, and can be relatively easily picked apart, their interested nature exposed, and opened up to dispute once again.[10]

Strategy II: Inclusion, participation, and transparency

The obverse, diametrically opposite, strategy is for the government and regulatory science to cleanse the taint of political or industry bias by including lay members of the public in the deliberations of expert advisory bodies, especially in matters directly relevant to them, thereby rendering decision-making processes more accountable, transparent and responsive. This strategy has been especially evident in medicine, where it ranges from mandatory inclusion of patients or patients' advocates in the deliberations of advisory bodies and the design of clinical trials; through the increased purview and influence these groups were afforded in the drug approval process; all the way to state-sponsored yet vaguely worded schemes for "patient-centered medicine."[11]

This strategy is clearly analogous to the position – in the debate about expertise – of those sociologists who discovered "lay expertise." Arguably, the discovery of lay expertise came *after* health authorities – especially the NHS in Britain in the mid 1980s – have initiated a set of reforms targeted at including patients and their families in medical decision-making. Thus, while the sociologists of lay expertise focused on the struggles of embodied health movements as the key factor in forcing public health authorities and the medical profession to adopt inclusion and transparency strategies, there were other, no less important reasons for this shift. Partly, the reforms were a conscious reaction by government agencies and professional associations to the perception of legitimacy crisis and declining trust. They were, thus, a "strategy with a strategist," designed with the specific aim of addressing the crisis of legitimacy. Partly, they were designed to secure the cooperation of patients and their families in the context of chronic budget pressures and personnel shortage. Partly, also, these strategies of inclusion were coopted by corporate interests to gain another lever over the regulatory process. Finally, the inclusion of lay stakeholders alongside experts in advisory and decision-making bodies was also partly motivated by the interests and worldviews of the experts themselves. This was especially the case with relatively subordinate and marginalized professions in the 1960s and 1970s, who drew on patients and their advocates as allies in their jurisdictional struggles with dominant professions – psychology against psychiatry, nursing against medicine, the therapies (physical, occupational, speech) against both.[12]

Inclusion and transparency strategies, indeed, are not unique to the field of medicine, nor do they date only from the mid 1980s. A concern with citizen participation was central to the establishment of the Environmental Protection Agency in 1969. The law establishing the agency, the National Environmental Policy Act of 1969 (NEPA), set a framework of rules for public involvement in technical decisions affecting the environment, a "social contract" between citizens and government. The EPA's first Director, William Ruekelshaus, was strongly committed to communicating with the public and empowering local decision-making about health and environmental hazards: "the question is not whether there is going to be a sharing, whether we will have participatory democracy with regard to the management of risk, but how." The key regulatory mechanism employed by the EPA – the Environmental Impact Statement (EIS) – requires numerous public hearings, though they often tend to be dominated by commercial interests. The UK Food Standards Agency, created in the wake of the BSE crisis, incorporates similar inclusion and transparency mandates, and they are also reflected in EU legislation. The French mechanism of "citizens' conferences" is an especially well-designed and elaborate institutionalized procedure to involve ordinary citizens in discussions and decision-making regarding technical matters of concern, for example the use of GMOs in agriculture and food production.[13]

All inclusion strategies, however, are caught on the horns of a dilemma. Including members of the public in consultation and decision-making can generate legitimacy, but it also reduces the likelihood of consensus. "Transparency may exacerbate rather than quell controversy ... Participation ... becomes an instrument to challenge scientific points on political grounds." Thus, the most effective mechanisms of participation in terms of securing consensus, such as negotiated rule-making, tend to limit participation to representatives of organized interests. In contrast, the most inclusive mechanisms, such as ballot initiatives that are open to all adult citizens, do not "provide an institutional forum for deliberation and debate." They merely poll public opinion at one point in time, are particularly vulnerable to manipulation by orators and sophisticated public relations campaigns, and can be decided by merely a few votes' difference. As Michel Callon puts it, they can become a bit like a game of "Russian Roulette" with decisions of incredible import (Brexit opponents will surely nod their assent here).[14]

Successful inclusion strategies must negotiate this tension. They need to create deliberative forums that are bounded, yet are not perceived to be limited to only "special interests." Within these forums, they must perform an increasingly delicate dance. To reach a consensus, it is necessary to *persuade*. If the means of persuasion, however, are highly scripted and pre-formatted, inclusion begins to appear as window dressing, merely "going through the motions." The "force of the better argument" devolves into force, pure and simple. The key difference is in the framing, especially temporal framing. The problem is "that [persuasion] often occurs prematurely, when people should be listening or gathering information rather than attempting to gain agreement."[15]

When the US Army sought to build chemical munitions disposal facilities, it convened public hearings in nearby communities. As Robert Futrell shows, the attempt at securing legitimation via inclusion backfired spectacularly, when local residents felt that the officers and experts representing the army at the hearings were intent on conveying technical information top-down and dismissive of residents' questions and concerns. Consequently, the crowd got the sense that the decision was already made, and the hearing was merely for show. This meant that every persuasive argument the experts made, however technically sound, was immediately perceived as an attempt to quash debate. The temporal framing was decisive. Even when the army relented and agreed to fund Citizens Review Teams (CRT) that would write their own report, what mattered most in the end was the fact that the report was due a mere month before the final decision was to be taken in an EIS process that has already taken four years. CRT members, therefore, had no faith that their report would have any impact on the final decision. They were left with the sense that it was merely a means of placating a concerned public, rather than genuine participation in decision-making. In short, without careful temporal framing, inclusionary measures will fail to generate legitimacy and will backfire: "They were like a parent scolding a kid, who keeps asking why something is the way it is, saying 'because I said so.'"[16]

On the other hand, if consultation is too open-ended and loosely formatted, it is unlikely to yield consensus. In the 1970s, for example, the US Army Corps of Engineers experimented with a process of "open planning," but had to abandon it because, tellingly, "it did not lead to consensus on the substance of the projects." As government agencies have come under fire for their heavy-handedness and sought to design ever more carefully calibrated participatory formats, and as these often failed to secure consensus, the tendency has been for government officials or industry representatives to step back, limit themselves to "listening" and abandon any attempt to persuade citizens, lest it be perceived as seeking to end debate prematurely. The temporal formatting of participatory deliberations is so focused on avoiding premature persuasion, that it ultimately censors persuasion altogether. The Assembled Chemical Weapons Assessment (ACWA) program at the Department of Defense (DoD), which in 1997 replaced the failed attempts to secure support for chemical munitions disposal sites, avoided trying to persuade citizens that incineration would be safe. Instead, it has left the decision not only about siting, but also about the method of disposal, to face-to-face consensus meetings organized by an environmental mediation group, the Keystone Center, and composed of citizens from affected communities, state regulators, relevant DoD staff and EPA staff, and environmental advocacy organizations. ACWA even paid for Citizens Advisory Technical Teams (CATT) of experts, who provided the local residents with technical advice regarding alternative disposal technologies. This participatory process was much more successful in terms of generating legitimacy. It was even more efficient, time-wise, than the earlier heavy-handed approach, because the latter provoked such resistance as to stretch the process over thirteen years. Yet, by the time Futrell published his article in 2003, the all-important decisions about siting and disposal methods were not yet made.[17]

In cases such as these, the extraordinary lengths to which agencies go to construct an "ideal speech situation," unencumbered by any appeal to expert authority, inevitably sacrifice the staff's ability to persuade, to bring the debate to an end, or to direct the process towards what they consider a technically superior solution. This not only demoralizes the staff, who are reduced to the status of facilitators; it not only increases the degree of "inclusion friction," a damaging slowing-down of the knowledge production process; but it also creates the distinct possibility that the process will be hijacked (as Weinberg worried along ago) by whoever is best able to present themselves as authentic representatives of citizens' interests. The legitimacy gains may prove short-lived if it is discovered – as has happened in numerous cases since – that the patients' group, for example, was funded by industry, or that residents were swayed by a charlatan like Wakefield.[18]

Strategy III: Mechanical objectivity

A different strategy seeks to reconstitute the credibility of regulatory science by reducing as much as possible its reliance on both expert judgment and lay participation, replacing it with objective procedures, quantitative measures, and standardized tests. This is, as noted earlier, a strategy of "mechanical objectivity," in the sense that it aims to remove as much as possible the element of human judgment, human error, and bias, by replacing it with strict – "mechanical" – adherence to formal, explicit, and transparent rules, and by quantitative

measurement of performance or "impact." As the judgment
of experts came to be seen as profoundly biased by their ideological preconceptions, disciplinary assumptions, the hubris of
"seeing like a state," or their interests and ties to industry, the
alternative for state agencies is to cultivate "trust in numbers."[19]

The most outstanding example of this response is the 1962
legislation requiring the FDA to conduct randomized controlled
trials (RCTs) as part of the drug approval process. Since then,
there has been a push to require the use of RCTs, impact evaluation and "measurable results" in medicine more broadly, as
well as in domestic public policy planning (especially in education, with the "No Child Left Behind" emphasis on objective
tests of students' performance; as well as in welfare-to-work
programs such as the "Wisconsin Model"), and as a condition
for the approval of international development aid projects
by the Bush Administration's Millennium Challenge Corporation, the World Bank, the Gates Foundation, and similar
donor organizations. This response is clearly analogous to the
position of "expert systems" in the debate about expertise.[20]

The FDA's objectivity campaign began at least a decade
before the 1962 legislation. Previously, jurisdiction over the
evaluation of drugs was shared between the FDA – nominally
limited to evaluating safety – and the medical profession,
which through the AMA claimed the sole authority to evaluate efficacy. Drug manufacturers distributed newly developed
medications to physician-investigators, whose research was
submitted to the FDA as part of the drug approval process.
In practice, companies often submitted impressionistic reports
written by physicians, who testified that they have administered
the new drug to their patients with satisfactory results. The
FDA's attempts to claim de jure jurisdiction over evaluating
and regulating efficacy, as explained earlier, were thwarted by
the Courts because they would have been tantamount to letting
the state pick winners and losers in competition among manufacturers. Nonetheless, throughout the 1940s and 1950s the
FDA was gradually expanding its role by various bureaucratic
routes to become a de facto efficacy regulator.[21]

When it became a de jure efficacy regulator, as empowered
by the 1962 legislation, this was in no small part by recruiting
to its side the emerging discipline of clinical pharmacology.
Kelsey was trained as clinical pharmacologist and drew on

its ethos of "rational therapeutics" and its "impulse to pro-tocol" when assessing the gaps in the evidence submitted by the manufacturer about Thalidomide. Clinical pharmacology formed itself against what it perceived as the subjectivity and unscientific nature of American medicine. It entertained a "pervasive institutional distrust of the capacities of the mid-century American physician." Not only were most doctors, including those conducting drug "research," untrained in statistics or toxicology, their shoddy research design was highly vulnerable to placebo effects, the "dynamic nature of the disease state," and the "psychological biases of the doctor–patient relationship." In a context of growing public distrust of the AMA, the perception that it was too cozy with industry, phar-macologists moved to dismiss physicians' research as "a form of [drug] promotion" and their reports in consequence as subjective, "merely testimonial." In contrast, pharmacologists promised that strict adherence to RCT protocol – prospective study designs, detailed procedures, centralized administration of experimental assignment, randomization, control of placebo effects – would eliminate subjectivity. "Winners and losers" would not be picked by the whim of state bureaucrats, nor through collusion between self-interested corporations and venal physicians, but by an objective mechanism that will determine incontrovertible facts about safety and efficacy. The three-phase structure of clinical trials became the objective procedure for picking winners and losers. It even organizes the disclosure of information used in the financial valuation of companies. The results of trials are publicized to investors before they are published in medical and scientific journals. The three-phase system also defines the basic structure of legal contracts between companies and venture capital. Since unex-pected changes in clinical trial results can create huge swings in company stock prices or invalidate venture capital contracts, the mechanical objectivity of RCTs is essential for the whole system to work and for preserving the legitimacy of the FDA.[22]

As a legitimation strategy, mechanical objectivity is highly attractive because of the apparent simplicity and transpar-ency of interpreting the results of RCTs and of standardized, quantitative measures, which seems to guarantee their inher-ent fairness and unassailability (to criticism). Over the last decade, a group of economists has been advocating, with

semi-religious zeal, the use of RCTs to evaluate international
development projects. Their leaders – Abhijit Banerjee and
Esther Duflo of MIT's "Poverty Lab" – have been spreading
the gospel of RCTs through numerous TED talks, interviews
and speeches. Among the converted is the Bill and Melinda
Gates Foundation, as well as other "philanthro-capitalists,"
who have made RCTs a cornerstone of their ethos of "effective altruism," conditioning funding on "measurable results."
The US and UK Governments, as well, the first through the
Millennium Challenge Corporation (more about it later), and
the second through the Behavioral Insights Team, have also
integrated RCTs into their policy development and evaluation
processes. The economists' winning pitch has dwelled, most
often, on the apparent simplicity and transparency of the results
delivered by RCTS: "the beauty of randomized evaluations is
that the results are what they are: we compare the outcome
in the treatment with the outcome in the control group, see
whether they are different, and if so by how much." Since "the
results are what they are," there seems to be no possibility of
bias. The self-effacing, virtuous expert merely conducts the
experiment and then steps aside so the skeptical audience can
see the results for themselves (a ploy which truly appeals to
the philanthro-capitalists). As Esther Duflo says about herself:
"One of my great assets of being in this business, or maybe
I've developed it over time, is I don't have many opinions
to start with [...] I have one opinion – one should evaluate
things – which is strongly held. I'm never unhappy with the
results. I haven't yet seen a result I didn't like."[23]

The main weakness of the strategy of mechanical objectivity, Duflo notwithstanding, is simply that *it promises more
than it can deliver*. As should be clear from the discussion in
Chapter 2, the simplicity and transparency of RCTs or of
quantitative measures are more apparent than real. They depend
on following a protocol, a set of explicit and detailed procedures, yet it is impossible to "follow a rule" without interpretation, hence without subjectivity, assumptions, tacit
knowledge, and expert judgment. FDA medical reviewers still
need to exercise judgment in interpreting the results of clinical
trials and in deciding whether to approve or reject a new drug
application. Their judgments about efficacy and safety inevitably involve balancing perceived benefits against estimated

risks, and therefore contain an irreducible political calculation. They can be accused, therefore, and have been accused, of "bias" (whether in favor of industry or against it).

Additionally, RCTs and other quantitative tests depend on transforming qualitative judgment into clear-cut quantitative comparisons, yet it is impossible to make numerical measurements valid without standardization, that is, without a large-scale political project of disciplining people, organizations and processes: "quantitative technologies ... work best if the world they aim to describe can be remade in their image." The ability to conduct clinical trials depends on the vast regulatory bureaucracy of the FDA, which reaches all the way into the laboratories of pharmaceuticals, hospital wards, physician offices, and pharmacies. This project of disciplining provokes multiple new political contestations and legitimacy problems at its margins: Should dietary supplements, which make vague promises about health improvements, also be regulated as drugs? (the FDA lost this battle); Should protocols be relaxed for terminally ill patients?; Who qualifies as terminally ill and on what basis can medications be deemed potentially life-saving experimental drugs? Are placebo arms always necessary and is it ethical to deny efficacious medications to experimental subjects? The contentious politics of clinical trials erupted into public consciousness in the 1980s with ACT-UP's assault on the FDA, but they were percolating much earlier in struggles over experimental cancer treatments. They demonstrated beyond doubt that mechanical objectivity was no panacea for beleaguered regulatory science.[24]

To this must be added all the, by now, well-rehearsed limitations of RCTs and similar approaches. RCTs testing the safety and efficacy of drugs, or the performance of development projects, promise clear-cut results, but in reality are quite limited because they cannot monitor long-term effects (e.g. lifetime "body burden" of chemicals or the political fortunes of a social policy); because the trial conditions are unrealistic (e.g. we are usually exposed to multiple chemicals at one and the same time); because the experimental and control groups are typically not representative of the affected population (e.g. most of our drugs have been tested on white males); and because the very attempt to control substitution and drop out biases (namely, when people in the control group use good substitutes for the experimental intervention; and when people in the experimental group drop out to pursue substitutes) prevents assessing how multiple conditions and interventions (e.g. taking several medications at the same time) interact with one another in the real world. Put differently, RCTs are so focused on removing the purported biases of the experts that they sacrifice the precision (namely how close to the real value) and validity (how generalizable) of their results.[25]

Perhaps most damningly for the use of RCTs to monitor the safety of medications and chemicals, they are unable to detect rare, but extremely serious, adverse effects. When these limitations were exposed in tragic fashion in the Vioxx debacle – FDA clinical pharmacologists, relying on evidence from clinical trials, approved Vioxx, overruling epidemiologists, who expressed reservations about the drug based on observational studies (namely aggregate reports on actual usage by patients) – RCTs themselves became polluted, called a "tarnished gold standard." It did not help that the FDA was perceived as too cozy with the manufacturer, Merck, and overly accommodating because of the political clout of arthritis patients. Finally, the spectacular growth of commercial Contract Research Organizations (CROs) since the 1990s, now conducting more than two thirds of all clinical trials, has further tarnished the gold standard and reduced the usefulness of mechanical objectivity strategies.[26]

While it promises more than it can deliver, and ultimately becomes tarnished itself, mechanical objectivity also undermines trust in the trained judgment of experts, threatening to nullify the legitimacy gains from exclusion strategies. As others have noted, the current enthusiasm for RCTs reflects a climate of mistrust of experts, and contributes to it. Even RCT champions among economists admit that RCTs are not an optimal research strategy for a Bayesian experimenter who "places little weight on persuading her audience." When, however, experimenters as a community are faced with "an adversarial audience who may be able to veto [their] choices … then randomized experiments allowing for prior-free inference become optimal." This adversarial audience with a veto power includes legislators, executives, and obviously also the philanthro-capitalists, who have settled on "performance monitoring," impact evaluation, and "measurable results" as a

short-term strategy to defeat political opponents and to deal
with their own legitimacy deficits – short term because, as
we saw above, these techniques promise more than they can
deliver; short term also because they respond to the incredible speed-up and short attention span imposed by new communication technologies. Yet, for their part, RCTs reinforce
mistrust of experts and ultimately exacerbate the legitimacy
crisis: "In cases where there is good reason to doubt the good
faith of experimenters, as in some pharmaceutical trials, randomization will indeed be the appropriate response. But we
believe such arguments are deeply destructive for scientific
endeavor and should be resisted as a general prescription for
scientific research."[27]

The more general point is that objectivity is a profoundly
negative concept, its meaning ultimately deriving from whatever facet of *subjectivity* is problematized as dangerous or
misleading. As Lorraine Daston and Peter Galison write:
"Objectivity is related to subjectivity as wax to seal, as hollow
imprint to the bolder and more solid features of subjectivity.
Each of the several components of objectivity opposes a distinct form of subjectivity; each is defined by censuring some
(by no means all) aspects of the personal." Objectivity encodes
a specific set of ascetic values – "painstaking care and exacti-
tude, infinite patience, unflagging perseverance," self-restraint,
humility, even some forms of deliberate ignorance (recall Duflo's
"asset" of "not having too many opinions to begin with")
– which characterize the virtuous expert, and which function
as weapons in struggles against other experts. Thus, pharmacologists championing RCTs problematized physicians' clinical
experience as anecdotal, unsystematic and biased. Similarly,
the advocates of governance indicators and development RCTs
in the Millennium Challenge Corporation problematized the
subjectivity of State Department experts and sector specialists
in developing countries, accusing them of "clientitis" (namely
of being so well-versed with the country and leaders assigned
to their desk, that they have become identified with them,
perhaps even "captured" by them, so they are unable to distinguish between the client's and the US's interests). This problematization of expert subjectivity echoed the neo-conservative
critique of government experts coming at the time from the
Bush White House. The "adversarial audience with veto power"

was pleased and rewarded the champions of RCTs with funds and political support.[28]

Strategy IV: Expertise spun-off, outsourced, and reassembled

Less than a coherent strategy, this is more of a hodge-podge of different arrangements that nonetheless have several characteristics in common, which also set them apart from the three other responses to the legitimacy crisis of regulatory science. More precisely, what they have in common is that they come, relatively speaking, *after* the three other responses – exclusion, inclusion, and mechanical objectivity – and represent a reaction to their perceived shortcomings. In this sense, outsourcing arrangements are analogous to the "co-production" position in the debate about expertise. These arrangements could be perhaps organized on a continuum from the more genuine grassroots "hybrid forums" composed of local residents, and supported by sympathetic advocates and experts, who are conducting "popular epidemiology," all the way to transparently spun-off semi-independent governmental agencies, modeled after the private sector, such as the Millennium Challenge Corporation with its "chief executive" and Board of Directors. In between, one finds attempts to independently organize scientific consensus, the most visible example being the Intergovernmental Panel on Climate Change (IPCC), as well as voluntary arrangements whereby private entities (companies and non-profits) collaborate to "set, implement and monitor standards concerning ... the ways to define and address [risks]."[29]

The first and most important common characteristic of these arrangements is a quasi-spatial framing device that inverts and challenges the terms under which most inclusionary strategies operated previously. Outsourcing strategies are similar to inclusionary strategies in that they aim to generate legitimacy by involving a wide variety of stakeholders, lay experts, and ordinary citizens in the processes by which risks are detected, assessed, and addressed. Yet, the "invitation" frame of previous inclusionary arrangements, whereby members of the public are brought *in* to participate in the deliberations of regulatory agencies (as when parents of children with autism are included in the deliberations of the Federal Interagency Autism Coordinating Committee; or when the jury of randomly selected French citizens is brought to a "citizens' conference" at the premises of the National Assembly), is inverted by an *out*sourcing frame, whereby the conduct and/or coordination of regulatory science and sometimes even regulatory enforcement is sub-contracted *out*, to interstitial entities that exist on the margins of the state, or that are at least held at arm's length from the centers of decision-making. This semi-privatization or spinning-off is a quasi-spatial frame that aims to combat the perception that inclusionary policies are merely "window-dressing." It seeks to create the appearance as well as the substance of a more genuinely collaborative sharing in the processes of research and policy formulation. No less importantly, in the spirit of the age, it is "state-phobic." *Out*sourcing rather than inviting *in* aims to cleanse the pollution incurred by association with the state. Paradoxically, it even aims to cleanse the state from association with itself.[30]

A good example is the response of European authorities to the BSE ("Mad Cow") affair. This was a classic crisis of symbolic pollution, in which the credibility of scientific experts was stained by their involvement in regulatory policy, with the rebound effect threatening the very legitimacy of UK and EU governmental institutions. At issue was the perception that government veterinary experts were too protective of the interests of their agro-industrial clients, that they let these considerations cloud their judgment regarding the potential hazard to public health. This was taken as a failure not merely of individuals, but of the previous system of scientific advice, wherein scientific committees were embedded in policy-directing Ministries and in the European Commission Directorate. Given their proximity, and the administrative focus on inspection and enforcement, the mechanisms and frames that were supposed to separate risk assessment from risk management, science from politics, failed. Armed with this diagnosis, European authorities responded to the crisis by spinning-off a "self-standing and arguably more visible and transparent" European Food Agency, limited to conducting risk assessment. The autonomy and independence of the new agency would serve to restore the credibility of its scientific experts, not least

in their own eyes. No less importantly, however, the focus of
the new agency was no longer on inspection and enforcement,
but on post-market monitoring of adverse events. By its very
nature, a system of monitoring and reporting of adverse events
is further removed from policy decisions – unlike clinical trials,
it doesn't declare a food or a drug "safe" or "effective," but
merely alerts to the presence of risks – and thus better separates risk assessment from risk management.[31]

The second common characteristic follows directly from
this state phobia. Outsourcing strategies are similar to exclusionary strategies in that they, too, seek to generate legitimacy
by organizing scientific consensus. The mechanisms they develop
for this purpose, however, and how these mechanisms have
evolved over time, reflect a conscious rejection of the gate-
keeping practices I surveyed earlier (whether the institutional
credentialing practiced by the FDA, or the "walls within walls"
built by the judge in the Silicon Implants litigation). Outsourcing arrangements often arise "from below" and seek to tap
and assemble together diverse and complementary sources of
expertise, many of which exist outside the institutional frame-
works of the state and academic science, or in the interstices
between them. Moreover, under constant pressure to generate
legitimacy, they evolve into ever more diverse and distributed
forms of pooling and vetting expertise. While exclusionary
strategies seek to generate legitimacy by contraction, outsourcing strategies seek to do so by extension.

The IPCC is a good example of these outsourcing arrangements and how they evolve. While it has been set up by
the United Nations Environment Program, it is essentially a
self-organized global network of literally thousands of vol-
unteer scientists. Moreover, neither does it conduct scientific
research on climate change, nor does it set climate policy. Its
chief role is to review the existing research, synthesize it, and
formulate a consensus view (or represent the main contending views) of its significance. In short, its principal task is to
organize scientific consensus. The IPCC report communicates
this consensus as expert assessment and advice to the periodic Conferences of Parties to the Framework Convention
on Climate Change. In this sense, it is a spun-off, independent organization strictly limited to organizing the scientific
consensus on risk assessment, with the proverbial "firewall"

separating it from risk management. The credibility of its conclusions, however, is guaranteed not by the sort of gate-keeping mechanisms employed by the judge in the Silicone Breast Implants case, but by "independent self-governance." Moreover, under constant pressure by critics and the periodic manufacture of "scandals" (e.g. Climategate), the IPCC has responded by undertaking extraordinary efforts to broaden its pool of participants, to guarantee a diversity of views and the inclusion of dissenting voices, as well as offer more transparency into its own processes. IPCC rules require that its teams of reviewers and authors "should reflect a range of views, expertise and geographical representation." A draft of the report is peer reviewed not only by a broad range of scientists, but also by "stakeholders" – national governments, environmental groups, and corporations – who can submit comments and criticisms. Independent review editors, uninvolved in the work of drafting the report, are assigned the task of ensuring that the final report is responsive to these comments and criticisms, and to the concerns of dissenters.[32]

Similarly, the concepts and standards underlying the European Food Agency's system of post-market monitoring came from below, the work of a self-appointed commission of independent food microbiologists and toxicologists, while the system itself relies on multiple stakeholders, especially businesses, for reporting and self-regulation. In this respect, it is similar to the earlier, far-flung, loosely coordinated networks of Adverse Drug Reaction (ADR) reporting. These were initially private, developing outside the state in the US, UK, and France, typically as a collaboration between the pharmaceutical industry and the medical profession, hospitals and especially pharmacologists. Even as they became public in the 1970s – in the US, the FDA joined as a third side to the agreement between the AMA and the industry; but in France, the Centre set up by the industry was integrated into the Health Ministry – they remain decentralized and dependent on the cooperation between public and private entities. Unlike the centralized administration of clinical trials, reporting systems are knowledge infrastructures that depend on soliciting and combining input from multiple local sources. They combine statistical and epidemiological expertise with the "experiential knowledge of physicians in the field," as well as with the reports of

pharmacists and the patients themselves; or, in the field of
food safety regulation, they combine the abstracting and standardizing concepts of food microbiologists and toxicologists
with the practical, hands-on knowledge of inspectors and
business owners. The resulting forms of expertise – PharmacoVigilance Planning (PVP), Hazard Analysis Critical Control
Point (HACCP), Post-Market Monitoring (PMM) – are collective, hybrid endeavors.[33]

The third common characteristic of outsourcing strategies
is that they foreground uncertainty rather than certainty,
experimentalism rather than decision, precaution rather than
prevention. This quality is clearly a reaction to strategies of
mechanical objectivity. While they share with these a healthy
lack of phobia regarding quantification and standardization,
they are less sanguine about "trust in numbers" and are not
as quick to negate the experiential knowledge and trained
judgment of experts (lay or credentialed). Instead of conveying
the certainty of mechanical objectivity, they seek to generate
legitimacy by admitting uncertainty, opening up black boxes,
providing alternative scenarios and including dissenting views
(as we saw with the IPCC). It goes without saying that this
kind of response to the crisis of legitimacy, *because it is also a
response to all the other responses,* lacks resources for bringing debate even to a resting point, let alone a provisional
end. Indeed, in the most forceful formulations it essentially
denies that bringing debate to a provisional end is a viable
or desirable goal. It thus skirts very closely to giving up on
generating legitimacy altogether. The hope is, nonetheless, that
debate could be brought to a provisional end, at least from the
point of view of the staff, by reiterative *weighting* – in terms
of degrees of confidence, breadth of support – of the different
positions in the debate. Dewey's experimentalism plus Bayes'
Theorem, hopefully equals conditional legitimacy. The well-
dressed and well-heeled Bruno Latour, conducting his own
friendly audit of a climate monitoring station atop a mountain
in the French Alps, reported and photographed in gorgeous
colors in the *New York Times Magazine*, embodies the same
hope that legitimacy could be conjured by experimentalism.[34]

Climate science, as described by Edwards, and as practiced
by the IPCC, provides a good example of how the foregrounding of uncertainty works. It is a good place to consider its

evident limitations. While climate science originated in the efforts of the post-World-War-II American State to gain the ability to control and predict the atmosphere and the oceans, it has become by now a far-flung, thoroughly inter-disciplinary, outsourced endeavor. At its heart, what holds all its different disciplines, institutions, and cliques together is what Paul Edwards calls a "knowledge infrastructure" – a complex network of measuring devices, data bases, standards, and techniques of analysis. This knowledge infrastructure furnishes detailed measurements that are used by the IPCC to run several alternative models, essentially simulations identifying the "likely climatic impacts for several alternative scenarios of future greenhouse-gas emissions." The core practice of climate science is what Edwards calls "infrastructural inversion," namely "examining and re-examining the past [data] and constantly looking for possible sources of error and new ways to correct them …" Simulations, alternative scenarios, re-examining the data, applying new ways of correcting the data (namely weighting, smoothing, fitting curves, filling in expected values, using trained judgment to assess goodness of fit), all these bespeak a practice that not only operates under conditions of uncertainty, but which constantly manufactures uncertainty. What is "infrastructural inversion" if not experimentalism in Dewey's sense: "a reconstruction or reorganization of experience which adds to the meaning of experience and which increases ability to direct the course of subsequent experiences." Similarly, the precautionary principle finds its justification for mandating constant vigilance and experimentation in a situation of uncertainty. Rather than a decisive "test" as in RCTs, or a single authoritative number as in the use of composite indicators, the alternative simulations, constant inversion, and vigilant precaution are meant to secure legitimacy, in the face of fierce political opposition, by foregrounding uncertainty, comparing alternative assumptions and weights, constantly modifying one's claims, and highlighting the reliance on the trained judgment of experts.[35]

The weaknesses of this response should be obvious to the reader, since they replicate the weaknesses of the other approaches, and since the public controversy over the IPCC's reports, for example, has been fierce and unrelenting. The transparency and inclusivity of outsourcing strategies has often backfired by encouraging controversy. However careful their procedures of organizing scientific consensus, especially the reliance on broad peer review, they are vulnerable to being depicted as stacking the deck, prematurely cutting off debate and practicing "tribalism," as became painfully clear in the course of the "Climategate" affair. The independence of spun-off agencies, however meticulously hedged around with fire-walls, or even of genuinely distributed regulation "from below," can never be taken for granted. It is vulnerable to political takeover (witness the Consumer Financial Protection Bureau) or to cooptation by industry. Additionally, as has become clear in the course of the climate controversy, the reliance on trained judgment and simulation models makes it exceedingly difficult to bring debate to an end – indeed, it is calculated to keep it open in *reversible time*, as shown by the climate science practice of "infrastructural inversion" – and thus is especially vulnerable to the tactic of "reasonable doubt" and claims that its results are speculative and "more research' is needed. The well-known abuses of this tactic by tobacco companies no doubt merit to be characterized as "agnotology" – the social construction of ignorance by injecting doubt and denying that a scientific consensus exists – but this merely demonstrates how vulnerable are outsourcing strategies to this tactic, since they possess no reliable mechanism for bring-ing debate to an end in *repeatable time*, and no test to dis-tinguish between reasonable and unreasonable doubt. The valiant and often ingenious attempts of social scientists to come to the aid of their regulatory science colleagues by devel-oping such a test are, unfortunately, vulnerable to the same tactics.[36]

Not only do all four responses have their weaknesses, but they often undermine each other, representing sources of implicit, and often explicit, criticism of one another. Inclusion strategies have been formulated in direct opposition to exclusion strategies. Worse. Once inclusion has been institutionalized, it represents an irreversible barrier and it becomes impossible to revert to full-blown exclusion strategies. Mechanical objectivity strategies, for their part, are animated by a problematization of expert trained judgment. Worse. They can be used by interested parties to sow mistrust in experts. For their part, outsourcing strategies aiming for as broad and heterogeneous mobilization as possible by foregrounding uncertainty constitute veritable refutations of the promise of certainty offered by mechanical objectivity strategies. The examples of tensions and contradictions can be multiplied further, but the point hopefully is clear: the responses to the legitimacy crisis backfire and exacerbate it, especially as they spar with one another. Science itself becomes infected, and the attempts to organize, pluralize, mechanize, or outsource expertise are all caught in a self-reinforcing vortex of mutual pollution and mutual undermining. Yet, albeit tension-ridden and crisis-prone, the entanglement of science and the state survives and even expands. However mistrusted or doubted, expertise is even more indispensable and essential than ever before. It is time, therefore, to consider the countervailing forces.

7

Balaam's Blessing

In the *Book of Numbers*, we are told of the diviner and prophet Balaam, son of Beor, who was hired by King Balak of Moab to curse the Israelite tribes encamped on the Eastern Bank of the Jordan River. On the road, he is met by an Angel of God who bars his way. The Angel ultimately permits him to continue on his errand but warns him to speak only the words that God will put in his mouth. Having arrived at a high place, overlooking the encamped tribes, he meets with the King, makes the sacrifices and prophesies. His prophecy, however, turns out to be a divine blessing of the people of Israel for millennia to come. He repeats the blessing several times, at several different occasions and places, to Balak's great consternation. The story is captured by a succinct Hebrew idiom, of obscure origins – "בא לקלל ונמצא מברך" [*Ba'a Le-kalel Ve-Nimtza Mevarech*] – roughly translated as "having set out to curse, he found himself to be blessing." Modern Hebrew retains this idiom and permits its inversion for other purposes – "בא לברך ונמצא מקלל" [*Ba'a Le-varech Ve-Nimtza Mekalel*] – "having set out to praise, he found himself to be condemning."[1]

Combined, the two idioms are a commentary on the weak hold that the speaker's intention has on the actual (unintended) consequences of her words. They sensitize us to the tangle of relations within which utterances acquire their final meaning.

They recall the speed with which trust can turn into mistrust; the way in which symbolic pollution can infect the agents and acts of legitimation – recall how the British Government, by seeking to reassure the public that GMO products were safe, achieved the opposite and caused levels of confidence in GMO products to plummet. Having set out to praise, the government found itself condemning. Yet, the two idioms combined intimate that the opposite is also possible: expressions of mistrust, by their very nature, may become petitions for shoring up the founts of legitimacy; pollution accusations may serve to reaffirm the central position of the accused, the symbolic potency of purity.[2]

This recursive dynamic, whereby attack, criticism, and accusation end up strengthening the position of the accused, is the other side of contemporary controversies over regulatory science and expertise. In controversies about climate change, for example, while "scientists are treated as proxies for interest group," *science* itself "is held up as universal and impartial." For understandable reasons, those who have sounded the alarm about the assault on experts have tended to emphasize the former dynamic, the tagging of scientists with impurity, and to ignore the latter. To the extent that they made note of it, they tended to see it as mere lip service, delaying tactic ("more research is needed"), or sheer ignorance about how science really works. While often true, this is hardly the full story.[3]

Daniel Carpenter's masterful history of the FDA – *Reputation and Power* – contains numerous examples of how "the continuous crystallization of an organizational reputation … relied upon constant criticism of particular decisions and actions." Critics of the Agency, modern Balaams, set out to condemn its failings, only to find themselves ultimately reinforcing its centrality, extending its reach, validating its regulatory science, and shoring up its reputation:[4]

- 1963. In the midst of Congressional testimony providing a "shocking indictment" of the FDA, John Nestor of the Bureau of Medicine nonetheless reaffirmed the centrality of the FDA's procedures for drug approval: "American society and American physicians could not trust any drug that had been put on the market 'without the benefit of a New Drug

Application.'" The press, even the normally hostile *Wall
Street Journal*, attributed many of the failures exposed by
Nestor to the weakness of the FDA's formal powers, thereby
building a case for their strengthening.[5]

- 1968. Clinical pharmacologists, incensed by the FDA's
attempts to dictate drug dosages via package inserts, ultimately tempered their accusations of overreach by com-
miserating with FDA experts: "there are no villains in the
FDA, only victims of inadequate public support." If only
it were provided with adequate funding and staffing, they
effectively said, the FDA would not need to resort to heavy-
handed regulatory measures. They thus supported the FDA's
leadership's petitions to Congress for more resources.[6]

- 1971. Another fierce critic of the agency, who called the
demand for RCTs "scientifically unreasonable," sought
to defend himself against accusations of industry bias by
pointing that the FDA consulted him and relied on his
research, thus implicitly acknowledging the FDA's conceptual authority.[7]

- 1976. The withering rebukes to which Senator Ted Kennedy
submitted the FDA over its failure to govern early clinical
trials properly, played a key role in the eventual projection
of FDA "veto power to universities, institutes, contract
research organizations" via Institutional Review Boards.
Having set out to condemn the Agency, Kennedy ended up
blessing the multiplication of its powers and the extension
of its arms.[8]

- 1978. However trenchant and resonant are conservative
attacks on the "drug lag" – namely the delay in market
introduction of new medications, caused by the FDA's cumbersome procedures – they also have the unintended effect
of reminding the public "that the administration had regulated with prudence and deliberation," and has lived up to
its reputation as "a protector of citizens."[9]

- 2004. Even the Vioxx episode, which, as I noted in the
previous chapter, seriously damaged the reputation of FDA
experts and tagged them with impurity, was not without its
moments of blessing and reaffirmation. The very metaphor
of pollution used by the critics referring to a "tarnished gold
standard," also implied a petition to the agency to cleanse
its polluted image and restore its prowess as gatekeeper.

Then-Senator Hillary Clinton, previously "a frequent FDA critic," called on the FDA to "nominate a leader with vision and drive to ensure that the FDA upholds its gold standard of drug regulation." The industry group Pharmaceutical Research and Manufacturers of America (PhRMA) echoed Clinton by calling the FDA the "gold standard of drug safety regulation." Even long-time critic of the FDA, the consumer advocate Sidney Wolfe, reminisced about a time, a decade earlier, when "the FDA was the gold standard." For many of these critics, the implication was that the fall from grace, the tarnishing of the protective shield, was due to political meddling in the Agency by the Bush Administration. If the FDA could be buffered from such interference and its autonomy restored, no doubt the gold standard would also be re-polished to its previous reassuring brilliance.[10]

In the biblical story, it was divine intervention that turned the curse into a blessing. God literally put words in Balaam's mouth. The reasons we can glean from Carpenter's account are more prosaic. The pharmaceutical industry may have complained for years about the FDA's intrusiveness, overbearing regulation, and "drug lag," but when it contemplated a future without the FDA's imprimatur, it baulked. The Chief Medical Officer of Pfizer warned that "there has been a loss of public confidence in the FDA, and we can't afford to have that." Put differently, the reputation of the regulator and the credibility of its scientific methods have become an integral part of the product the pharmaceuticals are selling. If the FDA and its scientific officers were to be permanently stained by their proximity to business, the pollution would rebound back upon drug manufacturers, destroying consumer trust in their products. It would also leave them exposed to the wrath of injured patients and their lawyers if something went wrong.[11]

The same holds for conservative politicians. Republicans may have called the FDA "number one job killer," but when they passed the FDA Modernization Act in 1997, they uncharacteristically opted not for "direct and statutory" deregulation, but for "behind the scenes, under the radar" administrative deregulation (increasing the proportion of the FDA budget funded by user fees, namely by industry). In other words, they sought to weaken the FDA, to make it more accommodating to pharmaceuticals, while preserving as much as possible its reputation for scientific rigor and zealous protection of the public's safety. The reasons are not difficult to fathom. If public opinion surmised that the FDA was "acting more as a political body than a scientific one," its standards "dictated by the existing political parties," any failure of drug regulation, any widespread adverse effects, would be laid at the politicians' door with disastrous consequences to legitimacy. Put differently, just as the FDA's imprimatur became part of the product pharmaceuticals were selling, similarly, the credibility of its methods has become an integral part of how political actions were made accountable to the public as rational and fair.[12]

Clinical pharmacologists may chafe against the Agency's control over scientific careers and its procedural approach to expert judgment, but they are also keenly aware that the very existence of their discipline, the most distinctive characteristics of their expertise, are entangled with the institutions of regulatory science, of which the FDA is the most prominent. It goes without saying that doctors, patient advocacy groups (some funded and organized by industry, some authentic grassroots organizations) and public health watchdogs, even as they assailed the FDA from opposing sides, are invested in restoring its image as the public's protector, since they purport to speak in the name of said public. And they are also keenly aware of the extent to which the FDA's expert system – for example, in the form of drug labels and package inserts – has worked its way into the fabric of everyday life and has become part of the *doxa*, the ubiquitous expertise of patients and caregivers. While ordinary individuals may be open to criticism of this or that decision by the FDA, they are not prepared for life without its seal of approval, which has insinuated itself into their embodied practices of prudence and responsibility. For ordinary individuals, indeed, "there is no acceptable alternative." For them, every criticism automatically becomes an appeal to the state to restore the proper order of things.[13]

Taken together, these reasons no longer seem all that prosaic, and they are certainly not accidental. They demonstrate that public actions in our society – political, commercial, civic – take place within a densely woven web of legitimation from which they derive their credibility. Taken together, they tell a story about a recursive dynamic of legitimation, mutual

pollution, and mutual shoring up within "a networked congeries of audiences – [pharmaceuticals,] pivotal professional
and scientific networks, Congressional committees, consumer
representatives, and media organizations," and one should
include among these audiences also the staff of the Agency
itself (composed of clinical pharmacologists, epidemiologists,
statisticians, and career bureaucrats). At the center of this
network of audiences is what Carpenter calls the FDA's "reputation," namely "a set of symbolic beliefs about an organization." Every attack on the FDA, every condemnation, inevitably
also reactivated these beliefs and images, thereby mobilizing
a counter-audience invested in them. It is worth quoting Carpenter at length here:

> In part, however, the Administration's reputation persisted
> because of the acrimony itself. The ceaseless contestation of
> the organization's power and its image yielded not an abiding
> uncertainty about the Administration, but instead a persistence
> of the metaphors representing it. ... Every criticism embedded
> a portrait. And every portrait displayed an organizational
> capacity that someone in the pluralistic soup of American
> national politics could admire.[14]

When activists complained about "industry bias," they reinforced the FDA's image as protector of the public. When
industry complained of "over caution," it reinforced the perception of the agency as composed of careful medical specialists. When medical specialists complained of interference in
their autonomy, they reinforced the FDA's reputation for tough
and stringent procedural regulation.

This "reputation," however, these beliefs, images, and metaphors, are not purely empirical psychological phenomena, as
we learned from Weber and Habermas. If they are able to
turn the condemnations of modern Balaams into a blessing,
this is because they derive their force from a heterogeneous,
yet networked together, set of mechanisms and frames orches-
trating the defensibility of commands – the pivotal command
being the approval or rejection of new drug applications, with
all the attendant implications for public safety, the distribution
of risks, the well-being of individual patients, and the picking
of winners and losers in the marketplace. These mechanisms
include, among many others, the apparatus of distinct phase 1,

2, and 3 clinical trials, culminating in double-blind, placebo-armed, randomized controlled trials; the "protocol" submitted by drug manufacturers defining hypotheses and measures *before* they are tested; the designation of industry actors as "sponsors" for the purpose of a new drug application, thus enforcing a separation of research from drug promotion; the credentials, experience, and autonomy of drug review officers; the administrative buffer between the drug review process and the political appointees at the Agency; the institutional credentialing that requires companies to hire qualified and approved clinical pharmacologists and statisticians; the regulation of doctors via drug labels and inserts. These mechanisms orchestrate the interests of the different audiences, the repeat players, harnessing them, sometimes one against the other in a delicate balance, in the overall production of defensibility. They may chafe against this or that command, this or that mechanism or framing device, but they have a stake in the continued operation of the whole set, in the framing devices that hold pollution at bay, in the procedures that certify actions – even those actions that challenge and disobey the command – as publicly accountable. And they are conscious that they are acting within margins defined by the "ontological complicity" between the practical sense of ordinary individuals and the reputation or "symbolic power" of the FDA, acting as their protector and insinuating itself into their *doxa*. So, like modern Balaams, they find themselves at the end of the day blessing the agency, hoping the blessing will redound to them as well.[15]

I do not think this dynamic of Balaam's blessing is unique to the FDA, though among the agencies of regulatory science it may have been the most successful in exploiting it. At the risk of appearing naive, I would suggest that we should reassess, from this perspective, the significance of even those strategies that have been branded as "agnotology" – the manufacturing of ignorance, doubt, and uncertainty (where none should exist, so goes the implicit rider) – in the debates about the link between smoking and cancer, climate change, and so on. These strategies typically involve recruiting "high proof" scientists (namely, scientists or even citizen-scientists speaking in the name of "the scientific method" and demanding rigorous proof) to cast doubt on findings accepted as state-of-the-art by most relevant scientists. These skeptics usually point out uncertainties regarding how the evidence was collected and how it should be interpreted (and in some cases, they outright accuse other scientists of fraud, cherry-picking the evidence, or conspiring to block out dissenting voices). The doubt and uncertainty injected are leveraged to support claims that "more science is needed," that there is a legitimate debate on the matter between an entrenched scientific orthodoxy and a small minority of heretics and skeptics. The criticisms usually highlight small inconsistencies in the evidence, as well as the conventions and expert judgment necessary to transform the evidence into a manipulable format, or the models and theories necessary to interpret it. They fuel calls for "sound science" – in the words of a Republican Member of Congress skeptical of the evidence regarding climate change: "theories or speculation about it are not sufficient. We need science, not pseudo-science."[16]

By amplifying and leveraging uncertainties, at least some of these strategies are calculated to throw sand in the gears of the political and administrative institutions charged with addressing risks. To the extent that they are successful, they do untold damage to public health, perhaps even to the very fabric of life on Planet Earth. Yet, it is important to recognize that they are not an "assault on science." They are hand-to-hand combat *within* the tunnels and corridors of the labyrinth of regulatory science. The attacks on the IPCC in the wake of "Climategate," for example, may have diminished some of its authority, but they have also attracted more attention and increased the significance attached to its reports. "This is because all the parties involved act as if climate policy will be decided by science alone." For that very reason, these are risky strategies, because if they fail, if they lose the local struggle, they end up reinforcing and lending legitimacy to their opponents' key advantage, their claim to represent scientific consensus.[17]

The Republican call for "sound science" cited above was immediately picked up by the Union of Concerned Scientists (UCS) to serve as its own slogan and to draw the skeptics into a debate they were likely to lose, about the relation between data and theory in modern science. The skeptics may launch a challenge by contrasting their own "actual measurements"

with their opponents' reliance on estimates and simulations,
as happened in the controversy about temperature readings
from Microwave Sounding Units (MSUs) mounted on satellites,
but in the course of hand-to-hand scientific combat they will
be forced to adjust their analysis algorithms, to admit that
their measurements were also modeled, and to accept multiple
"new corrections, adjustments, comparisons to other data and
analysis techniques." If they were playing for *time*, we could
call this success (and some, like tobacco companies, *were* evidently playing for time), but if they set out to condemn climate
science as inherently biased and speculative, they failed. Like
a modern Balaam, they blessed their enemy, reinforcing the
process of "infrastructural inversion" by which climate science
constantly reanalyzes its data, making "new versions of the
atmosphere" that are then plugged into political debates.[18]

Or take the case of SurfaceStations.org, which organized
an impressive citizen-science survey of all 1,221 US stations
measuring surface temperatures. The point was to document
factors that could bias temperature readings at these stations
(a nearby asphalt surface, for example, would inflate readings; a shady tree would lower them) and to assess the impact
of these distortions on the overall estimate of temperature
trends. Perhaps, the organizers of the survey conjectured,
after we correct for all these shoddy readings, we will find
that there is no global warming trend. To call this project
"agnotology," because the organizers were "climate skeptics,"
would be to practice double standards. In many respects, this
project is no different from the multiple cases noted earlier
in which citizens, activists, and supporting scientists mobilize
to document industrial pollution, to contest biased measurements of its impact on local residents, or to resist the siting
and method of disposal of hazardous materials imposed by
government scientists claiming that there are no other choices.
More importantly, this project is one of a piece with climate
science's "infrastructural inversion": "to find out more about
the past, you keep digging into exactly how the data were
made." What else were SurfaceStations.org doing but finding
out "how the data were made"? In retrospect, however, it
seems that the risky gambit undertaken by SurfaceStations.
org failed. The research yielded no smoking gun, no major
bias in reported temperature trends. Their website is dormant

and has not been updated since 2012. At the same time, the campaign mounted by SurfaceStations.org did serve to improve the quality of government climate data, either directly, or by forcing government agencies to re-examine "how the data were made," and to correct obvious failures. It thus had the unintended consequence of adding to the credibility of climate models based on surface temperature measurements. Having set out to condemn climate science, the critics ended up blessing the reliability of its methods and findings. Having set out to destroy Carthage, they ended up adding to its fortifications.[19]

The example of SurfaceStations.org is useful because – unlike the pharmaceuticals, for example – in this case the critics had no material interest in the workings of regulatory or policy science. Theories of "regulatory capture" cannot make sense of this example. Nor should we think about it as a fortuitous result, caused simply by the fact that in this case the measurements happened to accord with what climate scientists were saying all along. What would have happened if the activists of SurfaceStations.org *did find* major problems with surface temperature readings pointing away from a global warming trend? The results would still have needed to be compared and reconciled with other methods of measurement (like the MSU readings, ocean temperature levels, etc.) They would still have needed to be plugged into models and simulations (with all the necessary corrections and weightings that constitute the expertise, the "trained judgment" of climate scientists). Even more importantly, the findings would underscore the importance of obtaining accurate measurements. They would prompt investment to overhaul the system of climate surveillance. Ultimately, they would demonstrate that climate monitoring (like drug approval) is an integral, by now inseparable, part of accountable government action in the face of uncertainty. It is extremely unlikely that any results obtained by SurfaceStations.org, however discordant, would have undone the mutual relations between climate science and state agencies. These relations, and the resulting system of climate surveillance, are woven into the very fabric of state action. They preceded the discovery of global warming and are rooted, for example, in the needs of military planners for accurate atmospheric and oceanic predictions (i.e. both data, and the models and theories that transform these data into predictions). Global warming was discovered within the fabric of these relations, and remains integral to them. As the gaze of military planners extends into the future, and as they need to justify budgetary projections and investments in preparedness, the trend of global warming becomes an integral part of the calculus of state agencies, even though their principals may purport to ignore it.[20]

The countervailing forces, therefore, are formidable. Even as regulatory and policy science is besieged on all sides (and torn from within), its sworn enemies find themselves at times blessing it with longevity and even greater centrality. The two-headed *pushmi-pullyu* pulls to the brink, then retreats from it, because it is impossible to carry out the modern work of government, the daily issuing of commands, directives, regulations, advisories, forecasts, appropriations, disbursements, mandates, without relying on the whole machinery of defensibility that makes it publicly accountable.

Moreover, this work of governing is not carried out solely in government offices, only by government officials, nor is it external to private entities, ordinary individuals, and communities. Government economic statistics, for example, the system of national accounting discussed earlier, the indicators and business tools provided by the US Commerce Department, are compiled through the reporting and participation of multiple non-state actors as well as economists in corporations and banks. By the same token, however, government economic statistics form the knowledge infrastructure for privately interested or corporate economic action, as well as for key branches of the discipline of economics. Like other forms of regulatory and policy science, economic expertise is, as I said earlier, plugged into the body of the Leviathan by means of a permanent port, the traffic along which is two-way. Just as FDA approvals are part of what pharmaceuticals sell, so the indicators published by the Commerce Department form an integral part of the self-interested rational calculation of private economic actors. For this reason, a critique of their integrity can do little more than reinforce the need for even more economic expertise in government. To put it metaphorically, the critique does not unplug the port, but flows through it.[21]

Being aware of the countervailing dynamic of Balaam's blessing, however, does not mean that we should do nothing.

Riding the vortex still requires strenuous efforts to keep one's head above water and is no easy matter, nor does it guarantee escaping its fatal pull. Many have heeded the advice of lifeguards not to fight the vortex, and yet drowned. This is not an argument for sitting back and waiting until the *pushmi-pullyu* swings back and the attacks rebound upon themselves and combust. While the attacks cannot dislodge policy and regulatory science, they do significant damage to its autonomy, authority, and prestige, as evidenced by the declining levels of reported public trust in the FDA or by the effects of "Climategate." Moreover, there is often not enough time to wait for the countervailing forces to assert themselves and for the *pushmi-pullyu* to swing back. The window of opportunity to reverse global warming trends may be closing. Lives are lost and public health is compromised when the FDA is weak. Being aware of Balaam's blessing, however, is a reminder, even in the midst of seeming weakness and retreat, that the defenses built by modern expertise are ultimately, in the long run, stronger than their opponents. The conflict takes place on their home turf, in familiar tunnels and corridors, equipped with multiple devices for channeling the opposition to points where it can be decisively defeated or made to bless what it set out to condemn.

Conclusions

Trans-Science as a Vocation

I did not write this book to offer a solution to the crisis of expertise. I do not have one. In fact, if I had a solution, if there was one to be had, I would not have written this book because it is unlikely that the solution would be a book, a work of dry scholarship. When it comes to public, political debate, the main contribution of such work cannot be to offer solutions, or to tell people what they ought to do, but, as Max Weber said in his 1918 lecture, "Science as a Vocation," to force the different sides to "recognize inconvenient facts — I mean facts that are inconvenient for their party opinions." Alvin Gouldner called this "bringing the bad news." A dangerous mission, by all accounts, as we know what the proverb says about the fate of messengers bearing ill-tidings. Faced with inconvenient facts, people lash out. Even more dangerously, the mission can succeed only if the teaching is applied to the teacher herself. You teach students (or fellow experts, or civil servants, or other stakeholders, or the lay public) how to recognize inconvenient facts by recognizing them yourself, recognizing and grappling with precisely those facts that are inconvenient to *your* party opinion. Yet, if one manages to make even a small contribution towards developing in others the faculty of recognizing, acknowledging, even seeking out the inconvenient facts, then it may be reckoned as nothing less than a "moral achievement."[1]

So what are these "inconvenient facts" one can learn from this book? Which are the sides that should pay attention to them? What are the responsibilities they entail? On the one hand, Weber himself, or more precisely all those today who knowingly or unknowingly speak Weber-ish, who seek to draw a clear line where science ends and politics begins, must reckon with the inconvenient fact that almost everything that is in dispute and at stake in current struggles is, as Alvin Weinberg put it in 1972, "trans-scientific." By this he meant, strangely sounding like Luhmann, "questions which can be asked of science and yet which cannot be answered by science." Note that "trans-scientific" does not mean "extra-scientific." We are not simply talking about matters of value and politics, of which Weber thought scientists should steer clear in the lecture hall and the laboratory. Values and politics pose many questions that *should not be* asked of science. Weber was certainly right about this. Trans-scientific questions, in contrast, "arise in the course of the interaction between science or technology and society." They are "epistemologically speaking, questions of fact and can be stated in the language of science." Weinberg's somewhat non-committal "can" should be corrected to "will." These are questions that *should* and *will be* asked of scientists; matters in which scientists *have a responsibility* to intervene, not least because they concern problems that were caused by scientific and technological development itself. Yet, "they are unanswerable by science; they transcend science."[2]

Any Weberian hopes that a closer scrutiny of the trans-scientific will reveal the line where the scientist's statement of facts and advice about means could stop and give way to an extra-scientific debate about values and ultimate ends, is dispelled by Weinberg's examples, which include things such as the biological effects of low-level radiation insults, and the probability of "extremely improbable events" such as nuclear reactor accidents (written long before Chernobyl and Fukushima). The reasons why they cannot be answered by science are not because *in principle* they shouldn't be asked, because they are somehow questions about values and not facts. No. They cannot be answered because, *as a practical matter*, one cannot calculate them and because there is a mismatch between the temporality of scientific investigation and the nature of these problems. One simply cannot build a thousand nuclear reactors and wait 10,000 years to compile the data necessary to estimate with some degree of confidence the probability of an accident. To estimate, at 95 percent confidence level, whether low-level radiation causes cancer, Weinberg says, you'd need eight billion mice![3]

This is why I began this book thinking about expertise. Expertise is our name for this realm of trans-science, where questions are asked that *should* be asked but *cannot* be answered. Or, put differently, they cannot be answered without resorting to this ineffable thing called "expert judgment." This is clear from Weinberg's discussion. He includes the whole field of engineering as trans-scientific because engineering projects, as a practical matter, require making decisions on the basis of incomplete data, and rely, therefore, on "engineering judgment": "this ability, as well as necessity to come to good decisions with whatever scientific data are at hand."[4]

Expert judgment is not naked, unaided. It comes equipped with all the methods that have been devised over the last half century to discipline and support it and to shield it from criticism – Bayesian statistics is the foremost and the most honest about the dodginess of the whole business, but one should include also operations research, decision theory, risk analysis, global circulation models, simulations, scenario analysis, resilience analysis and preparedness, stress testing, adverse events surveillance and monitoring, military intelligence assessment – the list could be extended. At the end of the day, however, these methods overcome the incompleteness of the data by means of all these things that, as Weber knew, involve choice between values because they are designed, first and foremost, to bring debate to a provisional end – presuppositions, assumptions, "priors," heuristics, conventions, "acceptable levels," cutoffs, and so on. It is easy to demonstrate, as Ulrich Beck did, that these are chockfull of implicit values. The same holds for the newest form of mechanical objectivity that is now all the rage – algorithms. Most importantly, these methods were developed in the interface between science and the state because they are designed to answer – in a manner of speaking, using the rhetorical device of probability, framing the answer as provisional – precisely the question that Weber, quoting Tolstoy, said science does not answer and should not be asked: "what shall we do and how shall we live?" The inconvenient fact is that *there will never be a place* where scientists, wielding these methods and principles or others, can stop, secure in the conviction that they have not crossed the line into politics, and pass the baton of collective decision-making to others (decision-makers, judges, politicians, "the public"). Their very starting point has already transgressed the line and they come into the controversy already entangled. Trans-science, regulatory science, expert judgment and all its auxiliary methods, are first and foremost about the production of legitimacy.[5]

On the other hand, those who reject the Weberian distinction and embrace the hybridity of trans-science; who preach the virtues of participatory science and "hybrid forums" composed of experts and laypeople; who put their trust in the foregrounding of uncertainty; they must reckon with the inconvenient fact that openness, inclusion, transparency, and participation do not, by themselves, secure legitimacy. Just as often, they may undermine it. As I argued in Chapter 6, without careful temporal framing, inclusionary measures will fail to generate legitimacy and will backfire. Conversely, if these measures are too open-ended and loosely formatted, they will never produce a decision, let alone a consensus. Trans-science is a delicate dance between the horns of this dilemma. Already Weinberg was worried about the possibility that the new procedures for public participation in trans-scientific matters will be abused – though he thought there was "no choice but to welcome public participation" – and that they were "marred by their lack of discipline, even unruliness." He was right to worry. In the near half century that passed since he wrote, the appearance of the "merchants of doubt," whose interest is to prolong the controversy; the funding and recruitment of patients' groups by pharmaceuticals to essentially highjack the FDA's consultative process; the megaphone handed by the internet to charlatans and peddlers of outlandish theories; all have demonstrated the various ways in which participatory procedures can be abused, "inclusion friction" increased, and the experts' ability to persuade severely curtailed. Legitimacy depends on the ability to bring reasoned debate to an end, or at least a temporary halt (while keeping its potential continuation in sight). The inconvenient fact is that participatory and inclusive hybrid forums lack mechanisms for doing so, or they are extremely vulnerable to strategies which exploit the weaknesses of whatever mechanisms they possess.[6]

Such are the inconvenient facts that must be faced by all those who have made trans-science their vocation. Stating them as I have done – perhaps in a somewhat exaggerated manner – should not lead to paralysis. If one looks at them unflinchingly, the challenge they pose is formidable, but also cut in our measure. The challenge they pose can be expressed, in Dewey's phrase, as "(re)discovery of the state," a process of collective experimentation bent on reinventing how trans-scientific controversies are framed, organized, and led towards a legitimate conclusion.

What are the responsibilities that this challenge imposes on scientists and experts? Their response cannot be purely defensive, retreating behind the reinforced boundaries of "science." Weinberg tried this route, but did not stick to it for too long. His first attempt at formulation sounds very Weberian: "What the scientist can do in clarifying matters of trans-science differs from what he can do in clarifying matters of science. In the latter case, he can bring to bear his scientific expertise to help establish scientific truth; in the former case, he can, at most, help delineate where science ends and trans-science begins. We scientists sometimes refuse to concede that science has limits. The debate on risks versus benefits would be more fruitful if we recognized these limits." This could have been written by Max Weber himself. The job of scientists, it would seem, is to identify for decision-makers what can and cannot be answered by science, to draw a line, and then leave trans-scientific matters for public deliberation.[7]

Having read this far, the reader should be able to appreciate the pitfalls of this formulation. The act of "conceding that science has limits" is itself part of trans-science. Arguing about where lie the limits of what scientists can say with confidence – as evidenced by the struggles over climate change or second-hand cigarette smoke – is trans-scientific through and through. Weinberg quickly admits this. He says that the border between science and trans-science is inherently "elusive," and that consequently "trans-scientific debate ... inevitably weaves back and forth across the boundary between what is and what is not known and knowable."[8] Perhaps a more straightforward way of expressing this objection is to say that the argument is not about what scientists *can say with confidence*, but about what they *should say without confidence*. To put it with Michel Callon, if there are risks, there is no question in the matter. Our duty is to prevent them. If there are no risks, similarly there is no question in the matter. But trans-science is about *uncertainty*, about "acting in an uncertain world," about when are precautionary measures justified even if we cannot be confident in our detection and assessment of a correlation or a causal link. Too often now, to do one's "damned duty," as Weber would have said, means to resist the strategies of the "merchants of doubt" by insisting, contra Weinberg, that the trans-scientist can and should speak about these questions as a scientist or an expert, even though she cannot answer them conclusively, even though she has to admit the uncertainties; she must nonetheless add the weight of her instruments, evidence and judgment to unbalance the scales. In the face of these challenges, the vocation of the trans-scientist cannot be to simply retreat and leave the public and decision-makers without scientific advice. [9]

But neither could the scientist-qua-trans-scientist refuse to admit the limits of scientific knowledge. Hubris cannot be the vocation of trans-science. As Weber says: "the device of 'letting the facts speak for themselves' is the most unfair way of putting over a political position to the student." Weinberg warned that scientists should be candid about "the limits to the proficiency of their science," or they will lose their credibility with the public. Given all that has transpired in recent decades, I agree. This stance is extremely unlikely to inspire much trust in scientists, experts and regulatory science. One wonders, however, whether candor about uncertainty and the limitations of knowledge will be rewarded with credibility. It is more likely to be seen as "waffling" or obfuscation. "Damned if you do and damned if you don't," seems to be the predicament of the experts and scientists in trans-scientific controversies. [10]

At this point, Weinberg sees a more expansive vocation for scientists-qua-trans-scientists. It should be "to inject discipline and order into the often chaotic trans-scientific debate," and to contribute to the "development of better institutions for conducting trans-scientific debates." This is also where Weinberg's paper ends and leaves us with a challenge and a responsibility: what kind of institutions could these be? What would the republic of trans-science look like?[11]

Very briefly, I'd like to say something about what kind of institutions they *cannot be*, and draw from this some implications about the principles that should underlie the desired institutions for the republic of trans-science, based on the quasi-Weberian insight that trans-science is primarily about the production of legitimacy. Coming at the end of this book, I can only hope to begin a discussion.

First, the republic of trans-science cannot be modeled after the republic of science. The "long-termism" of the latter, the crucial role played by trust in the skilled judgment of the members of a small core-set, these are a sure recipe for a legitimacy crisis, as was evident in the Climategate debacle, which pulled the curtain back and let the public see how the scientific sausage gets made. If we want people not to be astounded by what they see, they need to be there, behind the curtain, much earlier and throughout the process. This is the valid insight of the inclusionary and outsourced responses to the crisis. A good example is the IPCC's effort to create an extended form of peer review, which includes not only scientists but various other organizations and stakeholders. By the same token, the temporal frames that organize scientific inquiry – reversible time, "in the long term it all comes out in the wash" – are not appropriate for trans-scientific inquiry. Trans-scientific inquiry and discussion need to be framed by something similar to the precautionary principle, which foregrounds the political, legal, and ethical irreversibility of certain decisions, and which marks out in time a period of heightened vigilance and concerted action.

Yet, by the same token, I also have my doubts about the ideals of maximal openness, inclusion, and transparency recommended by the advocates of "participatory science" and "lay expertise." I have a strong Weberian gut reaction. These are attractive ethical ideals, but poor machineries for producing legitimacy. They possess no mechanisms for bringing debate to an end, and no defenses against abuse by the merchants of doubt and other determined and interested parties. Those who would build the institutions of trans-science must shed the state-phobia of outsourcing strategies. The republic of trans-science cannot be modeled on the open *agora*. It should be much more like Carpenter's "networked congeries of audiences," namely composed of the relations of trust and mutual support between the *repeat players*, though every effort should be made to expand their ranks. And at the core of this network there should be, as Justice Breyer suggested, a dedicated and autonomous state agency. The fuzzy, permeable boundaries of the republic of trans-science will quickly lose any discernible shape without a strong backbone, indeed a skeletal structure, provided by a revalued, rededicated, professionalized, and emboldened *civil service*.

Finally, I do not believe that the republic of trans-science can be modeled upon the Anglo-American model of the institutionalization of partisanship as in the political process, or the think-tanks field, or the legal adversary system. Weinberg considered this possibility, rejected it, and yet returned to it in the absence of alternatives: "confrontation between scientists of opposing ethical or political positions is desirable." It is perhaps desirable in principle (Weber would certainly have condoned it), but right now this is the *status-quo* and we are well aware of its limitations, indeed of its destructive potential. The institutionalization of partisanship can work as a mechanism for producing legitimacy only if the battle is joined before an authority (judge and jury) that is able to ratify the result. There is no such authority at the moment. As Mary Douglas said, there is no Solomon. In the absence of Solomon, institutionalized partisanship is a recipe for polarization and paralysis. Perhaps we should draw from this the conclusion that the recipe for "better institutions for conducting trans-scientific debate" is to invert the principle of partisanship, to institutionalize the opposite of partisanship, which is not passive neutrality but active, combative *irony*. This is probably the most enduring, moving, and relevant message of Weber's, now ancient, lecture. It is certainly the one that I have found the most useful myself. The republic of trans-science would need to be one where "bringing the bad news," teaching others how to recognize "inconvenient facts," is established as a routine, yet honorable and well-regarded vocation.

Notes

Introduction: The Crisis

1 *Financial Times*, "Britain has had Enough of Experts, says Gove," June 3, 2016. https://www.ft.com/content/3be49734-29cb-11e6-83e4-abc22d5d108c. The whole interview can be watched at https://www.youtube.com/watch?v=GGgiGtJk7MA. See also Michael Deacon, "Michael Gove's Guide to Britain's Greatest Enemy ... The Experts," *Telegraph*, June 10, 2016. http://www.telegraph.co.uk/news/2016/06/10/michael-goves-guide-to-britains-greatest-enemy-the-experts/; Fraser Nelson, "Michael Gove was (Accidentally) Right about Experts," *Spectator*, January 14, 2017. https://www.spectator.co.uk/2017/01/michael-gove-was-accidentally-right-about-experts/; Ian Katz, "Have We Fallen out of Love with Experts?" *BBC Newsnight*, February 27, 2017. http://www.bbc.com/news/uk-39102840.

2 For the Union of Concerned Scientists' warning about an "assault on science," see Union of Concerned Scientists, "Stop this Assault on Science: The Regulatory Accountability Act." http://www.ucsusa.org/take-action/stop-dangerous-deceptive-assault-science-regulatory-accountability-act#.WYyZPFWG-PIW; Jimmy Tobias, "A Brief Survey of Trump's Assault on Science," *Pacific Standard*, July 24, 2017. https://psmag.com/environment/a-brief-survey-of-trumps-assault-on-science. For the attack on the CBO, see Philip Klein, "Mick Mulvaney: The Day of the CBO has Come and Gone," *The Washington Examiner*, May 31, 2017. http://www.washingtonexaminer.com/

mick-mulvaney-the-day-of-the-cbo-has-probably-come-and-gone/
article/2624609. For the transparency rule, see EPA Press Office,
"EPA Administrator Pruitt Proposes Rule to Strengthen Science
Used in EPA Regulations," April 24, 2018. https://www.epa.gov/
newsreleases/epa-administrator-pruitt-proposes-rule-strengthen-
science-used-epa-regulations. For speculations that attribute the
decline of trust in experts to the internet and social media, see
Gillian Tet, "Why We no Longer Trust the Experts? *Financial Times
Magazine*, July 1, 2016, https://www.ft.com/content/24035fc2-
3e45-11e6-9f2c-36b487ebd80a. Post-modernism and relativism
were mentioned in Sean Coughlan, "What does post-truth mean
for a philosopher?" *BBC News: Education and Family*, January
12, 2017. www.bbc.co.uk/news/education-38557838. Experts
themselves were given a stern talking-to by Julia Shaw, "The
Real Reason that We don't Trust Experts Anymore," *Independent*, July 8, 2016. http://www.independent.co.uk/voices/the-real-
reason-that-we-don-t-trust-experts-a7126536.html. The strategy
of cultivating doubt and ignorance is analyzed in Robert N.
Proctor and Londa Schiebinger (eds.) *Agnotology: The Making
and Unmaking of Ignorance* (Stanford, CA: Stanford University
Press, 2008); and Naomi Oreskes and Eric Conway, *Merchants
of Doubt* (London: Bloomsbury Press, 2010).
3 Tom Nichols, *The Death of Expertise: The Campaign against
Established Knowledge and Why it Matters* (Oxford University
Press, 2017).
4 For a similar formulation of what needs to be explained, see
Weibe E. Bijker, Roland Bal, and Ruud Hendriks, *The Paradox
of Scientific Authority: The Role of Scientific Advice in Democracies* (Cambridge, MA: MIT Press, 2009), 1.
5 Nichols, 232–233; Richard Hofstadter, *Anti-Intellectualism in
American Life* (New York: Vintage Books, 1962), 6–7, 37.
6 The Cyclamate example is in Anthony Giddens, *The Consequences
of Modernity* (Stanford, CA: Stanford University Press, 1990),
148. Many more examples could be added (e.g. eggs and cholesterol). Cyclamate is currently banned in the US, but approved for
use in the EU. https://en.wikipedia.org/wiki/Sodium_cyclamate.
The parable of the lambs and the birds of prey is in Friedrich
Nietzsche, 1887, *On the Genealogy of Morals* (New York: Vintage
Books, 1990), 44–46.
7 John Dewey, *The Public and its Problems* (New York: Henry Holt
and Company, 1927), 3; Hofstadter, *Anti-Intellectualism*, 23.
8 Ibid.
9 Bruno Latour, *The Pasteurization of France* (Harvard University
Press, 1988), 216. For the plurality of scientific methods, cultures,
and epistemic virtues, see Peter Galison and David J. Stump

(eds.) *The Disunity of Science: Boundaries, Contexts, and Power* (Stanford, CA: Stanford University Press, 1996); Karin Knorr-Cetina, *Epistemic Cultures: How the Sciences Make Knowledge* (Cambridge, MA: Harvard University Press, 1999).

10 On the peculiar nature of legal facts and the differences between legal and scientific abstraction, see Bruno Latour, *The Making of Law: An Ethnography of the Conseil d'Etat* (Cambridge: Polity, 2010). On the problems with eyewitness testimony, see Dan Simon, *In Doubt: The Psychology of the Criminal Justice Process* (Harvard University Press, 2012).

11 On regulatory science, see Sheila Jasanoff, *The Fifth Branch: Science Advisers as Policymakers* (Harvard University Press, 1990). As Jasanoff says, the decision to approve or ban a particular chemical combines scientific content with regulatory power. It is a hybrid unlike "normal science." Collins and Evans make an essentially similar point by distinguishing the "historical sciences" from normal science. "Historical sciences deal with unique historical trends [e.g. climate change] rather than repeatable laboratory tests." What they fail to note is that the need to arrive at a decision cuts off the repetition of laboratory tests and transforms regulatory science into a sort of historical science. See Harry Collins and Robert Evans, "The Third Wave of Science Studies: Studies of Expertise and Experience," *Social Studies of Science*, 32, 2 (April 2002): 268. On the "long termism" of normal science, see Gilbert, G. N., and Mulkay, M., *Opening Pandora's Box* (Cambridge University Press, 1984), 90–111; and Steven Yearly, 1994. "Understanding Science from the Perspective of the Sociology of Scientific Knowledge: An Overview," *Public Understanding of Science*, 3 (1994): 245–258.

12 In a Turing test, one tries to guess who is the real expert (or the real human, rather than a computer), solely on the basis of written answers to a set of questions. Collins and Evans, "The Third Wave," 254–256; Harry Collins and Robert Evans, *Rethinking Expertise* (Chicago: University of Chicago Press, 2007); Harry Collins, "Three Dimensions of Expertise," *Phenomenology and the Cognitive Sciences*, 12, 2 (June 2013): 253–273; Harry Collins, *Are We All Scientific Experts Now?* (Cambridge: Polity, 2014).

13 Walter Lippmann, *The Phantom Public* (New Brunswick: Transaction Publishers, 1927 [2004]), 30–43, 57–58. About Lippmann's influence as syndicated columnist, see Craufurd Goodwin, "The Making of a Public Economist: Walter Lippmann (1889–1974) in Peace and War," *HOPE*, vol. 45, Issue 5, *The Economist as Public Intellectual* (Durham, NC: Duke University Press, 2013).

1   Expertise

1 John Earle, *English Prose: Its Elements, History, and Usage* (New York: G. P. Putnam's Sons, 1891), 218–223.
2 Evan Selinger and Robert P. Crease (eds.) *The Philosophy of Expertise* (New York: Columbia University Press, 2006); K. Andres Ericsson and Jacqui Smith (eds.) *Towards a General Theory of Expertise: Prospects and Limits* (Cambridge: Cambridge University Press, 1991); Merim Bialić, *The Neuroscience of Expertise* (Cambridge: Cambridge University Press, 2017); Guy Benveniste, *The Politics of Expertise* (San Francisco: Boyd & Fraser, 1977); Bruce Bimber, *The Politics of Expertise in Congress* (State University of New York Press, 1996); Frank Fischer, *Democracy and Expertise* (Oxford: Oxford University Press, 2009); Tal Golan, *Laws of Men and Laws of Nature: The History of Scientific Expert Testimony in England and America* (Cambridge, MA: Harvard University Press, 2004); Sheila Jasanoff, *Science at the Bar: Law, Science, and Technology in America* (Cambridge, MA: Harvard University Press, 1995); Edmond, Gary, and David Mercer, "Experts and Expertise in Legal and Regulatory Settings," in Gary Edmond, *Expertise in Regulation and Law* (Burlington: Ashgate Publishing, 2004); Steven Epstein, "The Construction of Lay Expertise: AIDS Activism and the Forging of Credibility in the Reform of Clinical Trials," *Science, Technology and Human Values*, 20(4) (Autumn 1995): 408–437; Collins and Evans, *Rethinking Expertise*; Collins and Evans, "The Third Wave"; Steven Epstein, *Impure Science: AIDS, Activism and the Politics of Knowledge* (University of California Press, 1998); Vololona Rabeharisoa and Michel Callon, "Patients and Scientists in French Muscular Dystrophy Research," in S. Jasanoff (ed.) *States of Knowledge: The Co-Production of Science and Social Order* (London: Routledge, 2004), 142–160; Lindsay Prior, "Belief, Knowledge and Expertise: The Emergence of the Lay Expert in Medical Sociology," *Sociology of Health and Illness*, 25 (2003): 41–57; Paul Feltovich, Kenneth M. Ford, and Robert R. Hoffman, *Expertise in Context* (Boston, MA: MIT Press, 1997); Michelene T. H. Chi, Robert Glaser, and M. J. Farr (eds.) *The Nature of Expertise* (Laurence Erlbaum Publishers, 1988).
3 Sir Robert Harry Inglis Palgrave (ed.) *The Dictionary of Political Economy*, vol. 1 (London: Macmillan, 1894), 793; Robley Dunglison, MD, *Dictionary of Medical Science* (Philadelphia: Henry C. Lea, 1874); Albert Tougard (ed.) *Une expertise en écriture (1748–1749): Au sujet de deux morceaux rimes* (Rouen: Société Rouennaise de bibliophiles, 1899); Dr. Emmanuel Regis, *A Practical Manual of Mental Medicine*, translation from the

French (Utica, New York: Press of the American Journal of Insanity, 1894), 654; *The Bulletin of the Metropolitan Museum of Art*, 8(6) (June 1913): 120; W. J. Stillman, "letter." *Literature*, 72 (March 4, 1899): 242; "Art experts on the defensive," *The Nation*, 89(2297) (1909): 40; Montgomery Schviler, "The New York State House and its Site," *The Architectural Record* 36(1) (July 1914): 7; Graham Walas, *Our Social Heritage* (Yale University Press, 1921), 68–69; H. L. Mencken, *The American Language: An Inquiry into the Development of English in the United States* (New York: Alfred A. Knopf, 1936), 193.

4 My thanks to Larry Au for explaining how "expertise" would be translated to Mandarin.

5 Based on the data made available by Google Books Ngram Viewer. https://books.google.com/ngrams/graph?content=expert% 2Cexpertise%2C+professions&year_start=1800&year_ end=2000&corpus=0&smoothing=3&share=& direct_url=t1%3B%2Cexpert%3B%2Cc0%3B. t1%3B%2Cexpertise%3B%2Cc0%3B.t1%3B%2Cprofessions %3B%2Cc0.

6 Nico Stehr, *Knowledge Societies* (London: Sage, 1994); Grenot Bohme and Nico Stehr, *The Knowledge Society: The Growing Impact of Scientific Knowledge on Social Relations* (D. Reidel Publishing Company, 1986); Burton R. Clark, *Educating the Expert Society* (Chandler Publishers, 1962).

7 Felix Frankfurter, *The Public and its Government* (New Haven: Yale University Press, 1930); "Foreword," *Yale Law Journal*, 47, 4 (1938): 515–518; Robert M. Cooper, "Administrative Justice and the Role of Discretion," *Yale Law Journal*, 47, 4 (1938): 577–604; Ralph F. Fuchs, "Concepts and Policies in Anglo-American Administrative Law Theory," *Yale Law Journal* 47, 4 (1938): 538–576; Wilson K. Doyle, *Independent Commissions in the Federal Government* (UNC Press, 1939); James M. Landis, "Crucial Issues in Administrative Law: The Walter-Logan Bill," *Harvard Law Review*, 53, 7 (May 1940): 1077–1102; J. Forrester Davison, "Administrative Technique – The Report on Administrative Procedure," *Columbia Law Review*, 41 (1941): 628–645; Franklin Delano Roosevelt, "Logan–Walter Bill Fails," *American Bar Association Journal*, 27(1) (January 1941): 52–54. This dispute, importantly, has never been resolved and is likely to come again before the US Supreme Court, where the recently appointed Neil Gorsuch is known to be a fierce opponent of the doctrine requiring that judges defer to administrative agencies' interpretations of the law. This is "the most distinctive aspect" of his jurisprudence and played no small role in conservatives' enthusiasm for his appointment. Emily Bazelon and Eric Posner,

"The Government Gorsuch Wants to Undo," *New York Times*, April 1, 2017. https://www.nytimes.com/2017/04/01/sunday-review/the-government-gorsuch-wants-to-undo.html.

8 John Dickinson, "Judicial Control of Official Discretion," *American Political Science Review*, 22, 2 (1928): 275–302.

9 W. J. Butler (1946). "The rising tide of expertise," *Fordham Law Review*, 15: 19–61.

10 Butler, 21–23, 35–36.

11 For the claims of early AI research, see E. A. Feigenbaum and J. Feldman, *Computers and Thought* (McGraw-Hill: New York, 1963); Richard O. Duda and Edward H. Shortlife, "Experts Systems Research," *Science*, 220(4594) (April 1983): 261–268; Robert R. Hoffman, Paul J. Feltovich and Kenneth M. Ford, "A General Framework for Conceiving of Expertise and Expert Systems in Context," in their *Expertise in Context*, 543–580. The most influential critique was articulated by Hubert Dreyfus, *What Computers Can't Do: A Critique of Artificial Reason*. Harper & Row Publishers, 1972. See also Dreyfus, Hubert, *What Computers Still Can't Do* (Boston, MA: MIT Press, 1992); Dreyfus, Hubert and Stuart E. Dreyfus, "Peripheral Vision: Expertise in Real World Contexts," *Organization Studies*, 26(5) (2005):779–792. For the debate about lay expertise, see Epstein, "The Construction of Lay Expertise"; Epstein, *Impure Science*I; Phil Brown, Stephen Zavestoski, Sabrina McCormick, Brian Mayer, Rachel Morello-Frosch, and Rebecca Gasior Altman, "Embodied Health Movements: New Approaches to Social Movements in Health," *Sociology of Health and Illness*, 26(1) (January 2004): 50–80; Rabeharisoa and Callon, "Patients and Scientists in French Muscular Dystrophy Research"; Prior, "Belief, Knowledge and Expertise"; Brian Wynne, "Misunderstood Misunderstandings: Social Identities and the Public Uptake of Science," in Allan Irwin and Brian Wynne (eds.) *Misunderstanding Science: The Public Reconstruction of Science and Policy* (Cambridge: Cambridge University Press, 2004): 19–46; Collins and Evans, "The Third Wave," 238.

12 For the history of scientific expert testimony see Tal Golan's magnificent *Laws of Men and Laws of Nature*. For the courts' reliance on the professions, see ibid., 257. For the debate leading to the *Daubert* decision, see Edmond and Mercer, "Experts and Expertise"; Jasanoff, *Science at the Bar*; Sheila Jasanoff, "Science and the Statistical Victim: Modernizing Knowledge in Breast Implant Litigation," *Social Studies of Science*, 32(1)(2002): 37–69; Carpenter, *Reputation and Power*, 265–66. For the debates about risk assessment see Jakob Arnoldi, *Risk* (Cambridge: Polity, 2009); Ulrich Beck, *Risk Society: Towards a New Modernity* (London: Sage, 1992).

13 Benveniste, *The Politics of Expertise*; Stephen Breyer, *Breaking the Vicious Circle: Towards Effective Risk Regulation* (Cambridge, MA: Harvard University Press, 1993); Noortje Marres, "Issues Spark a Public into Being: A Key but Forgotten Point of the Lippmann-Dewey Debate," in Bruno Latour and Peter Weibel, *Making Things Public: Atmospheres of Democracy* (Boston, MA: MIT Press, 2005), 208–217.

14 Namely, "concepts the proper use of which inevitably involves endless disputes about their proper uses on the part of their users" (Gallie, 1956), 169.

2   The Debate about Expertise

1 Raymond Williams, *Keywords* (New York: Oxford University Press, 2014), 129. For the plumber example, see Hoffman et al., "A General Framework," 552.

2 Claims to expertise and jurisdictional struggles are studied by the sociology of professions: Andrew Abbott, *The System of Professions: An Essay on the Division of Expert Labor* (Chicago: University of Chicago Press, 1988); Eliot Freidson, *Professional Powers: A Study of the Institutionalization of Formal Knowledge* (Chicago: University of Chicago Press, 1986); Magali Sarfatti Larson, *The Rise of Professionalism: A Sociological Analysis* (Berkeley: University of California Press, 1977). For an example of how one group of experts prevails over another not because of any advantages in knowledge, but because they do also "scat" work and cultivate informal relations with their clients, see Ruthanne Huizing, "To Hive or to Hold? Producing Professional Authority through Scut Work," *Administrative Science Quarterly* 60(2) (2014): 263–299.

3 Collins and Evans, *Rethinking Expertise*, 15–18; Harry Collins, *Artificial Experts: Social Knowledge and Intelligent Machines* (Cambridge, MA: MIT Press, 1990); Dreyfus, *What Computers Still Can't Do*; Dreyfus and Dreyfus, "Peripheral Vision"; Harold Garfinkel, *Studies in Ethnomethodology* (Cambridge: Polity, 1968). Alfred Schutz, "Common Sense and Scientific Interpretation of Human Action," *Collected Papers*.

4 Collins and Evans, *Rethinking Expertise*, 17; Butler, "The Rising Tide," 34. Dreyfus and Dreyfus, "Peripheral Vision."

5 Harry Collins, *Tacit and Explicit Knowledge* (Chicago: University of Chicago Press, 2010).

6 Brian Wynne, "May the Sheep Safely Graze? A Reflexive View of the Expert–Lay Knowledge Divide," in Scott Lash, Bronislaw Szerszynski and Brian Wynne, *Risk, Environment and Modernity:*

Towards a New Ecology (London: Sage, 1996); Brian Wynne, "Misunderstood Misunderstandings: Social Identities and Public Uptake of Science," in Alan Irwin and Brian Wynne, *Misunderstanding Science? The Public Reconstruction of Science and Technology* (Cambridge: Cambridge University Press, 1996), 19–46; Brian Wynne, "Uncertainty and Environmental Learning: Reconceiving Science and Policy in the Preventive Paradigm," *Global Environmental Change* 2(2) (1992): 111–127.

7 Niklas Luhmann, quoted in Gotthard Bechmann, "The Rise and Crisis of Scientific Expertise," in his and Imre Hronzsky (eds.) *Expertise and its Interfaces* (Berlin: Edition Sigma, 2003), 23.

8 Duda and Shortlife, "Expert Systems," 262–263; Colleen M. Zeitz, "Some Concrete Advantages of Abstraction: How Experts' Representations Facilitate Reasoning," in Feltovich et al., *Expertise in Context*, 43–65. The first artificial intelligence program was Newel and Simon's "Logic Theory Machine": Allan Newell and Herbert A. Simon, "The Logic Theory Machine: A Complex Information Processing System," *IRE Transactions, Information Theory*, 2(3) (1956): 61–79. A useful account of the early history of AI and expert systems is David Alan Greer's interview with Edward Feigenbaum in *IEEE, Annals of the History of Computing*, 35(4) (2013): 74–81.

9 Duda and Shortlife, "Expert Systems," 265; K. Anders Ericsson and Neil Charness, "Cognitive and Developmental Factors in Expert Performance," in Feltovich et al., *Expertise in Context*, 35–36; Hoffman et al., "A General Framework," 548.

10 Dreyfus and Dreyfus, "Peripheral Vision"; Dreyfus, *What Computers Can't Do*. See also Michael Lynch, Eric Livingston, and Harold Garfinkel, "Temporal Order in Laboratory Work," in Knor-Cetina and Mulkay (eds.) *Science Observed* (London: Sage, 1983).

11 Ford, "Preface," in Feltovich et al., *Expertise in Context*, ix–xi; Hoffman et al., "A General Framework," 547–551; Collins, *Artificial Experts*; Sarah Sachs, "The Algorithm at Work: Algorithmic Expertise and the Construction of Meaning in Art Data" (Unpublished Manuscript).

12 Abbott, *System of Professions*, 8–9. Friedson, *Professional Powers*, 73–87; Everett Hughes, "Professions," *Daedalus* 92, 4 (Fall, 1963): 655–668.

13 Abbott, *System of Professions*, 8–9.

14 The classic analysis of distributed cognition in the cockpit is Edwin Hutchins, "How a Cockpit Remembers its Speeds," *Cognitive Science*, 19 (1995): 265–288. Other key texts in this line of work are Jean Lave, *Cognition in Practice* (Cambridge:

Cambridge University Press, 1988); Lucy Suchman, *Plans and Situated Actions* (Cambridge: Cambridge University Press, 1987).

15 Dewey, *The Public*, 190. The analysis of how the manual ventilator "withdraws" and becomes an extension of the expert's body is in Cornelius Schubert, "Making Sure. A Comparative Micro-Analysis of Diagnostic Instruments in Medical Practice," *Social Science and Medicine*, 73 (2011): 851–857. Similar arguments have been developed, from a slightly different angle, by ANT scholars, especially Michel Callon, *The Laws of the Markets* (Oxford: Blackwell, 1998); and Donald Mackenzie, *Material Markets: How Economic Agents are Constructed* (New York: Oxford University Press, 2009).

16 Latour, *Science in Action*; Latour, *The Making of Law*; Bruno Latour, "Circulating Reference," ch. 2 in *Pandora's Hope* (Cambridge, MA: Harvard University Press, 1999); Andrew Lakoff, *Pharmaceutical Reason* (Cambridge: Cambridge University Press, 2005).

17 Hoffman et al., "A General Framework," 551–554; Zeitz, "Some Concrete Advantages," 44; Kenneth Ford, "Preface" in Feltovich et al., *Expertise in Context*, ix–xi; Feltovich et al., "A Preliminary Tour of Human and Machine Expertise in Context," in their *Expertise in Context*, xiv.

18 Collins and Evans, *Rethinking Expertise*, 2–3, 14, 30–35. See also Harry Collins and Robert Evans, "Expertise Revisited, Part I: Interactional Expertise," *Studies in the History and Philosophy of Science, Part A*, 54 (December 2015): 113–123; Harry Collins, Robert Evans, and Martin Weinel, 2016. "Expertise Revisited, Part II: Contributory Expertise," *Studies in the History and Philosophy of Science, Part A*, 56 (April): 103–110.

19 Collins and Evans, *Rethinking Expertise*, ibid.; Collins, *Artificial Experts*.

20 Gil Eyal, "For a Sociology of Expertise," *AJS*, 118(4) (January 2013): 863–907. See also Gil Eyal, *The Disenchantment of the Orient: Expertise in Arab Affairs and the Israeli State* (Stanford, CA: Stanford University Press, 2006), 185–188. On "optimal abstraction," see Abbott, *The System of Professions*, 102–103. On the challenge of lay expertise, see Epstein, "The Construction of Lay Expertise."

21 Collins and Evans, "The Third Wave," 240; Epstein, "The Construction of Lay Expertise"; Brian Wynne, 'May the Sheep Safely Graze? A Reflexive View of the Expert–Lay Knowledge Divide', in Scott Lash, Bronislaw Szerszynski, and Brian Wynne (eds.) *Risk, Environment and Modernity: Towards a New Ecology* (London: Sage, 1996), 44–83; Bruno Latour, "From Realpolitik to Dingpolitik," in his and Peter Weibel's, *Making Things*

Public: Atmospheres of Democracy (Boston, MA: MIT Press, 2005), 14–41; Michel Callon, "Disabled Persons of All Countries, Unite!" in Latour and Weibel, *Making Things Public*, 308–313; Michel Callon, Pierre Lascoumes, and Yannick Barthe, *Acting in an Uncertain World: An Essay on Technical Democracy* (Cambridge, MA: The MIT Press, 2009), 11.

22 Collins and Evans, *Rethinking Expertise*, 10; Collins and Evans, "The Third Wave," 235–236; Callon, "Disabled Persons," 308; Marres, "Issues Spark a Public into Being."

23 On the modern condition of trust in "expert systems," see Anthony Giddens, *The Consequences of Modernity* (Stanford, CA: Stanford University Press, 1990). On the political conditions and trade-offs involving mechanical objectivity as against expert judgment, see Theodore M. Porter, *Trust in Numbers: The Pursuit of Objectivity in Science and Public Life* (Princeton, NJ: Princeton University Press, 1995).

24 On EBM, see Stefan Timmermans and Marc Berg, *The Gold Standard: The Challenge of Evidence-Based Medicine and Standardization in Health Care* (Philadelphia: Temple University Press, 2003).

25 The analysis of AFM's model of co-production is in Vololona Rabeharisoa and Michel Callon, "Patients and Scientists in French Muscular Dystrophy Research," in Sheila Jasanoff (ed.) *States of Knowledge: The Co-Production of Science and Social Order* (London: Routledge, 2004), 142–160, see especially 150–157.

26 This criticism of the concept of interactional expertise was formulated by Evan Selinger and John Mix, "On Interactional Expertise: Pragmatic and Ontological Considerations," in Evan Selinger and Robert P. Crease, *The Philosophy of Expertise* (New York: Columbia University Press, 2006), 305–306.

3 Trust

1 On the "moral equivalence of the scientist," see Steven Shapin, *The Scientific Life: A Moral History of a Late Modern Vocation* (Chicago: University of Chicago Press, 2008), 47–92. On science's strengths and how they are perceived by the public see Yearly, "Understanding Science," 252.

2 On "virtual witnessing," see Steven Shapin, 1988. "The House of Experiment in 17th Century England," *Isis*, 79(3): 373–404.

3 The results of the reproducibility project are reported in Brian Nosek et al., 2015. "Estimating the Reproducibility of Psychological Science," *Science*, 349 (6251): aac4716. Tellingly, the Trump Administration cited the "replication crisis" as justification for

new rules that effectively diminish the role of scientific research in its decision making: EPA Press Office, "EPA Administrator,"; Coral Davenport. "In the Trump Administration, Science is Unwelcome. So is Advice," *New York Times*, June 6, 2018. Of Ioannidis' prodigious output, the following are especially relevant: John P. A. Ioannidis, 2005. "Why Most Research Findings are False," *PLoS Medicine*, 2(8): e124; David Robert Grimes, Chris T. Bauch and John P. A. Ioannidis, 2018. "Modelling Science Trustworthiness under Publish or Perish Pressure," *Royal Society Open Science*, 5: 171511. http://dx.doi.org/10.1098/rsos.171511; and John P. A. Ioannidis et al., 2001. "Replication Validity of Genetic Association Studies," *Nature Genetics*, 29: 306–309.

4 Yearly, "Understanding Science," 252. On "trained judgment," see Lorraine Daston and Peter Galison, *Objectivity* (Cambridge, MA: Zone Books, 2007), 309–362. On "normal science," see Thomas Kuhn, *The Structure of Scientific Revolutions* (Chicago: University of Chicago Press, 1962).

5 The litany of problems of conflict-of-interest in drug research is in Ray Moyinhan, "REALITY CHECK: It's Time to Rebuild the Evidence Base," *British Medical Journal*, 342, 7808 (2011): 1183. The former BMJ editor is Richard Smith, "Medical Journals Are an Extension of the Marketing Arm of Pharmaceutical Companies," *PLoS Med* 2(5) (2005): e138. The damning findings are reported in G. Rattinger and L. Bero, "Factors Associated with Results and Conclusions of Trials of Thiazolidinediones," *PLoS ONE* 4(6) (2009): e5826. doi:10.1371/journal.pone.0005826; L. Bero, F. Oostvogel, P. Bacchetti, and K. Lee, "Factors Associated with Findings of Published Trials of Drug–Drug Comparisons: Why Some Statins Appear More Efficacious Than Others," *PLoS Med* 4(6) (2007): e184. doi:10.1371/journal.pmed.0040184; Erick H. Turner, MD, Annette M. Matthews, MD, Eftihia Linardatos, BSc, Robert A. Tell, LCSW, and Robert Rosenthal, PhD, "Selective Publication of Antidepressant Trials and its Influence on Apparent Efficacy," *New England Journal of Medicine*, 358 (2008): 252–260; Michelle Roseman, BA, Katherine Milette, BSc, Lisa A. Bero, PhD, James C. Coyne, PhD, Joel Lexchin, MD, Erick H. Turner, MD, and Brett D. Thombs, PhD, "Reporting of Conflicts of Interest in Meta-analyses of Trials of Pharmacological Treatments," *JAMA*, March 9, 305(10) (2011): 1008–1017.

6 Cary Funk, "Mixed Messages about Public Trust in Science," *Pew Research Center*, December 8, 2017. http://www.pewinternet.org/2017/12/08/mixed-messages-about-public-trust-in-science/; Yu Xie and Alexandra Killewald, *Is American Science in Decline?* (Cambridge, MA: Harvard University Press, 2012), 64–75; Friederike Hendriks, Dorothe Kienhues, and Rainer Bromme, "Trust

in Science and the Science of Trust," in B. Blobaum (ed.) *Trust and Communication in a Digitized World* (Switzerland: Springer International Publishing, 2016), 148–149.

7 Fink, "Mixed Messages."

8 Xie and Killewald, *Is American Science in Decline?*, 71.

9 Gordon Gauchat, "Politicization of Science in the Public Sphere: A Study of Public Trust in the United States, 1974 to 2010," *American Sociological Review*, 77(2) (2012): 167–187.

10 Anne M. Price and Lindsey P. Peterson, "Scientific Progress, Risk, and Development: Explaining Attitudes Toward Science Cross-Nationally," *International Sociology*, 31(1) (2016): 57–80. The trends among Republicans and Democrats were obtained by using the GSS *Data Explorer* tool, https://gssdataexplorer. norc.org/trends/Politics?measure=consci.

11 Science Barometer, 2017, https://www.wissenschaft-im-dialog.de/en/our-projects/science-barometer/science-barometer-2017/; The Pew Questionnaire can be accessed at http://www.pewinternet.org/datasets/2016/.

12 Funk, "Mixed Messages"; "What do we Know about Public Trust in Science?" ch. 3 of The National Academies of Sciences, Engineering, and Medicine. *Trust and Confidence at the Interfaces of the Life Sciences and Society: Does the Public Trust Science?* A Workshop Summary (Washington, DC: The National Academies Press, 2015). https://www-ncbi-nlm-nih-gov.ezproxy.cul.columbia.edu/books/NBK321981/.

13 Hendriks et al., "Trust in Science," 148–153; Science Barometer, 2017, https://www.wissenschaft-im-dialog.de/en/our-projects/science-barometer/science-barometer-2017/.

14 Peter Barton Hutt, "The State of Science at the FDA," *Administrative Law Review*, 60(2) (Spring 2008), 443.

15 The Harris Poll, February 26, 2015, "US Mint and FAA Receive Highest Rating of 17 US Agencies," https://theharrispoll.com/eight-in-ten-79-u-s-adults-who-understand-what-the-u-s-mint-does-rate-the-job-its-doing-positively-i-e-excellent-or-pretty-good-making-it-the-highest-rated-of-17-government-agencies-tested/; Teresa A. Myers, John Kotcher, Ashley A. Anderson, Edward Maibach, Lindsey Beall, and Anthony Leiserowitz, "Predictors of Trust in the General Science and Climate Science Research of US Federal Agencies," *Public Understanding of Science* 26(7) (2017): 843–860.

16 On the British Monsanto study, see Eric Millstone and Patrick van Zwanenberg, "A Crisis of Trust: for Science, Scientists, or Institutions?" *Nature Medicine*, 6(12) (2000): 1307–1308; Hans Harbers, "Trust in Politics, Science and Technology: Breaching the Modernist Constitution," in Frank R. Ankersmit, and Henk

Te Velde, *Trust: Cement of Democracy?* (Leuven: Peeters, 2004), 146; Hendriks et al., "Trust in Science," 150–151, 155. It goes without saying that valiant attempts to separate the different components of trust – to measure, for example, trust in "the scientific method" separately from "trust in scientific institutions" – are doomed from the start, and typically rely on questionable and tendentious reading of the significance of survey questions. For an example, see Peter Achterberg, Willem de Koster, and Jeroen van der Waal, "A Science Confidence Gap: Education, Trust in Scientific Methods, and Trust in Scientific Institutions in the United States, 2014," *Public Understanding of Science* 26 (6) (2017): 704–720.

17 Myers et al., "Predictors of Trust," 848–850.
18 The characterization of trust as "tacit acceptance" is by Giddens, *Consequences*, 90. This critique of trust measures dovetails Jerolmack and Khan's argument: Colin Jerolmack and Shamus Khan, "Talk is Cheap: Ethnography and the Attitudinal Fallacy," *Sociological Methods and Research*, 43 (2014): 178–209.
19 Harbers, "Trust in Politics, Science and Technology," 146; Myers et al., "Predictors of Trust," 844; Alonzo Plough and Sheldon Krimsky, "The Emergence of Risk Communication Studies: Social and Political Context," *Science, Technology and Human Values* 12: 3–4 (1987): 4–10; Matthias Koring, "Misunderstanding trust in science: a critique of the traditional discourse on science communication," *Journal of Science Communication* 15, 5 (2016): 1–4.
20 Giddens, *The Consequences*, 88–89.
21 Julie Bronwlie and Alexandra Howson, "Leaps of Faith and MMR: An Empirical Study of Trust," *Sociology*, 39(2) (2005): 226. Wakefield's results were published as Andrew Wakefield et al., "Ileal-Lymphoid-Nodular Hyperplasia, Non-Specific Colitis, and Pervasive Developmental Disorder in Children," *Lancet*, 351 (1999): 637–41. The parents' study was published Sally Bernard et al., "Autism: A Novel Form of Mercury Poisoning," *Medical Hypotheses*, 56(4) (2001): 462–471.
22 Giddens, *The Consequences*, 27–29, 99–100.
23 Harold Garfinkel, "A Conception of, and Experiments with, "Trust" as a Condition of Stable Concerted Actions," in *Motivation and Social Interaction: Cognitive Approaches*, O. J. Harvey, edn (New York, Ronald Press, 1963), 187–238.
24 Niklas Luhmann, 1973, *Trust and Power* (Cambridge: Polity, 2017); Niklas Luhmann, "Familiarity, Confidence, Trust: Problems and Alternatives," in Diego Gambetta (ed.) *Trust: Making and Breaking Cooperative Relations* (London: Basil Blackwell, 1988), 94–107; Giddens, *Consequences*, 92–100; Hendriks et

al., "Trust in Science," 153; Georg Simmel, *The Philosophy of Money* (London: Routledge, 2004), 178.

25 Giddens, *Consequences*, 33; Hendriks et al., "Trust in Science," 152–3.

26 On trust as a "leap of faith" or "suspension," see Guido Mollering, *Trust: Reason, Routine, Reflexivity* (Amsterdam: Elsevier, 2006),105–126.

27 Brownlie and Howson, "Leaps of Faith," 227–231.

28 Pierre Bourdieu, *Pascalian Meditations* (Cambridge: Polity, 2000), 191–202. See also the discussion in Michel Callon, "Introduction: The Embeddedness of Economic Markets in Economics," in his *The Laws of the Markets* (Oxford: Blackwell, 1998), 13–15.

29 Mollering, *Trust*, 115–117; Bourdieu, *Pascalian Meditations*, 192; Luhmann, *Trust and Power*, 27. On trust as the cement of modern, liberal societies see Adam Seligman, *The Problem of Trust* (Princeton, NJ: Princeton University Press, 1997); Brownlie and Howson, "Leaps of Faith," 228–231. Stephen Breyer, too, though for somewhat different reasons, doubts that transparency is the solution to rebuilding trust in regulatory risk management: Breyer, *Breaking the Vicious Circle*, 78.

30 Brownlie and Howson, "Leaps of Faith," 228–231; Giddens, *Consequences*, 80–87.

31 Simmel, *The Philosophy of Money*, 178.

32 Paul Slovic, 1999. "Trust, Emotion, Sex, Politics, and Science: Surveying the Risk-Assessment Battlefield," *Risk Analysis* 19(4): 689–701; Emile Durkheim, *The Elementary Forms of Religious Life* (New York: The Free Press, 1995); Mary Douglas, *Purity and Danger* (London: Routledge, 1966).

4 Risk

1 Over the same years, there was also a small increase in the use of the term "uncertainty," but nowhere near proportionally to the increases in "risk" and "expertise." Based on the data made available by Google Books Ngram Viewer. https://books.google.com/ngrams/graph?content=expertise%2Crisk&year_start=1900&year_end=2000&corpus=15&smoothing=3&share=&direct_url=t1%3B%2Cexpertise%3B%2Cc0%3B.t1%3B%2Crisk%3B%2Cc0.

2 Beck, *Risk Society*, 29.

3 On political risk analysis, see Gil Eyal (with Grace Pok), "What is Security Expertise?: From the Sociology of Professions to the Analysis of Networks of Expertise," in Trine Villumsen Berling and Christian Bueger (eds.) *Capturing Security Expertise* (London:

Routledge, 2015). On the multidisciplinary nature of risk analysis and the eclipse of toxicology, see David Demortain, *Scientists and the Regulation of Risk: Standardizing Control* (Cheltenham, UK: Edward Elgar, 2011), 2011, 1–2, 14–15, 40–59.

4 Dominic Golding, "A Social and Programmatic History of Risk Research," in Sheldon Krimsky and Dominic Golding (eds.) *Social Theories of Risk* (Westport, CT: Praeger, 1992), 23–52. Beck, *Risk Society*, 28–29.

5 Dyson's quote is from Freeman Dyson, 2007. "Heretical Thoughts about Science and Society," Edge.org https://www.edge.org/conversation/heretical-thoughts-about-science-and-society. On the problem of "body burden" as an "overflow" not captured by toxicological expertise, see Norah MacKendrick, "Media Framing of Body Burdens: Precautionary Consumption and the Individualization of Risk," *Sociological Inquiry* 80(1) (2010): 126–149.

6 Beck, *Risk Society*, 28–30; Brian Wynne, "Uncertainty and environmental learning: Reconceiving science and policy in the preventive paradigm," *Global Environmental Change* 2(2) (1992): 111–127; Callon et al., *Acting in an Uncertain World*, 18–26. On "systemic risk," see Onur Ozgode, "Governing the Economy at the Limits of Neoliberalism: Toward a Genealogy of Systemic Risk Regulation in the United States, 1922–2012" (PhD Dissertation, Department of Sociology, Columbia University, 2014).

7 Wynne, "May the Sheep Safely Graze"; Callon et al., *Acting in an Uncertain World*, 19.

8 Demortain, *Scientists and the Regulation of Risk*, 2.

9 On insurance as a political technology that utilizes uncertainty as a collective resource, see François Ewald, "Insurance and Risk," in Graham Burchell, Colin Gordon, and Peter Miller (eds.) *The Foucault Effect* (Chicago: University of Chicago Press, 1991). When assumptions and boundary conditions are shared by all relevant actors and hard-wired into technology, sociologists say that they are "performative," i.e. they shape the reality they govern so it confirms the correctness of the assumptions. But even in these cases, they produce ignorance and indeterminacy that can undo them. Donald MacKenzie, Fabian Muniesa, and Lucia Siu, "Introduction," in their *Do Economists Make Markets? On the Performativity of Economics* (Princeton, NJ: Princeton University Press, 2007), 1–19; and Donald MacKenzie, "Is Economics Performative?: Options Theory and the Construction of Derivatives Markets," in MacKenzie et al., *Do Economists Make Markets?*, 54–86.

10 Wynne, "Uncertainty and Environmental Learning"; Callon et al., *Acting in an Uncertain World*, 18–26; Beck, *Risk Society*, 64–68.

11 Beck, *Risk Society*, 68.

12 Chauncey Starr, "Social Benefit versus Technological Risk," *Science*, 165 (3899) (1969): 1232–8.
13 Malcolm M. Feeley and Jonathan Simon, 1992. "The New Penology: Notes on the Emerging Strategy of Corrections and its Implications," *Criminology*, 30 (4): 449–474; Robert Castel, "From Dangerousness to Risk," in Colin Gordon (ed.) *The Foucault Effect: Studies in Governmentality* (Chicago: University of Chicago Press, 1991), 281–298; Adam Reich, 2012. "Disciplined Doctors: The Electronic Medical Record and Physicians' Changing Relationship to Medical Knowledge," *Social Science and Medicine*, 74: 1021–1028. On "intellectual jurisdiction," see Abbott, *The System of Professions*, 69–79. On commensuration, see Wendy Espeland and Mitchell Stevens, "Commensuration as a Social Process," *Annual Review of Sociology*, 24 (1998): 313–343.
14 Paul Slovic, "Perceptions of Risk," *Science*, 236 (17) (1987): 280–285; Paul Slovic, "Trust, Emotion, Sex, Politics, and Science: Surveying the Risk-Assessment Battlefield," *Risk Analysis*, 19(4) (1999): 689–701. On "herd immunity" and how it figures in debates about vaccination, see Eula Biss, *On Immunity: An Inoculation* (Minneapolis, Graywolf Press, 2014).
15 Slovic, "Perceptions of Risk"; Slovic, "Trust, Emotion, Sex, Politics, and Science"; Golding, "A Social and Programmatic History," 39; Demortain, *Scientists and the Regulation of Risk*, 3–4, 16, nos. 5–6.
16 The cultural analysis of risk was pioneered by Mary Douglas, whose approach was adopted by ecologists and political scientists. See Mary Douglas, *Risk and Blame: Essays in Cultural Theory* (London: Routledge, 1992); Douglas and Wildavsky, *Risk and Culture*; Michiel Schwarz and Michael Thompson, *Divided We Stand: Redefining Politics, Technology and Social Choice* (New York: Harvester Wheatsheaf, 1990); Steve Rayner, "Cultural Theory and Risk Analysis," in Krimsky and Golding, *Social Theories of Risk* (Westport, CT: Praeger, 1992), 83–115.
17 Golan, *Laws of Men*, 2.
18 Ibid., 46–54, 128–129.
19 Ibid., 211–253.
20 Ibid., 211–253, 258–260, 263. The concept of "truth-producing practices" is obviously taken from Foucault. Indeed, his work on criminal psychiatry is concerned precisely with the question of how, despite all the tensions and competition between them, the interface between law and psychiatry was stabilized and the improbable (he calls it ludicrous) expertise of the forensic psychiatrist became a regular feature of legal proceedings. See Michel Foucault, *Abnormal. Lectures at the Collége de France, 1974–1975* (New York: Picador, 2003); Michel Foucault, "About

the Concept of the 'Dangerous Individual' in 19th Century Legal Psychiatry," in James D. Faubion (ed.) *Essential Works of Michel Foucault*, vol. 3: *Power* (New York: The New Press, 2000), 176–200.

21 Interpretations of the process leading to the *Daubert* decision and its significance are in Golan, *Laws of Men*, 258–64; Jasanoff, *Science at the Bar*, 42–68; Jasanoff, "Science and the Statistical Victim," 45–52; Edmond and Mercer, "Experts and Expertise in Legal and Regulatory Settings."

22 This interpretation of the *Daubert* decision is mine alone. Tal Golan tells me that I am wrong. *Daubert*, he says, is no doubt a "reaction to the rise of the statistical risk expert," but he does not see evidence that "risk analyzers posed a direct threat to the American judge. In fact, risk culture legitimated the new and more powerful judicial role: managerial, with an eye toward broad economic, social and political implications." Tal Golan, personal communication, 10/17/2018. He is the expert, and I have to defer to him. It is probably likely that the threat represented by risk analysis was quite minimal, and served instead as a foil against which American judges were able to assert new authorities and new gatekeeping powers for themselves. The Director of Oak Ridge was nuclear physicist Alvin Weinberg. He used the term "trans-science" to refer to "attempts to weigh the benefits of technology against its risks." These attempts, he said, "ask for the impossible: scientific answers to questions that are trans-scientific." Alvin Weinberg, "Science and Trans-Science," *Science*, 177(4045) (1972): 211. See also Jakob Arnoldi, *Risk* (Cambridge: Polity, 2009), 7–9. The description of American judges as pragmatists balancing the probabilities of different consequences is taken from Richard Posner, *How Judges Think* (Cambridge, MA: Harvard University Press, 2008), 78–121, 230–265.

23 Ewald, "Insurance and Risk"; Douglas, "Risk as Forensic Resource."

24 Biss, *On Immunity*, 23–50, 72–76; Claire Decoteau and Kelly Underman, 2015. "Adjudicating Non-Knowledge in the Autism Omnibus Proceedings," *Social Studies of Science*, 45, 4: 471–500.

25 Douglas, "Risk as Forensic Resource," 12.

26 Beck, *Risk Society*, 58; Douglas and Wildavsky, *Risk and Culture*; Starr, "Social Benefit versus Technological Risk."

27 Weinberg, "Science and Trans-Science."

28 Brian Wynne, "When Doubt Becomes a Weapon," *Nature*, 466 (7305) (2010): 441–442; Callon et al., *Acting in an Uncertain World*, 16, 18–27; Beck, *Risk Society*, 62; Proctor and Schiebinger, *Agnotology*; Oreskes and Conway, *Merchants of Doubt*. On "inclusion friction," see Edwards, *A Vast Machine*, 421–7.

5   Crisis, Take 2

1 Nichols, *The Death of Expertise*, 3–5, 11, 105–133, 216–217. On the concept of crisis as a device of historical narrative, see Janet Roitman, "The Stakes of Crisis," in P. Kjaer and N. Olsen (eds.) *Critical Theories of Crisis in Europe* (Rowman & Littlefield, 2016), 17–24; Elena Esposito, "Critique Without Crisis: Systems Theory as a Critical Sociology," *Thesis*, 11, 143(1) (2017): 18–27.

2 If you doubt that we've been here before, just read this litany written a decade ago: "During the George W. Bush administration ... even as the scientific consensus [about climate change] grew ever stronger, political appointees carried the manufacture of controversy to the point of criminal corruption. They censored scientists at Federal agencies, successfully blocked the reappointment of Robert Watson as IPCC Chair, and altered numerous government scientific reports in an attempt to conceal their most alarming conclusions." Paul Edwards, *A Vast Machine: Computer Models, Climate Data and the Politics of Global Warming* (Cambridge, MA: MIT Press, 2010), 409.

3 Nichols, *The Death of Expertise*, 5. Marx's Third Thesis reads as follows: "The materialist doctrine that men are products of circumstances and upbringing, and that, therefore, changed men are products of other circumstances and changed upbringing, forgets that it is men who change circumstances and that it is essential to educate the educator himself. Hence, this doctrine necessarily arrives at dividing society into two parts, one of which is superior to society." Robert C. Tucker, *The Marx–Engels Reader*, 2nd edn (New York: W.W. Norton & Company, 1978), 144. The thesis refutes a form of determinist materialism by asking how it would explain change and showing that the argument relies on an unacknowledged element of revolutionary practice – "it is essential to educate the educator himself." In the text, I have similarly tried to push Nichols' theory by asking how it would explain change from its dire predictions.

4 Jürgen Habermas, *Legitimation Crisis* (Cambridge: Polity, 1973), 95–108. On agnotology, see Proctor and Schiebinger, *Agnotology*.

5 Max Weber, "Domination and Legitimacy," in Guenther Roth and Claus Wittich (eds.) *Economy and Society*, vol. I (Berkeley: University of California Press, 1978), 212–215. My reading of this passage has been profoundly influenced by Ivan Szelenyi's lectures on Weber, and by his "Weber's Theory of Domination and Post-Communist Capitalisms," *Theory and Society*, 45 (2016): 1–24. The quote about forms of government being like machinery is from a letter Weber wrote, reported in Wolfgang Mommsen, *Max Weber and German Politics, 1890–1920*

(Oxford: Blackwell, 1984), 396. See the illuminating discussion in Svan Eliasson, "Constitutional Caesarism: Weber's Politics in their German Context," in Stephen Turner (ed.) *The Cambridge Companion to Weber* (Cambridge: Cambridge University Press, 2000), 131–148.

6 Weber, "Domination and Legitimacy," 212–215.

7 For the idea of "obligatory points of passage," see Latour, *The Pasteurization of France*, 43–49.

8 Habermas, *Legitimation Crisis*, 97–110.

9 Ibid.

10 Ibid.

11 On legibility and typifications, see James Scott, *Seeing Like a State: How Certain Schemes to Improve the Human Condition have Failed* (New Haven: Yale University Press, 1998), 76–83; Demortain, *Scientists and the Regulation of Risk*, 5–8.

12 The meaning of "discursive" employed here is taken from Michel Foucault, "Orders of Discourse," *Social Science Information*, 10, 2 (1971), 7–30; Michel Foucault, *The Archeology of Knowledge* (London: Tavistock, 1972). On the role of rhetorical mechanisms in legitimacy, see Yaron Ezrahi, *The Descent of Icarus: Science and the Transformation of Contemporary Democracy* (Cambridge, MA: Harvard University Press, 1990), 10–13. See also Rowan's "rhetorical model of risk communication": Katherine E. Rowan, "The Technical and Democratic Approaches to Risk Situations: Their Appeal, Limitations and Rhetorical Alternative," *Argumentation*, 8 (1994), 391–409. On legitimacy being created by repetition, see Carpenter, *Reputation and Power*, 194. I am also building on Carl Friedrich's influential critique of the opposition between rationality and tradition that underpins Weber's framework. Friedrich argues that Weber has conflated "authority" and "legitimacy." Authority is "the capacity to issue communications that can be elaborated by convincing reasons." It is an "art of authoritative reasoning," namely rhetoric, which is common to both traditional and rational-legal domination. Carl J. Friedrich, *Tradition and Authority* (New York: Praeger Publishers, 1972). Clearly, my reworking of legitimacy as "defensibility" essentially rebuilds it on the model of an "art of authoritative reasoning," i.e. rhetoric in Friedrich's sense. I eschew, however, Friedrich's distinction between authority and legitimacy because it implies that the latter term stands for some source or fount outside authoritative reasoning, essentially the political claim to rule in the name of tradition or the people, upon which the whole edifice rests. In contrast, in the approach I develop here – which is closer to Ezrahi's – there is a seamless transition (and often entanglement) from defending a command in terms of the correct

political procedures of representation to defending it in terms of
the correct scientific procedures of demonstration.

13 Franz Kafka, *The Trial* (New York: Alfred A. Knopf, 1937),
   267–268.

14 This image of legitimacy as a rhetorical maze was loosely inspired
   by Latour, *Science in Action*, and also by Weber's discussion of
   the revolution represented by Greek philosophy and its invention
   of the concept: "for the first time, appeared a handy means by
   which one could put the logical screws upon somebody so that
   he could not come out without admitting either that he knew
   nothing or that this and nothing else was truth, the eternal truth
   that never would vanish as the doings of the blind men would
   vanish." Weber says that this discovery "seemed to open the
   way for knowing and for teaching how to act ... as a citizen
   of the state; for this question was everything to Hellenic man,
   whose thinking was political throughout." Max Weber, 1918,
   "Science as a Vocation," in H. H. Gerth and C. W. Mills (eds.)
   From Marx Weber: Essays in Sociology (New York: Oxford
   University Press, 1946), 141. My reading of Kafka as speaking
   about legitimacy was also articulated by Pierre Bourdieu in his
   lectures on the state. *The Trial*, says Bourdieu, is animated by
   a "search for the place where the true identity of social agents
   is defined ... a sociological search for a central place where the
   resources of legitimate authority are concentrated, and which
   is accordingly the point where regression stops ... there is a
   moment at which you have to stop, and this place where you
   stop is the state." This stopping place exists only by virtue of
   "an extraordinary symbolic act of force," which Bourdieu depicts
   as the "coup d'état from which the state was born." Yet, this
   symbolic act of force, which is a "conforming transgression, a
   transgression within the proper forms," is also repeated with
   every act of *prosopopoeia*, every time a politician or a jurist
   speaks "for" a collective entity (the people, the state, public
   opinion) and thereby brings it into being as the "one point of
   view that is the measure of all points of view." Pierre Bourdieu,
   On the State: Lectures at the Collège de France, 1989–1992
   (Cambridge: Polity, 2014), 67–69.

15 Weber, "Domination and Legitimacy," 212–14; Szelenyi, "Weber's
   Theory of Domination," 3–5.

16 The analysis of symbolic pollution builds on Mary Douglas,
   Purity and Danger (London: Routledge, 1966). See also Eyal,
   The Disenchantment of the Orient, 153, 159–164.

17 Habermas, *Legitimation Crisis*, 71; Jürgen Habermas, "Technology and Science as Ideology," 81–127 in his *Towards a Rational
   Society* (Boston, MA: Beacon Press, 1970). An example of how

the post-World-War-II American state sought to integrate, predict and control the physical environment is provided by Zeke Baker, "Climate State: Science–State Struggles and the Formation of Climate Science in the US from the 1930s to 1960s," *Social Studies of Science*, 46, 7 (2017): 861–87.

18 Vibha Kapuria-Foreman and Mark Perlman, "An Economic Historian's Economist: Remembering Simon Kuznets." *Economic Journal*, 105 (433) (1995): 1524–1547; John W. Kendrick, *The New System of National Accounts* (Dordrecht: Kluwer, 1996); Zoltan Kennessey, *The Accounts of Nations* (Amsterdam: IOS Press, 1994); Kurabayashi, Yoshimasa, "Keynes' *How to Pay for the War* and its Influence on Postwar National Accounting," in Kennessey, 93–108; Simon Kuznets, "National Income, 1929–1932," *National Bureau of Economic Research Bulletin*, 49 (June 7, 1934): 1–12; André Vanoli, *A History of National Accounting* (Amsterdam: IOS Press, 2005).

19 On the system of national accounting and the construction of "the economy," see Timothy Mitchell, "Fixing the Economy." *Cultural Studies*, 12 (1) (1998): 82–101; Daniel Breslau, "Economics Invents the Economy: Mathematics, Statistics, and Models in the Work of Irving Fisher and Wesley Mitchell," *Theory and Society*, 32(3) (2003): 379–411; Gil Eyal and Moran Levy, "Economic Expertise and the Public Sphere," *HOPE*, vol. 45, issue 5, *The Economist as Public Intellectual* (Durham, NC: Duke University Press, 2013). On the ideological role of indicators of aggregate productivity in mediating the conflict between employers and unions, see Fred Block and Gene A. Burns, "Productivity as a Social Problem: The Uses and Misuses of Social Indicators," *American Sociological Review*, 51 (6) (1986): 767–80. On the exclusion of unpaid domestic labor from the GDP, see Nancy Folbre, "Women's Work and Women's Households: Gender Bias in the US Census," *Social Research*, 56 (3)(1989): 545–69. On the "governmentalization" of the state, see Michel Foucault, "Governmentality," in G. Burchell, C. Gordon, and P. Miller (eds.) *The Foucault Effect: Studies in Governmentality* (Chicago: University of Chicago Press, 1991); Gil Eyal, "Plugging into the Body of the Leviathan: Proposal for a New Sociology of Public Interventions," *Middle East – Topics and Arguments*, 1 (2013). http://meta-journal.net/article/view/1033/984.

20 Daniel Breslau, "What Do Market Designers Do When They Design Markets? Economists as Consultants to the Redesign of Wholesale Electricity Markets in the US," in Charles Camic, Neil Gross, and Michele Lamont (eds.) *Social Knowledge in the Making* (Chicago: University of Chicago Press, 2011), 379–404; Michel Callon, "Introduction: The Embeddedness of Economic Markets

in Economics," in Michel Callon (ed.) *The Laws of the Markets* (Oxford: Blackwell, 1998), 1–57; Marion Fourcade, *Economists and Societies* (Princeton, NJ: Princeton University Press, 2009); MacKenzie, Donald, and Yuval Milo, "Constructing a Market, Performing Theory: The Historical Sociology of a Financial Derivatives Exchange," AJS, 109(1) (2003): 107–45; MacKenzie, Donald, Fabian Muniesa, and Lucia Siu, *Do Economists Make Markets? On the Performativity of Economics* (Princeton, NJ: Princeton University Press, 2007); Markoff, J. and Veronica Montecinos, "The Ubiquitous Rise of Economists." *Journal of Public Policy*, 13 (1) (1993): 37–68; Gil Eyal, "Anti-Politics and the Spirit of Capitalism: Dissidents, Monetarists and the Czech Transition to Capitalism," *Theory and Society* 29(1) (February 2000): 49–92.

21 Peter Weingart, "The Paradoxes of Expert Advising," in Gotthard Bechmann and Imre Hronszky, *Expertise and its Interfaces* (Berlin: Edition Sigma, 2003), 43–89. In a sense, Weingart's extremely insightful argument can be seen as synthesizing, against the grain, the opposing analyses of Habermas ("scientization of politics") and Beck ("politicization of science"). My refurbishing of the "legitimation crisis" concept draws on the insights of all three, but adds to them the missing element of attention to boundaries, hybridity and pollution supplied by Mary Douglas and further developed by Bruno Latour: Douglas, *Purity and Danger*; Mary Douglas, *Risk and Blame: Essays in Cultural Theory* (London: Routledge, 1992); Mary Douglas and Aaron Wildavsky, *Risk and Culture: an Essay on the Selection of Technological and Environmental Dangers* (Berkeley, CA: University of California Press, 1982); Bruno Latour, *We've Never Been Modern* (Cambridge, MA: Harvard University Press, 1991). The imagery of a "vicious spiral" owes to Breyer, *Breaking the Vicious Circle*. On "pharmacovigilance," see Demortain, *Scientists and the Regulation of Risk*, 17, n.12.

22 Habermas, "Technology and Science as Ideology"; Beck, *Risk Society*, 64–69; Weingart, "Paradoxes," 58–59.

23 Carpenter, *Reputation and Power*, 16–18, 228–297.

24 Ibid. On "mechanical objectivity" as a means of combating bias and generating trust, see Lorraine Daston and Peter Galison, "The Image of Objectivity." *Representations*, 40 (1992): 81–128; Porter, *Trust in Numbers*.

25 Rory O'Kelly, "Prescribing Diseases: The Industrial Injuries Advisory Council," in Roger Smith and Brian Wynne (eds.) *Expert Evidence: The Interpretation of Science in Law* (London: Routledge, 1989), 131–150. On the distinction between mechanical and disciplinary objectivity, see Porter, *Trust in Numbers*, 3–8.

26 Beck, *Risk Society*, 29, 59–69.

27 O'Kelley, "Prescribing Diseases," 144–147.
28 Sheila Jasanoff, "The Problem of Rationality in American Health and Safety Regulation," in Brian Wynne and Roger Smith (eds.) *Expert Evidence*, 151–183; Demortain, *Scientists*, 1.
29 Weingart, "Paradoxes," 78–79.
30 Carpenter, *Reputation and Power*, 342–345.

6 Inside the Vortex

 1 The idea of "strategy without strategist" is common to both Bourdieu and Foucault; see Loïc J. D. Wacquant, "Towards a Social Praxeology: The Structure and Logic of Bourdieu's Sociology," in Pierre Bourdieu and Loïc J. D. Wacquant, *An Invitation to Reflexive Sociology* (Chicago: University of Chicago Press, 1992), 25; Hubert Dreyfus and Paul Rabinow, *Michel Foucault: Beyond Structuralism and Hermeneutics* (Chicago: University of Chicago Press, 1982). The concept of "overflowing" is key to Callon et al., *Acting in an Uncertain World*, 9.
 2 Weingart, "Paradoxes," 80–81; Decoteau and Underman, "Adjudicating Non-Knowledge in the Autism Omnibus Proceedings."
 3 Carpenter, *Reputation and Power*, 160–161, 346–348, 410–414.
 4 Bijker et al., *The Paradox of Scientific Authority*, 47–55.
 5 Ibid., 46.
 6 Jasanoff, "Science and the Statistical Victim," 52–58, 60–63.
 7 Ibid.
 8 Breyer, *Breaking the Vicious Circle*, 48–67.
 9 The concept of "boundary work" was developed in Thomas F. Gieryn, "Boundary Work and the Demarcation of Science from Non-Science: Strains and Interests in Professional Ideologies of Scientists," *American Sociological Review*, 48 (1983): 781–795. It was applied to case of the *Gezondheidsraad* by Bijker et al., *The Paradox of Scientific Authority*, 40–41, 47–67. My critique of this concept draws on my own earlier work, as well as my reading of Foucault, Latour and Mitchell. Gil Eyal, *The Disenchantment of the Orient: Expertise about Arab Affairs and the Israeli State* (Stanford, CA: Stanford University Press, 2006), 7–8; Michel Foucault, "Preface to Transgression," in Paul Rabinow (ed.) *Aesthetics, Method and Epistemology*, vol. 2 of *Essential Works of Michel Foucault, 1954–1984* (New York: The New Press, 1998), 73; Bruno Latour, *We've Never Been Modern* (Cambridge, MA: Harvard University Press, 1993); Timothy Mitchell, 1991. "The Limits of the State: Beyond Statist Approaches and their Critics," *American Political Science Review* 85, 1: 77–96.
10 Bijker et al., *The Paradox of Scientific Authority*, 64–65.

11 Lindsay Prior, 2003. "Belief, Knowledge and Expertise: The Emergence of the Lay Expert in Medical Sociology," *Sociology of Health and Illness* 25: 41–53; Carpenter, *Reputation and Power*, 396–8; John Abraham and Courtney Davis, 2011. "Rethinking Innovation Accounting in Pharmaceutical Regulation: A Case Study in the Deconstruction of Therapeutic Advance and Therapeutic Breakthrough," *Science, Technology and Human Values* 36 (6): 791–815.

12 Carpenter *Reputation and Power*, 730–743; Epstein, *Impure Science*; Phil Brown et al., 2004. "Embodied Health Movements: New Approaches to Social Movements in Health," *Sociology of Health and Illness* 26 (1); 50–80; Gil Eyal et al., *The Autism Matrix* (Cambridge: Polity, 2010); Charles Hersch, 1968. "The Discontent Explosion in Mental Health," *American Psychologist* 23: 497–508; Callon and Rabeharisoa, "Patients and Scientists"; Paul Starr, 1982, *The Social Transformation of American Medicine* (New York: Basic Books, 2017), 485–491. On the concept of "jurisdictional struggles," see Abbott, *The System of Professions.*

13 Sheila Jasanoff, "Technologies of Humility: Citizens' Participation in Governing Science, *Minerva* 41(3) (2003): 223–244; The quote from Ruckelshaus is in Rowan, "The Technical and Democratic Approaches," 397–398. On the French Citizens' conferences, see Callon et al., *Acting in an Uncertain World*, 169–176.

14 Jasanoff, "Technologies of Humility," 237; Daniel Fiorino, 1990. "Citizen Participation and Environmental Risk: A Survey of Institutional Mechanisms," *Science, Technology and Human Values*, 15 (2): 230–236; Callon et al., *Acting in an Uncertain World*, 155–157. On how transparency can heighten suspicion, confusion and friction, see also Edwards, *A Vast Machine*, 398, 421–430.

15 Rowan, "The Technical and Democratic Approaches," 401.

16 Robert Futrell, 2003. "Technical Adversarialism and Participatory Collaboration in the U.S. Chemical Weapons Disposal Program," *Science, Technology and Human Values* 28 (4): 456, 460–462, 465–471. For a similar case where perfunctory inclusionary measures failed for similar reasons, see Callon et al., *Acting in an Uncertain World*, 13–18.

17 Rowan, "The Technical and Democratic Approaches," 400–401;Futrell, "Technical Adeversarialism," 464–471; Fiorino, "Citizen Participation," 231.

18 Abrahama and Davis, "Rethinking Innovation." On "inclusion friction," as well as cases where inclusion and transparency lead to a process driven by "ideological and political strategies," see Paul Edwards' account of the practice of "climate auditing" by citizen scientists: Edwards, *A Vast Machine*, 421–427.

19 Porter, *Trust in Numbers*, viii-ix, 4–5; Scott, *Seeing Like a State;* Carpenter, *Reputation and Power*, 256–297; Lorraine Daston and Peter Galison. 1992. "The Image of Objectivity." *Representations* 40:81–128.
20 Timmermans, Stefan, and Marc Berg. 2003. *The Gold Standard: The Challenge of Evidence-Based Medicine and Standardization in Health Care.* Philadelphia: Temple University Press; Judith M. Gueron and Howard Rolston, 2013. *Fighting for Reliable Evidence* (New York: Russell Sage Foundation, 2013); Jigar Bhatt, "Politics by Other Means: Economic Expertise, Power and Global Development Finance Reform" (Unpublished Doctoral Dissertation, Columbia University, 2018); Donovan, Kevin. 2018. "The Rise of Randomistas: on the Experimental Turn in International Aid," *Economy and Society* 47(1): 27–58. Luciana de Souza Leao and Gil Eyal, "Experiments in the Wild: A Historical Perspective on the Rise of Randomized Controlled Trials in International Development" (Unpublished Manuscript).
21 Carpenter, *Reputation and Power*, 118–264, 294–5.
22 Ibid.
23 The first quote is from Abhijit Banerjee, Silvain Chassang, and Eric Snowberg. 2016. "Decision Theoretic Approaches to Experiment Design and External Validity." *NBER Working Paper 22167.* Duflo is quoted in Ian Parker, 2010. "The Poverty Lab." Published in *The New Yorker*, on May 17, 2010. http://www.newyorker.com/magazine/2010/05/17/the-poverty-lab. The Behavioral Insights Team "started life inside 10 Downing Street," but is now "a social purpose company...jointly owned by the UK Government; Nesta (the innovation charity); and our employees," i.e. like the Millennium Challenge Corporation, it is an example of the "outsourcing" strategy to be discussed later. https://www.behaviouralinsights.co.uk/about-us/ (last accesed 12/4/2018).
24 Porter, *Trust in Numbers*, 6–48; Carpenter, *Reputation and Power*, 387–390, 393–410, 476–492, 508–509.
25 Deaton, Angus, and Nancy Cartwright. 2016. "Understanding and Misunderstanding Randomized Controlled Trials." *NBER Working Paper Series*, 22595; Rodrik, Dani. 2008. "The New Development Economics: We Shall Experiment, But How Shall We Learn?" *HKS Faculty Research Working Paper Series*, RWP08–055; James Heckman et al., 2000. "Substitution and Drop Out Bias in Social Experiments: A Study of an Influential Social Experiment," *The Quarterly Journal of Economics* 115(2): 651–694; Demortain, *Scientists and the Regulation of Risk*, 53–57.
26 Carpenter, *Reputation and Power*, 736–747; Miriam Schuman, 2007. "Commercializing Clinical Trials – Risks and Benefits of

the CRO Boom," *New England Journal of Medicine* 357(14): 1365–8.

27 Banerjee et al., "Decision Theoretic Approaches," 11–15; Deaton and Cartwright, "Understanding and Misunderstanding," 16–17.

28 Lorraine Daston and Peter Galison. 1992. "The Image of Objectivity." *Representations* 40:81–128; Carpenter, *Reputation and Power*, 142–6, 219; Bhatt, *Politics by Other Means*, 78, 186–8.

29 On "popular epidemiology" and "hybrid forums," see Callon et al., *Acting in an Uncertain World*, 153–189; Phil Brown, "Popular Epidemiology Revisited," *Current Sociology* 45(3) (1997): 137–156. On the Millenium Challenge Corporation, see Bhatt, *Politics by Other Means*, 8–9. On the IPCC, see Edwards, *A Vast Machine*, 17–20, 398–404; Silke Beck, 2012. "Between Tribalism and Trust: The IPCC under the 'Public Microscope'," *Nature and Culture* 7(2), 151–172. On these arrangements of voluntary regulation in the areas of adverse reactions to medications and food safety, see Demortain, *Scientists and the Regulation of Risk*, 8–11.

30 On state phobia, see Mitchell Dean and Kaspar Villadsen, *State Phobia and Civil Society: The Political Legacy of Michel Foucault* (Stanford, CA: Stanford University Press, 2016). On the French Citizens' Conferences, see Callon et al., *Acting in an Uncertain World*, 169–174. On the Interagency Autism Coordinating Committee, see Adrianna Bagnall, 2012. *Storytelling or the Story Itself: Forming an Institutional Narrative of Autism in the Interagency Autism Coordinating Committee* (Unpublished Manuscript, Department of Sociology, Columbia University).

31 Demortain, *Scientists and the Regulation of Risk*, 44–47, 53–59, 66–67.

32 Edwards, *A Vast Machine*, 398–404; Beck, "Between Tribalism and Trust."

33 Demortain, *Scientists and the Regulation of Risk*, 44–47, 53–59, 66–67.

34 The virtues of uncertainty and an experimental approach, as embodied, for example, in the precautionary principle, are articulated most forcefully by Callon et al., *Acting in an Uncertain World*, 191–223. Bayes' Theorem treats probability not as objective distribution in a given population, but as subjective degree of belief. It describes how to reiteratively update the degree of confidence attached to a subjective belief in light of new evidence. It is a way, therefore, of combining judgment (including prior assumptions common among a community of experts – known as "priors") with whatever pieces of incomplete and uncertain evidence are at hand. Sharon Bertsch McGrayne, *The Theory That Would Not Die* (New Haven: Yale University Press, 2011).

The article announcing Latour's mobilization on behalf of climate science is Ava Kofman, "Bruno-Latour, the Post-Truth Philosopher, Mounts a Defense of Science," *New York Times Magazine*, October 25, 2018.

35 On the military origins of climate science, see Baker, "Climate State." On infrastructural inversion, see Edwards *A Vast Machine*, 404–430. On the precautionary principle and its foregrounding of uncertainty, see Callon et al., *Acting in an Uncertain World*, 191–223. On "trained judgment," see Daston and Galison, *Objectivity*, 309–362. On the use of composite indicators, see Richard Rottenburg, Sally E. Merry, Sung-Joon Park and Johanna Mugler, *The World of Indicators: The Making of Governmental Knowledge through Quantification* (Cambridge: Cambridge University Press, 2015). Dewey's quote comes from John Dewey, *Democracy and Education* (New York: The Free Press, 1916), 76.

36 Edwards, *A Vast Machine*, 404–430. On "Climategate," see the Editorial, 2010. "Closing the Climategate," *Nature* 468 (November 10), 345. On the accusation of "tribalism" against the IPCC, see Silke Beck, "Between Tribalism and Trust: The IPCC Under the 'Public Microscope'," *Nature and Culture*, 7(2) (2012): 151–172. On the drawbacks of transparency and the "honest" foregrounding of uncertainty, see Stephen John, "Epistemic Trust and the Ethics of Science Communication: Against Transparency, Openness, Sincerity and Honesty," *Social Epistemology*, 32(2) (2018): 75–87. On agnotology and the tactic of "reasonable doubt," see Proctor et al., *Agnotology*; Oreskes and Conway, *Merchants of Doubt*. Two attempts to provide a test for scientific consensus are: Naomi Oreskes, "The Scientific Consensus on Climate Change: How do we Know We're not Wrong?" in J. F. DiMento and P. Doughman (eds.) *Climate Change: What It Means for Us, Our Children, and Our Grandchildren* (Cambridge, MA: MIT Press, 2007), 105–148; Uri Shwed and Peter Bearman, "The Temporal Structure of Scientific Consensus Formation," *American Sociological Review* 75(6) (2010): 817–840.

7   Balaam's Blessing

1 *Numbers*, 22–24.
2 Douglas, *Purity and Danger*; Millstone and van Zwanenberg, "A Crisis of Trust."
3 Edwards, *A Vast Machine*, 407.
4 Carpenter, Reputation and Power, 385.
5 Ibid., 335–336.
6 Ibid., 321–323.

7 Ibid., 331.
8 Ibid., 546–572.
9 Ibid., 379.
10 Ibid., 736–740.
11 Ibid., 730–740.
12 Ibid. For science as an integral component in turning political acts into public and accountable actions, see Ezrahi, *The Descent of Icarus*, 18–28.
13 On the state as the producer and guarantor of the *doxa*, see Lecture of February 7, 1991, in Pierre Bourdieu, *On the State: Lectures at the College de France, 1989–1992*. (Cambridge: Polity, 2014). For how expert systems work themselves into the fabric of everyday life, see Giddens, *The Consequences of Modernity*, 27–29, 83–92.
14 Carpenter, *Reputation and Power*, 16–18, 300–301.
15 Ibid., 276–283, 294–295, 301, 610–621. On "institutional credentialing" see Friedson, *Professional Powers*. On ontological complicity, see Pierre Bourdieu and Loic Wacquant, *An Invitation to Reflexive Sociology* (Chicago: University of Chicago Press, 1992), 128. On legitimacy working even through disobedience, even through the breaking of the law, as a "confirming transgression," see Bourdieu, *On the State*, 47.
16 Edwards, *A Vast Machine*, 407–412; Robert N. Proctor, "Agnotology: A Missing Term to Describe the Cultural Production of Ignorance (and its Study)" in Proctor and Shchiebinger, *Agnotology*, 1–33; Oreskes and Conway, *Merchants of Doubt*; David Michaels, *Doubt is Their Product: How Industry's Assault on Science Threatens Your Health* (Oxford University Press, 2008).
17 Silke Beck, "Between Tribalism and Trust: The IPCC Under the 'Public Microscope'," *Nature and Culture* 7(2) (2012): 152–4.
18 Edwards, *A Vast Machine*, 413–418.
19 Edwards, *A Vast Machine*, 424–426; Fall, S., A. Watts, J. Nielsen-Gammon, E. Jones, D. Niyogi, J. R. Christy, and R. A. Pielke Sr., "Analysis of the Impacts of Station Exposure on the US Historical Climatology Network Temperatures and Temperature Trends," *J. Geophys. Res.*, 116 (2011), D14120, doi:10.1029/2010JD015146; SurfaceStations.org. On the mobilization of scientists, residents and activists in "hybrid forums," see Callon et al., *Acting in an Uncertain World*, 25–34.
20 On the theory of "regulatory capture" and its limitations, see Carpenter, *Reputation and Power*, 36–43. On the military origins of climate science, see Baker, "Climate State." On how military planners continue to plan for global warming despite the Trump Administration's avowals to the contrary, see Tara Copp, "Pentagon is Still Preparing for Global Warming Even Though Trump

Said to Stop," *Military Times*, September 12, 2017. https://www.
militarytimes.com/news/your-military/2017/09/12/pentagon-is-still-
preparing-for-global-warming-even-though-trump-said-to-stop/;
Erika Bolstad, "Military Leaders Urge Trump to See Climate as a
Security Threat," *Scientific American*, November 15, 2016. https://
www.scientificamerican.com/article/military-leaders-urge-trump-
to-see-climate-as-a-security-threat/; Laura Parker, "Who's Still
Fighting Climate Change? The US Military," *National Geographic*,
February 7, 2017. https://news.nationalgeographic.com/2017/02/
pentagon-fights-climate-change-sea-level-rise-defense-department-
military/.
21 Eyal, "Plugging into the Body of the Leviathan"; Eyal and Levy,
"Economic Expertise and the Public Sphere."

Conclusions: Trans-Science as a Vocation

1 Weber, "Science as a Vocation," 147; Alvin Gouldner, "The Dark
Side of the Dialectic: Towards a New Objectivity," *Sociological
Inquiry* 46(1) (1976): 3–15.
2 Alvin Weinberg, "Science and Trans-Science," *Minerva* 10(2)
(1972): 209–222.
3 Ibid., 209–211.
4 Ibid., 211–212.
5 Weber, "Science as a Vocation," 143; Beck, *Risk Society*, 64–69;
On how Bayesian statistics, rejected by the luminaries of statistics as subjective and unscientific, found a fertile ground in
state agencies and policy circles, see Bertsch McGrayne, *The
Theory that would not Die*. On resilience, preparedness and
sentinel systems, see Stephen Collier and Andrew Lakoff, "Vital
Systems Security: Reflexive Biopolitics and the Government of
Emergency, *Theory, Culture and Society* 32(2) (2015); Andrew
Lakoff, "Real Time Biopolitics: The Actuary and the Sentinel in
Global Public Health," *Economy and Society* 44(1) (2015): 40–59.
On algorithms, see Virginia Eubanks, *Automating Inequality:
How High-Tech Tools Profile, Police and Punish the Poor* (New
York: St. Martin's Press, 2017); Frank Pasquale, *The Black Box
Society* (Harvard University Press, 2015).
6 Weinberg, "Science and Trans-Science," 211.
7 Ibid.
8 Weinberg, "Science and Trans-Science," 220.
9 Callon et al., *Acting in an Uncertain World*, 191–223.
10 Weber, "Science as a Vocation," 146.
11 Weinberg, "Science and Trans-Science," 211; Weinberg, "Science
and Trans-Science," 220.

Index

Abbott, Andrew, 31
Abraham, 58
abstract knowledge, 23, 25–36, 41
acceptable levels, 69, 71, 76, 98, 101
actor-network theory (ANT), 31–33, 37, 39–40
adjudication, 79, 149; *see also* judiciary; jury system
adverse drug reaction (ADR) reporting, 125–126
agnotology, 2, 81, 84, 128, 136
algorithms, 26, 30, 75, 144
American Language, The (Mencken), 12
American Medical Association (AMA), 116, 117, 125
anti-intellectualism, 4, 47
antinomy, 83–84
anti-vaxxers *see* vaccination
Aristotle, 58
Assembled Chemical Weapons Assessment (ACWA) program, 114–115

artificial intelligence (AI), 17, 23, 26–28, 29–30, 34
attribution (of expertise), 22, 25–26, 30–31, 34, 41
authority, 79, 83–84, 88–89, 90–91, 115, 149
autism, 55, 106

Balaam effect, 130–141
Banerjee, Abhijit, 118
Bayesian statistics, 126, 144
Beck, Ulrich, 64–65, 67, 70, 74, 101, 144
Behavioural Insights Team, 118
better argument, force of, 86, 87, 89, 93, 113
blame, 55, 56, 77–79
Bodmer report, 53
boundary mechanisms
  and legitimacy, 93–94, 108–111
  location of boundary work, 110–111
  and risk analysis, 68–70, 80
Bourdieu, Pierre, 59
Bureau of Medicine, 131–132

Brexit, 1–2, 3, 113
Breyer, Stephen, 108–109,
    149
British Medical Journal, 45–46
Brownlie, Julie, 55–56
BSE crisis, 51, 94, 112,
    123–124

Callon, Michel, 67, 68, 81,
    113, 147
Cameron, David, 1
capabilities, 36, 41
carcinogens, 5, 72, 101–102
Carpenter, Daniel, 131–135,
    149
Chernobyl, 24–25, 70, 143
citizens' conferences, 112–113,
    123
climate change, 2–3, 50,
    66–67, 80, 124–128, 131,
    136–140
Climategate, 125, 128, 137,
    148
clinical pharmacology, 116–
    117, 120, 132, 134, 136
clinical trials, 98–100, 102–
    103, 111, 116–122, 132,
    135–136
Clinton, Hillary, 133
closed facts, 7–8
codification, 26–28, 32–33
cognitive psychology, 12, 26,
    27, 31
Collins, Harry, 8, 9, 23, 24,
    34–35, 36, 37–38, 39, 40,
    105
competing claims (to expertise),
    16, 17–18, 21–22, 66
confirmation bias, 44, 50, 82
conflicts of interest, 44, 50
Congressional Budget Office,
    (CBO), 3
consensus, 97, 105–111,
    113–115, 122, 124–125,
    128

consultation
    of experts, 105–107, 110
    public see inclusion;
        participatory approaches
Consumer Financial Protection
    Bureau, 128
consumer price index (CPI), 95
Contract Research
    Organizations (CROs),
    120, 132
contributory expertise, 9, 17,
    105, 107–108
co-production model (public
    role of expertise), 40,
    122
credibility, 6, 17–18, 25, 43,
    73, 84, 97, 123–124; see
    also legitimacy; trust
cultural theory of risk, 73

Datson, Lorraine, 121
Daubert ruling, 18, 74, 76–77
decision-support systems,
    26–27
defensibility, 69, 75, 84, 86–94,
    135–136, 140
deficit model, 53–54
democracy, 4, 37–41, 85
democratic legitimacy, 75–76,
    81
Demortain, David, 102
denial, 6
deregulation, 96, 133–134
development aid, 116, 118,
    121
Dewey, John, 5, 32, 38, 126,
    127, 146
distributed cognition, 31–33
distributed regulation, 124,
    128
distribution (of expertise),
    29–30, 31–36, 41
Douglas, Mary, 63, 77, 78, 79,
    149
Dreyfus, Hubert, 29

drug approval, 98–100,
102–103, 111, 116–122,
131–136
drug lag, 103, 132, 133
drug reporting systems,
125–126
Duflo, Esther, 118
Durkheim, Émile, 63
Dutch Health Council *see*
Gezondheidsraad
dyslexia, 110–111
Dyson, Freeman, 66–67

Earle, John, 11
economics, 1–2, 3, 15–16,
94–97, 117–118, 120, 140
economy, 94–96
education, 116
Edwards, Paul, 126–127
efficient market hypothesis, 96
electronic healthcare records
(EHR), 71
engineering, 71, 72, 144
Environmental Impact
Statements (EISs), 112,
114
Environmental Protection
Agency (EPA), 2–3, 51,
112, 115
Eurobarometer, 46
European Commission, 46, 123
European Food Agency,
123–124, 125
Evans, Robert, 9, 34–35, 36,
37–38, 39, 40, 105
evidence *see* expert testimony
evidence-based medicine
(EBM), 39, 71
exclusion, as legitimation
strategy, 103, 104,
105–111, 128
experience model (public role
of expertise), 39, 40
experience-based knowledge, 9,
17

experimentalism, 126, 127
expert systems
as model for public role of
expertise, 39
and theories of expertise,
26–28, 29–30, 34, 36
trust in, 56, 61–62, 77–78
expert testimony
competing claims, 17–18
Daubert ruling, 18, 74,
76–77
determining credibility of,
12, 16, 17–18, 66,
74–77
Frye ruling, 17–18, 66, 74,
75–76, 108
general acceptability
criterion, 17–18, 66,
75–77, 108
and lie detector technology,
75
and risk, 17–18, 74–77
selection of experts, 107–108
weaponizing of, 74
expertise
appeals to, 8–9, 19
and artificial intelligence, 17
artificial scarcity of, 105
attribution of, 22, 25–26,
30–31, 34, 41
and authority, 79, 83–84, 88
and the Balaam effect,
130–141
and capabilities, 36, 41
competing claims to, 16,
17–18, 21–22, 66
and consensus, 97, 105–111,
122, 124–125, 128
and consultation, 105–106,
110
contributory expertise, 9, 17,
105, 107–108
death of, 3–4, 8, 82
debate on the nature of,
26–42

expertise (cont.)
determining possession of, 8–10, 12, 14–20
development of, 12, 25
distribution of, 29–30, 31–36, 41
and error, 1–2, 5, 25
as historically specific way of talking, 19–20, 21
interactional expertise, 9, 34–35, 40, 108
internal possession of, 22, 25–30, 34, 35, 41
and interpretation, 8–9, 44–45, 118–119
and jurisdictional struggles, 22, 24, 30–31, 35–36, 65, 70–73, 75–77, 97
and knowledge, 15–16, 17, 22–36, 41
lay expertise, 9, 12, 17, 35, 36–37, 40, 102, 111–112, 148
and legal testimony *see* expert testimony
and legitimacy, 82–85, 94–103, 104–129
meaning of, 12–13, 19, 21–42
origins of term, 12, 21
pejorative use of term, 3
and policy-making, 18–19, 94–103, 104–129
politics of, 12, 19
pragmatics of term, 14–20
and prediction, 1–2, 24–25
prescriptive approaches, 27, 36–37
and public opinion, 1–2, 3, 9–10, 43–54, 82–83
reliance upon, 4, 14
resentment of, 4–5
and risk, 64–77, 102
role in the public sphere, 37–41

selection of experts, 105–109
social recognition of, 22, 30–31
supply and demand, 30
trained judgment, 39–41, 44–45, 100–101, 120, 126–128, 139, 144
and trans-science, 143–149
and trust, 3–4, 38–41, 42, 43–63, 84
usage of term, 11–20, 97
expertise theory, the, 16
explication, 24, 27
extension, problem of, 37–41, 103
eyewitness testimony, 7

facts
appeals to, 5–6
closed, 7–8
inconvenient, 142–143, 145–146, 149
interpretation of, 5–6, 8–9, 44–45, 118–119
and law and policy, 7–8
open-forward, 7–8
and science, 6, 7–8
and values, 76, 93, 97, 105–106, 143–144
faith, 57–60, 62–63
fake news, 5, 93
Fama, Eugene, 96
Federal Trade Commission (FTC), 15
financial crisis, 1, 65, 68, 69, 94, 96, 97
financial risk, 65, 67, 69
Folkes v. Chadd, 74
food, 50, 51, 52, 112–113, 125, 126
Food and Drug Administration (FDA), 5, 51–53, 98–100, 102–103, 105, 116–120, 125, 131–136, 141, 145
Food Standards Agency, 112

forensic science, 75
Foucault, Michel, 90, 96
Framework Convention on
    Climate Change, 124
framing
    and legitimacy, 106–111,
        113–114, 122–123, 145
    of survey results, 46–48
    and trust, 57, 60–63
Frankfurter, Felix, 15–16
French Muscular Dystrophy
    Association (AFM),
    39–40
Frye ruling, 17–18, 66, 74,
    75–76, 108
Fukushima, 70, 143
Futrell, Robert, 113–115

Galison, Peter, 121
game theory, 89
Garfinkel, Harold, 56
Gates Foundation, 116, 118
general acceptability criterion,
    17–18, 66, 75–77, 108
General Social Survey (GSS),
    46, 47
genetically-modified organisms
    (GMOs), 49, 50, 51, 52,
    113, 131
Gezondheidsraad, 105–106,
    110–111
Giddens, Anthony, 54–55,
    56–57, 58
gift exchange, 59–60, 88–89
Glass–Steagall Act, 94
Golan, Tal, 74, 75
Google, 11, 14
Gouldner, Alvin, 142
Gove, Michael, 1–3, 97, 105
government agencies, 50–3, 66,
    94–103, 105–129,
    131–136
Great Depression, 94–95
gross domestic product (GDP),
    95

Habermas, Jürgen, 87–90, 93,
    95–96, 135
habitual trust, 52–53, 56–57
Harbers, Hans, 51
hazard analysis critical control
    point (HACCP), 126
Heidegger, Martin, 32
Hofstadter, Richard, 4, 5
Howson, Alexandra, 55–56
hybrid forums, 37, 80, 122,
    145–146

ignorance
    production of, 2, 81, 84,
        128, 136
    of the public, 82–83
    and risk, 67, 68, 69, 80,
        81
    and trust, 54–55, 56–57,
        59
inclusion
    and consensus, 113–115
    inclusion friction, 81, 115,
        145
    as legitimation strategy, 103,
        104, 111–115, 128,
        145–146
    and medicine, 17, 39–40,
        111–112
    as model for public role of
        expertise, 41
    and risk analysis, 80–81,
        112–113
    and science, 80–81
    see also participatory
        approaches
inconvenient facts, 142–143,
    145–146, 149
independent commissions,
    14–17
independent review, 125
indeterminacy, 67, 68, 69,
    80
Industrial Injuries Advisory
    Council (IIAC), 100–101

infrastructural inversion, 127, 128, 138–139
Institute of Medicine (IOM), 105
instruments, 31–33, 36
insurance, 68–69, 77–79
interactional expertise, 9, 34–35, 40, 108
Intergovernmental Panel on Climate Change (IPCC), 2, 122, 124–125, 126–128, 137, 148
internet, 82–83, 93–94, 145
interpretation, 5–6, 8–9, 44–45, 118–119
Interstate Commerce Act, 14–15
Interstate Commerce Commission (ICC), 15
Ioannidis, John, 44
Islam, Faisal, 1–3

Jasanoff, Sheila, 107–108
judicial review, 14–16
judiciary, 18, 74–77, 94
junk science, 18, 74, 75
jurisdictional struggles
  and abstract knowledge, 30–31, 35–36
  and expertise, 22, 24, 30–31, 35–36, 65, 70–73, 75–77, 97
  and risk, 65, 70–73, 76
  and law, 75–77
  and medicine, 71, 112
  and science, 97
jury system, 75

Kafka, Franz, 90–91
Kefauver–Harris amendments, 98–100
Kelsey, Frances, 98–99, 116–117
Kennedy, John F., 98–99
Kennedy, Ted, 132

Keynesianism, 96
knowledge
  abstract knowledge, 23, 25–36, 41
  codification of, 26–28, 32–33
  elicitation of, 26–27, 29–30
  experience-based knowledge, 9, 17
  expert knowledge, 15–16, 17, 22–36, 41
  explication of, 24, 27
  knowledge infrastructure, 127
  knowledge society, 14, 19
  specialized knowledge, 15–16, 22–23
  tacit knowledge, 17, 23–24, 25–36, 41, 45
Kuznets, Simon, 94–95

Lancet, 55
Latour, Bruno, 6, 33, 126
law
  defensibility of decisions, 75
  expert testimony see expert testimony
  eyewitness testimony, 7
  and facts, 7–8
  judicial review, 14–16
  judiciary, 18, 74–77, 94
  jurisdictional struggles, 75–77
  jury system, 75
  legitimacy of, 75, 77
  and lie detector technology, 75
  relation to science, 7–8, 20, 75–76
  tort litigation, 17–18, 76–77, 107–108
lay expertise, 9, 12, 17, 35, 36–37, 40, 102, 111–112, 148

legal facts, 7–8
legitimacy
  and authority, 83–84, 88–89,
    90–91, 149
  and the Balaam effect,
    130–141
  belief in, 85–7
  and boundary mechanisms,
    93–4, 108–111
  crisis of, 79, 82–103,
    104–129
  and defensibility, 69, 75, 84,
    86–94, 135–136, 140
  democratic, 75–76, 81
  and economics, 94–96
  and exclusion, 103, 104,
    105–111, 128
  and expertise, 82–5, 94–103,
    104–129
  and framing, 106–111,
    113–114, 122–123,
    145
  and inclusion, 103, 104,
    111–115, 128, 145–146
  of the legal system, 75,
    77
  meaning of, 85–94
  and medicine, 98–100,
    102–103, 111–112,
    116–122
  and objective procedures,
    98–100, 103, 104,
    115–122, 128–129
  and outsourcing, 103, 104,
    122–129
  political, 94–103, 134
  and repetition, 89–90, 92,
    149
  and science, 94–103,
    104–129, 145
  and staff, 91–93
  and the state, 94–103,
    123–124
  strategies for dealing with
    crisis of, 103, 104–129

  and symbolic pollution,
    92–93, 96–98, 100–103,
    107, 123–124, 131,
    134–135
  and time, 77, 88–94,
    113–114, 128, 145
  and trans-science, 145–146,
    148–149
  and truth, 86, 87–89
  and uncertainty, 126–127,
    128–129, 145
lie detector technology, 75
Lippmann, Walter, 9–10, 38,
    41
long-termism, 8, 45–46,
    148
Luhmann, Niklas, 25, 56–57,
    60, 67, 87–90, 93, 143

marketization, 96
Marx, Karl, 83
measles, 55
mechanical objectivity see
    objective procedures
Medical Hypotheses, 55
medical journals, 45–46, 55
medical research, 39–40, 44,
    45–46, 55
medicine
  clinical trials, 98–100,
    102–103, 111, 116–122,
    132, 135–136
  decision-support systems,
    26–27
  drug approval, 98–100,
    102–103, 111, 116–122,
    131–136
  drug reporting systems,
    125–126
  electronic healthcare records,
    71
  evidence-based medicine, 39,
    71
  inclusion of patient groups,
    17, 39–40, 111–112

medicine (cont.)
  and legitimacy, 98–100,
    102–103, 111–112,
    116–122
  jurisdictional struggles, 71,
    112
  research *see* medical research
  and trained judgment,
    100–101, 120
  and trust, 47, 55–56, 58–59,
    61–62, 112, 120–21
  vaccination, 2, 52, 55–56,
    58–59, 61–62, 78–79, 80,
    106
Mencken, H. L., 12
Merleau-Ponty, Maurice, 32
microwave sounding units
  (MSUs), 138, 139
Millennium Challenge
  Corporation, 116, 118,
  121, 122
mistrust, 43, 54–56, 58, 60–63,
  131
MMR vaccine, 55, 61, 106
Mollering, Guido, 60
Monsanto, 51
MYCIN system, 26–27

National Academy of
  Engineering (NAE), 105
National Academy of Sciences,
  5, 105
national accounting, 94–96
National Bureau of Economic
  Research (NBER), 94–95
National Research Council
  (NRC), 105
National Science Board, 46
National Science Foundation
  (NSF), 3
National Science Panel,
  107–108
neo-liberalism, 96
Nestor, John, 131
neutrality, 107–111

New Deal debate, 14–17, 19,
  22, 24
new penology, 71
New Public Management
  (NPM), 96
Nietzsche, Friedrich, 5
No Child Left Behind program,
  116
no-fault liability, 77–79
nuclear incidents, 24–25,
  67–68, 70, 72, 143–144

obedience, 85–86, 91–92
objective procedures
  as legitimation strategy,
    98–100, 103, 104,
    115–122, 128–129
  and trust, 39–41
occupational diseases, 100–101
open-forward facts, 7–8
Origgi, Gloria, 57
outsourcing, as legitimation
  strategy, 103, 104,
  122–129

panel selection, 105–109
Paris Climate Agreement, 3
participatory approaches
  and consensus, 113–115
  and legitimacy, 111–115,
    145–146
  and medicine, 17, 39–40,
    111–112
  participatory democracy,
    37–41, 112
  and risk analysis, 80–81,
    112–113
  and science, 80–81, 145, 148
  and time, 113–114, 145
  see also inclusion
partisanship, 149
patient groups, 17, 102,
  111–112, 134, 145
peer review, 18, 77, 128, 148
pesticides, 3, 49, 50

Pew Research Center, 46–48, 49

pharmaceutical companies, 45–6, 52, 98–100, 102–103, 116–120, 125, 133–136, 145

Pharmaceutical Research and Manufacturers of America (PhRMA), 133

pharmacovigilance planning (PVP), 97, 126

phenomenology, 22–23, 28–30

placebo effect, 117, 119, 136

policy
and facts, 7–8
and legitimacy, 94–103, 104–129, 134
relation to economics, 94–97
relation to science, 7–8, 20, 94–103, 104–129
role of experts, 18–19, 94–103, 104–129

policy science, 7–8, 64, 70–73, 96–129, 131–141

political risk, 65

political views
polarization of, 82–83
and risk, 79–80
and trust in science, 48–49, 51

pollution
acceptable levels of, 69, 98, 101
and breach of trust, 63
and clinical trials, 120
environmental, 18, 65, 67, 69–70, 72, 78, 98, 101, 102, 138
and legitimacy, 92–93, 96–98, 100–103, 107, 123–124, 131, 134–135
and risk, 69–70, 72, 78–79, 98, 102
and science, 96–98, 100–103, 123–124, 129

symbolic, 63, 70, 72, 78–79, 92–93, 96–98, 100–103, 107, 120, 123–124, 129, 131, 134–135

populism, 2–3

post-market monitoring (PMM), 124, 125, 126

post-truth, 82

precautionary principle, 127, 148

prediction, 1–2, 24–25

prescriptive approaches, 27, 36–37

prisons, 71

professional associations, 18, 75–76, 112

Pruitt, Scott, 3, 58

psychology, 72–73, 75

public opinion, 1–2, 3, 9–10, 43–54, 82–83, 113, 131, 134; see also survey research

public relations, 61, 107, 113–114

Public Understanding of Science, 53–54

radioactive contamination, 24–25, 67–68

randomized controlled trials (RCTs), 99–100, 116–122, 132, 136

regulatory science, 7–8, 18–19, 50–53, 64, 70–73, 77, 89, 96–141, 145

repetition, 89–90, 92, 149

Reproducibility Project, 44

reputation, 38, 44, 62, 84, 90–91, 102, 131–136

research see medical research; scientific research; survey research

research misconduct, 18, 44, 50, 55

resentment, 4–5

rhetoric, 90, 109–110
risk
  absence of experts on, 64–77
  acceptable levels of, 69, 71,
    76, 98
  backgrounds of risk analysts,
    65–66
  boundary mechanisms of risk
    analysis, 68–70, 80
  as camouflaged ethics and
    politics, 74–77
  and competing claims to
    expertise, 66
  as a de-differentiating
    concept, 70–74
  and expert testimony, 17–18,
    74–77
  financial risk, 65, 67, 69
  and ignorance, 67, 68, 69,
    80, 81
  impossibility of eliminating,
    69–70
  and indeterminacy, 67, 68,
    69, 80
  and insurance, 68–69, 77–79
  and jurisdictional struggles,
    65, 70–73, 76
  multi-disciplinary nature of,
    18, 65–66, 76
  no field of expertise
    specifically relevant to,
    66–70
  participatory approaches,
    80–81, 112–113
  political risk, 65
  and political views, 79–80
  proposed Federal Agency for
    risk regulation, 108–109
  public perceptions of, 71–73,
    79–80
  risk controversies, 66
  and symbolic pollution,
    69–70, 72, 78–79, 98, 102
  too many fields of expertise
    pertain to, 65–66, 76

  tort litigation about, 17–18,
    76–77
  and trust, 77–79
  and uncertainty, 67, 68–70,
    77–78, 80–81
  usage of term, 64–65
Roosevelt, Franklin D., 14
Royal Society, 53
Ruckelshaus, William, 112
rules, 23–24, 26–29, 32–33,
    115–116, 118

sacredness, 63
science
  appeals to, 6–8, 79
  assault on, 2–3, 4, 6–7, 43,
    131
  and the Balaam effect,
    130–141
  and consensus, 97, 105–111,
    122, 124–125, 128
  deficit model, 53–54
  and facts, 6, 7–8
  forensic science, 75
  junk science, 18, 74, 75
  jurisdictional struggles, 97
  and legal testimony see
    expert testimony
  and legitimacy, 94–103,
    104–129, 145
  and long-termism, 8, 45–46,
    148
  medical see medicine
  methodology, 4, 6, 44–45,
    136–137
  participatory approaches,
    80–81, 145, 148
  plurality of disciplines, 6–7
  policy science, 7–8, 64,
    70–73, 96–129, 131–141
  politicization of, 79, 94–103,
    134
  and public opinion, 43–54
  public understanding of,
    53–54

regulatory, 7–8, 18–19,
50–53, 64, 70–73, 77, 89,
96–141, 145
relation to policy and law,
7–8, 20, 75–76, 94–103,
104–129
research *see* scientific
research
and symbolic pollution,
96–98, 100–103, 123–124,
129
and time, 7, 148
and trained judgment,
44–45, 100–101, 120,
127–128, 139
trans-science, 76, 80,
143–149
and trust, 8, 43–63, 84
Science and Engineering
Indicators, 46
scientific journals, 44, 45–46
scientific research
by government agencies,
50–53
methodology, 4, 6, 44–45,
136–137
non-replication of, 44, 50
overstatement of, 44
peer review, 18, 77, 128, 148
publication of, 44, 45–46
pure research, 7–8
research misconduct, 18, 44,
50, 55
sponsorship of, 45–46, 50
see also medical research
Second World War, 95
Securities and Exchange
Commission (SEC), 15
selection processes, 105–109
silicone breast implants
litigation, 107–108, 110
Simmel, Georg, 57, 62–63
simulation models, 2, 127–128,
138, 139
Slovic, Paul, 73

social media, 82–83
social recognition, 22, 30–31
social welfare, 116
Society for Risk Analysis, 66,
72, 73
sociology of professions, 22,
30–31, 35–6
specialized knowledge, 15–16
sponsorship, 45–46, 50
staff, 91–93
state legitimacy, 94–103,
123–124
state regulation, 94–96
subjectivity, 121–122
Superior Health Council
(HGR), 105
SurfaceStations.org, 138–139
survey research
framing of results, 46–48
influence of political views,
48–49, 51
proliferation of, 46, 53–54
on trust in science, 46–54
wording of questions and
response options, 49–50, 53
see also public opinion
symbolic pollution *see*
pollution

tacit knowledge, 17, 23–24,
25–36, 41, 45
tacit trust, 52–53, 56–57
technocracy, 37–41, 96,
105–111
testimony *see* expert testimony;
eyewitness testimony
Thalidomide, 98–99, 117
time
and gift exchange, 59, 88–89
and the internet, 93–94
and legal or policy decisions,
7–8, 77
and legitimacy, 77, 88–94,
113–114, 128, 145
and outsourcing, 128

time (cont.)
  and participatory
    approaches, 113–114, 145
  and science, 7, 148
tobacco companies, 128, 138
tort litigation, 17–18, 76–77,
    107–108
toxicology, 65, 67, 72, 117
trained judgment, 39–41,
    44–45, 100–101, 120,
    126, 127–128, 139, 144
transparency, 3, 39–41, 61, 69,
    77, 97, 102, 106, 111–
    115, 117–118, 125,
    127–128, 145
trans-science, 76, 80, 143–149
Trump, Donald, 2–3
trust
  breach of, 54–55, 62–63
  in expert systems, 56, 61–62,
    77–78
  in experts, 3–4, 38–41, 42,
    43–63, 84
  and faith, 57–60, 62–63
  and framing, 57, 60–63
  habitual trust, 52–53, 56–57
  and ignorance, 54–55,
    56–57, 59
  loss of trust, 3–4, 43
  and medicine, 47, 55–56,
    58–59, 61–62, 112,
    120–121
  and mistrust, 43, 54–56, 58,
    60–63, 131
  in objective procedures,
    39–41
  problem of, 38–41, 103
  and public opinion, 43–54
  research on, 43, 46–54
  and responsibility, 54–56
  and risk, 77–79
  and science, 8, 43–63, 84
  and symbolic pollution, 63
  tacit trust, 52–53, 56–57
  and transparency, 61
  vigilant trust, 50–51, 57–60

truth, 6, 45, 59, 75–76, 86,
    87–89

uncertainty
  and facts, 6
  foregrounding of, 126–127,
    128–129, 145
  highlighted by critics of
    science, 136–137
  and legitimacy, 126–127,
    128–129, 145
  and risk, 67, 68–70, 77–78,
    80–81
  and trans-science, 145, 147
Union of Concerned Scientists
    (UCS), 2–3, 137–138
United Nations, 95, 124
US Army, 113–114

VA Barometer, 46
vaccination, 2, 52, 55–56,
    58–59, 61–62, 78–79, 80,
    106
validity, 86–94
values, 68, 76, 93, 97, 105–
    106, 143–144
vigilant trust, 50–51, 57–60
Vioxx, 53, 120, 132–133
Virginia Commonwealth
    University Life Sciences
    Survey, 49
virtual witnessing, 44

Wakefield, Andrew, 55, 61,
    106, 110, 115
Weber, Max, 75, 85–86, 87,
    91–92, 135, 142–149
Weinberg, Alvin, 76, 80, 81,
    115, 143–149
Wellcome Trust Monitor, 46
Wisconsin Model, 116
Wissenschaftsbarometer, 46, 49
Wittgenstein, Ludwig, 28
Wolfe, Sidney, 133
World Bank, 116
Wynne, Brian, 24–25, 67